A TIGER
ROSE
OUT OF
GEORGIA

A TIGER ROSE OUT OF GEORGIA

TIGER FLOWERS CHAMPION OF THE WORLD

Bob Mee

FONTHILL

I was coming home from visiting my aunt this weekend and decided to detour by Tiger Flowers Drive. I know that's not where Tiger lived but there were several people out and about. Out of curiosity I asked if anyone knew who Tiger Flowers was. They all said no. And such is the way of history, I suppose.
(Entry on an Atlanta website forum)

Theodore 'Tiger' Flowers was Atlanta's 1920s renaissance man. He was an immaculate dresser, a generous philanthropist and a ferocious boxer.
(Herman 'Skip' Mason, Black Atlanta in the Roaring Twenties*)*

No cleaner, more decent boxer ever has graced the prize ring than Theodore Flowers… a simple, unaffected lad, steward of a little Methodist Church in Georgia, Flowers once said: 'I never strike my opponent in anger'.
(Johnny Salak, Ring *Magazine)*

Fonthill Media Limited
Fonthill Media LLC
www.fonthillmedia.com
office@fonthillmedia.com

First published in the United Kingdom 2013
First published in the United States of America 2014

ISBN 978-1-78155-270-4

Typeset in 10pt on 13pt Sabon LT
Printed and bound in England

Connect with us

facebook.com/fonthillmedia   twitter.com/fonthillmedia

CONTENTS

Acknowledgements

Clay Moyle, for his help with the Henry Grady Edney book *Theodore Tiger Flowers*; Thomas Hauser, for his interest and willingness to offer encouragement during the long period of research; the descendants of Theodore Flowers who did their best to help me; Tris Dixon, for sharing the *Boxing News* file on Flowers; those friends and colleagues who, over the years, had to listen to my over-enthusiastic, drawn-out stories on the progress, or not, as was too often the case, of this book; and Janet, my wife, for her guidance and critical ability through the writing and editing process. More important than any of us, I acknowledge with, I hope, appropriate courtesy the ongoing, changing struggle of the African-American people from the moment they were put on slave ships in western Africa to the present day.

CHAPTER 1

A Moral Wilderness

On a hot, humid Thursday morning in June 2011, I took a cab to Harlem with work colleagues David Caine and John Rawling to find the house – 58 West 140th Street – where Tiger Flowers lived when he was world middleweight champion in 1926. The cab inched along West 140th, but the house was gone, replaced by high-rise, red brick buildings from the fifties or sixties. A church where this most Christian of men might occasionally have worshipped, the Zion African Methodist Episcopal on 138th, was still there. The front door was open, but the man behind the lobby desk refused to allow us inside. The church, he said, was open only on Wednesdays or Sundays. What Tiger Flowers might have made of that, I don't know, but it seemed to me to symbolise the problems of writing this book. Many doors have opened. One or two, to me at least, have remained tightly, resolutely shut.

Theodore 'Tiger' Flowers was the first black middleweight champion of the world. More than that, he was an African-American from the Deep South, where life could be at best difficult, at worst horrific. When I began this book, I felt I was exploring the life and career of a boxer, an athlete, a mysterious, enigmatic, Christian person who somehow, against expectations, rose to the top of a maverick, unpredictable, too often corrupt profession. Naïvely, too, I seemed to want to write a book about kindness and generosity in the middle of the vagaries of ordinary life, about an athlete for whom faith was not a crutch but a foundation upon which he built his life. As I searched and researched, I discovered I had only the vaguest notion of what I was doing, of what it must have been like to come out of the world Flowers knew and understood. In writing, I felt unworthy most of the way, and felt like giving up more than once. Perhaps along the journey the legend of Tiger Flowers led me, through a glimmer of understanding, to the edge of a moral wilderness masking as civilisation, a featureless place that seemed to have no end, no meaning, no way out. A place where Christ's message of, 'Do unto them as you would have them do unto you,' was cast aside in favour of, 'Do unto them exactly what you feel like doing for your own amusement or material benefit'. I found a place filled with pain, with the cries of the exploited, misunderstood, maimed, and with the wails of those who spent their last minutes in an agony inflicted by others in callousness and indifference.

Take Charlie Atkins. He was born in Georgia in 1907. His father, also Charlie Atkins, farmed a rented patch of land at Sun Hill, Washington County, roughly halfway between Augusta and Macon. They were sharecroppers, raising what they could to feed themselves on the understanding that a large percentage of what they grew would go to the landowner. By 1910 Charlie Sr., and his wife Ella had been married for eighteen years, since they were twenty-three and nineteen. They were approaching middle age, their family growing. Charlie Jr. was the youngest of their eight surviving children, and second son. As the children became old enough, they helped on the land.

Roll forward to 18 May 1922. Charlie Atkins is fifteen now and has just been rounded up in Davisboro, a small community a dozen miles away from where he was raised. A twenty-year-old rural mail carrier, a married white woman named Elizabeth Kitchens, has been found dead. Three other African-Americans, including his brother, are also in the hands of a mob of around 200 white people – men, women and children. There is no apparent evidence to suggest they are responsible, by accident or design, for Kitchens' death but the people of Davisboro are not interested in vague concepts like fair trials, evidence, due process of law, innocent until proven guilty, reasonable doubt. Nor by the fact that Charlie has a family, who will almost certainly be haunted for the rest of their lives by what is about to happen to him.

Charlie is bound and chained to a stake, which is laid above an open fire. He is roasted alive for fifteen minutes, one for each year of his life. Charlie shrieks in agony, in terror, and knowing there is no way back, with the boundaries of reality probably blurred to the point where truth and lies, wrong and right, are an irrelevance, at last he confesses to the killing, but has enough intelligence and strength to say his brother was not involved. The white people of Davisboro hammer the stake into the ground, rebuild the fire around him and feed it to turn it into a furnace. They shoot Charlie as he burns. They shoot 200 bullets into his body, one for roughly each member of the mob.

And this was the way it was. This was civilisation.

The grotesque murder of Charlie Atkins, for which nobody was ever prosecuted, was not committed in isolation. In just three weeks in that May of 1922 in Georgia there were ten other people whose lives were thoughtlessly destroyed by white people who felt ignoring the accepted process of law by lynching African-Americans was acceptable behaviour.

Roll back a little, to 1918, and go to Valdosta, in the south of Georgia near the border with Florida, where a white farmer with a reputation for cruelty, Hampton Smith, has repeatedly whipped a nineteen-year-old black worker,

Sydney Johnson, because he's too sick to work. What has been going through Johnson's mind we cannot know, but he has taken a gun and shot Smith dead, then gone on the run. A white mob has used Smith's slaying as an excuse to ride around the countryside, killing blacks who have had the misfortune to be in their way, who might or might not have been Sydney Johnson. Now they have found Hayes Turner, whose wife, Mary, is eight months pregnant.

Mary is not prepared to let them take her husband without defending him. She tells them Hayes has done nothing wrong and warns them that if they hurt him she will have them arrested. Hayes will be killed anyway, but for having the courage to attempt to protect him Mary is hauled away from her home, tied by her ankles and held beneath the waters of the Withlacoochie River. A crowd of several hundred white people gather as she is hung upside down in a tree, her clothes soaked in petrol and oil and then set alight. While she is still alive, a man steps forward and cuts open her belly. Her child falls to the floor, cries twice, and is stamped to death.

An Associated Press report says the people of Valdosta had taken exception to her remarks and her attitude. No one is put on trial for her murder, for the people who killed her are the law.

And, I say again, this was the way it was. This was civilisation.

This was Georgia. This was the South.

CHAPTER 2

What Kind of a Man was This?

It is Monday, 21 November 1927, and in the city auditorium on Courtland Street, Atlanta, Georgia, all 7,000 seats have been filled long before a burial service begins. Outside, thousands more folk, some sorrowful, some just curious, mill about and then stand and watch as the copper casket, silver-plated and inlaid with gold, bears the body through the heavy doors into the hall.

As the procession, led by the vested choir of the dead man's church, moves down the aisle, the congregation rises. Charles Sheldon, the city organist, play's Chopin's haunting Funeral March and members of the man's lodge in all their regalia sway, moving even more slowly than the music.

As the coffin is laid in front of the stage, surrounded by a bank of floral wreaths, the man's wife and daughter, brothers and sisters, mother and father, are ushered to seats reserved for them.

The service that follows lasts almost three hours, with six clergymen taking turn to pay tribute, solo vocal and violin performances by accomplished young musicians, and an address by an academic from the great seat of learning where the man's wife was a student in her youth, before closing remarks from a bishop.

Incredibly, the people of Atlanta are burying not a great politician or elder statesman from one of the powerful white business families, but a black man from a poor background who has earned his living in a trade that has made ordinary, straight-living, God-fearing folk uneasy, a trade that has demanded personal courage, certainly, but which has brought with it a reputation for bad money, corrupt business practices and degenerate admirers.

This man, about to be laid to rest in a new cemetery named after one of the nation's great presidents, is a prize-fighter – Theodore Flowers.

Flowers has died suddenly, in a New York City clinic, hours after surgery to remove a knot of gristle that had formed a lump on his forehead above his right eye. It had supposedly been routine, a tidying-up procedure designed to prolong his ring career and to restore him to the health required for him to challenge for the championship he had lost only twelve months earlier in dubious, possibly Mob-influenced circumstances.

Now it is a mark of the regard in which he is held that Atlanta has permitted both Caucasian and African-American people to sit in the hall to pay their respects. The balcony is reserved for whites. Black people have their seats on the main floor of the hall, along with some white dignitaries. General seating is not entirely segregated. As far as it has ever been up to that time in Georgia, this is a brief moment when people have laid to one side the colour of their skin and have given attention to the life of a man who has touched them all in one way or another.

At the front is his grief-stricken widow, Willie Mae, and their daughter, Verna Lee, along with his mother, Lula, and father, Aaron, and his brothers and sisters with their own families.

As the casket is placed in position, an anguished, sobbing scream rises above the sudden hush. It is the voice of his sister.

'No more Tiger, no more Tiger,' she cries. 'Hold the boat and let me go. I want to see him again.'

She is hushed and comforted and a quiet, almost stiff formality falls upon the gathering.

The service begins with a prayer by the Revd J. E. Wilson, a prominent figure in the ongoing battle to provide a proper education for African-Americans. The prayer is followed by a Bible reading from the Revd A. F. Bailey, of Atlanta's West Mitchell Street Colored Methodist Episcopal Church. Flowers' own pastor, G. L. Ward, also takes his turn.

After two musical solos, and addresses, the choir of the Butler Street CME Church, where Flowers had been a trustee, leads the congregation in the melodramatic, passionate old hymn, *Come Ye Disconsolate*.

And thousands of voices rise together to sing:

> Come, ye disconsolate, where'er ye languish
> Come to the mercy seat, fervently kneel
> Here bring your wounded hearts, here tell your anguish
> Earth has no sorrow that Heaven cannot heal.

Further solos follow, broken only by occasional sobs and cries from his family. A boy known as Stonewall Carruthers takes his turn, followed by John Herbert Wheeler, a violinist from Morehouse College, which has benefited from Flowers' financial support. Wheeler will eventually turn down a career as a professional musician to become a banker. In between them, the Revd William J. Faulkner, of the First Congregational Church, speaks for five minutes.

Particularly meaningful for Flowers' widow is the presence of Dr George Lake Imes, who for twenty-five years has worked at the Tuskegee Institute, the great educational centre for black people forged by Booker T. Washington in Alabama. Willie Mae Flowers was a teenager there in the closing years of Washington's life and, as one of its 15,000 students, a third of them female, would have known Dr Imes from that time.

His short talk is followed by the Morehouse College Quartet. Unlike Tuskegee, which is trade-based, Morehouse is one of the first great academic centres for black Americans in the South.

A violin solo from Professor Kemper Harrold leads into a tribute to the Tiger's boxing career from Morgan Blake, the (white) sports editor of the *Atlanta Journal*. Blake tells the crowd that the city has risen above prejudice to recognise Flowers' character, manhood and achievements. As Blake resumes his seat the crowd breaks into a 'long thunder of applause'. And finally, the closing remarks from the esteemed Bishop Randall A. Carter of the CME Church in Georgia.

We do not have a transcript of the message delivered by Bishop Carter, but he was probably selected as the right man to complete the ceremony because his teachings perhaps acted as a guide to the way Tiger Flowers had conducted his life. Four years earlier Carter had addressed the students at Paine College in Augusta, where he himself had studied in the 1880s. He had concluded that speech as follows:

> And now a last word about race prejudice. You will meet it at every turn and everywhere you go. Sad to say, it is growing steadily. Your color will be against you in almost every field of activity. Do not deceive yourselves into believing that anywhere in this country you will escape this curse of the age. Often it will be veiled and stealthy. Frequently, it will walk openly and unafraid, but it will be the same illogical and unreasoning thing. Learn to expect it, and face it, and conquer it. You may console yourselves, however, with the fact that the Negro race is not the only race which suffers from race prejudice. Deport yourselves in such a gentle and quiet and confident and unassuming manner that you will make those ashamed who practise it. Wherever you go, let people learn that a colored skin can cover just as much culture and refinement and decency as any other kind of skin. Also, I exhort you, try to make friends with and command the respect of those with whom you live. Do not depend upon friends who are far away. Whatever the color of the people with whom you deal daily, they will respect refinement, modesty, integrity, scrupulous honesty, industry, and money.

And so at last the body of Theodore Flowers is carried from the auditorium, and the cortège passes through downtown Atlanta, where people stand three and four deep, and out to the 100-plus acres of Lincoln Cemetery, with its fresh, clean air and sense of space, set back from Simpson Road, not far from where the Flowers family have lived in their luxurious fourteen-room house at number 1010.

Lincoln Cemetery, where Atlanta's African-Americans bury their dead, has been open only two years. The cemetery has responded rapidly to the boxer's death by donating a plot of 400 square feet for the exclusive use of the Flowers family.

The funeral procession is led by the band of the Negro Elks of America with Willie Mae and Verna Lee, and the rest of the family, following the hearse in cars. Walk Miller, Flowers' white manager, drives the boxer's car, or 'costly roadster', as the *Associated Press* report describes it. This, according to the writer is, 'a gesture of respect not unlike the riderless horse of an officer in a military funeral'. It takes seven cars to carry the floral wreaths to the graveside. With those who had been inside and outside the auditorium for the service following on, the procession stretches out more than a mile.

The whole city, the whole of Georgia, knows Tiger Flowers has gone.

. . . . .

Two days before he was buried, Flowers was given a glowing tribute in the *Atlanta Constitution* by Paul Stevenson, who described his death as a grievous blow.

> His head was never turned. He brought credit to the Negro race at home as well as abroad. He was a clean-living man, a man who loved his family and his home life, and who had the desire and the stamina to resist those temptations which have not always been resisted by the champions of our boxing ring, both those of the white race and the Negro race.

Stevenson praised Flowers as thrifty and frugal, and as a man who, with the money he earned from boxing, contributed liberally to the causes that were for the betterment of people in Atlanta. Stevenson also referred to the grand house on Simpson Road.

> He built for himself and his family a magnificent home and in its possession he had no envy from the persons of any race.

Yet within days the story had taken a more sinister turn. The outpouring of grief was replaced by confusion, suspicion, resentment and anger. For Walker Miller, the white man who had managed Flowers' career from their early days in Atlanta right up to the heady triumphs in Madison Square Garden, New York, had struck a devastating emotional blow that epitomised the relationship between white and black in Georgia in particular and America as a whole. Miller stunned Flowers' family by producing a will he claimed

Tiger had signed on the day of his death, hours before he went into the operating room at the clinic of Dr Wilford Fralick in Manhattan.

In this will, the boxer left Miller in charge of a $60,000 trust fund for his daughter, Verna Lee, under the terms of which Miller would have no restrictions on how to use the money. The will also appeared to allow Miller to act as executor in preference to any member of the boxer's family, or his lawyers.

Flowers had been dead little more than a fortnight when the newspaper for African-Americans, the *Atlanta Independent*, ran a long piece by its editor, Benjamin Davis, detailing Miller's harassment and intimidation of Willie Mae Flowers. Miller had threatened to put the grieving Willie Mae in an asylum and Verna Lee in an orphanage.

While Tiger had been a subscriber to the doctrines preached in the Colored (later Christian) Methodist Episcopal Church that change would come by example, that obedience and humility on earth led to eternal life, Davis was an advocate of outspoken resistance. And he used his voice as editor to investigate, to encourage his largely black readership to re-think their values, to consider how they should act to best effect. If he did attract any white readers, his writing challenged them to examine their perception of what justice was, of how society was being run.

Davis knew Miller's will did not ring true. Yet it was there, and had to be disproved.

It allowed Flowers' mother, Lula, to keep the house he had bought for her at 938 Simpson Road, and left $1,000 cash sums for his five brothers and sisters. Miller said there was little cash in the bank, but that the estate was worth between $100,000 and $125,000, and that the family home at 1010 Simpson Road was bequeathed to Willie Mae. Miller had, however, somehow managed to raise three mortgages of his own against it, according to a later report in the *Pittsburgh Courier*.

Miller said he was certain there was enough to keep Willie Mae comfortably for life, but strangely also spoke of special instructions left in a safe deposit box that had not yet been opened. 'These will be taken care of to the letter,' he said. And if Miller was in control of the $60,000 trust fund, then it did not take a mathematician to deduce that Willie Mae was under pressure.

In another bizarre twist, Miller said Flowers had also left $1,000 in cash to a supposed female friend, Mattie Jarrett. I can find no other trace of anyone by that name who might have been connected to Flowers. Did she exist, or was she a fiction, a part of Miller's plan to destabilise Willie Mae's position?

By losing Flowers, Miller had lost his meal ticket. He had managed other boxers, even briefly the hugely popular light-heavyweight contender William 'Young' Stribling, but none had provided him with anything like the status or financial reward that Flowers had done.

In learning to live among the rogues that inhabited boxing, it is entirely possible that Miller had learned to think like them, and that whatever affection he had for Flowers and all he stood for died with him. It is probable that Miller, in running an office and maintaining a home in Manhattan for the past couple of years, had been living hand-to-mouth. The sudden loss of Flowers may well have grieved him, but also rang the financial alarm bells in his head. And he knew that to protect himself, to survive in the world he had created for himself, he had to have access to ready money – and if that meant getting his hands on the dead fighter's estate, then so be it.

Casting doubt over the veracity of Miller's story was his previous, apparently contradictory evidence that on the day of Flowers' death, the boxer had spoken only three times. Each time in response to something that Miller had said – 'Yes, sir', 'Sure is' (written as 'sho is' at the time), and finally when Miller asked immediately before he walked in for surgery if there was anything he wanted to talk over, the fighter had replied 'No, sir'.

And so by introducing the 'new' will, Miller would have had people believe that in addition to those perfunctory remarks on the day he had gone in for what was supposed to be relatively routine surgery, this most Christian of fighters had made the momentous decision to exclude his wife of twelve years, his childhood sweetheart, from making any decisions over the financial well-being of their only daughter, and without discussing anything with her, to make a will that would put her in an untenable financial position. It is possible that Flowers was naïve and too trusting with regard to his manager's actions and intentions but highly unlikely, to the point of being incredible, that he would have preferred Miller to look after his estate and the well-being of his family in the event of his death.

Six days after the emergence of the Miller will, it was revealed in the *Atlanta Independent* by Benjamin Davis that Willie Mae had gone to court to establish her rights. Judge Thomas H. Jeffries, Fulton County Ordinary, appointed her temporary administrix of the estate. However, pending the outcome of the ruling on the new will, she was unable to dispose of any of the estate. The order simply gave her the right to continue with the day-to-day business of the estate, the value of which was now put at $120,000. Strangely, Miller remained for the time being executor of the trust fund for Verna Lee.

On 3 December 1927, the outspoken, extrovert Davis went on the attack on behalf of the up-to-now placid Willie Mae. He declared:

> The public is entitled to know the facts; and to know the import of Walk Miller's interest in The Tiger Flowers' Estate; and just why he nursed his corpse; stayed in the undertaker's shop with the dead body; advised his wife not to come to New York for the remains; why he sought and seeks to keep her from her friends; chose the undertaker and continues to visit

and threaten her with taking the child away from her and putting her in the asylum.

This was an astonishing accusation but Davis took things to their logical conclusion:

> We have always had a lurking suspicion of a white man who loves Negroes better than he does his own race, and who practises social equality with Negroes on the sly, and Mr Miller is no exception to the rule.

Davis insisted, with apparent justification, that Flowers had intended his wealth to be used, in the event of his death, for the benefit of his legal dependents and not his former manager. Flowers did have a trust fund for Verna Lee, but this was based on other property he owned and therefore did not pose any threat to Willie Mae; furthermore that he expected to administer the trust fund himself, or that were he to die or resign as trustee his successor would be selected by process of law. Davis also said Flowers had further protected Willie Mae's position, and perhaps helped their tax situation, by signing the family home over to her. In short, he had acted consistently with his character throughout his life in safeguarding the interests of his loved ones. And at no time had there ever been a suggestion or indication that Willie Mae was of an unstable or unsound mind.

Davis, tenacious and aggressive, said Miller's will effectively gave the manager absolute power.

> Under this will, Miller could sell the entire property, and put the proceeds in his pocket... Under Walk Miller's will, the little girl would not even come into possession of her property when she is twenty-one years old, but Mr Miller would hold it in perpetuity. The New York Will gives his wife all of his personal property, without naming it, and the income from all his real estate, without naming it, and $2,500 in cash.

Davis also reported that Willie Mae's lawyers had released details of her complaint about Miller's behaviour towards her.

> ... That Mr Miller continues to visit her, annoy and harass her by threatening to take the child away, put it in an orphan house, and put her in an asylum for the insane; that he has not settled with Tiger, nor her, for the last three fights; that he has taken from her one of her husband's $5,000 Lincoln automobiles; that he demanded that she turn over to him the keys to her husband's safe deposit box in the Fulton National Bank, and that she has been so intimidated by him that she is actually afraid to come out into the streets to attend to her business or to consult her attorneys. That she

is living in actual fear of her husband's manager, who has taken complete charge of the estate; that he has ordered her to move out of her own house, asserting that he is executor of the estate and trustee for her child, whom he would remove, and put her out of doors…

The evidence against Miller was damning, although he pointed out the car was in a garage in Atlanta and was to be used as a security bond in a $3,000 civil law suit relating to a crash Flowers had been a part of in Harrisonburg, Virginia, the previous October. It may simply have been that Willie Mae had not been made aware of either the whereabouts of the car or the civil claim that was pending. The *Pittsburgh Courier* also said the house was not worth what Flowers had paid to have it built as he had died before it had chance to accumulate its value. Christmas 1927 would have been traumatic enough for Willie Mae and Verna Lee Flowers, but here they were, with Tiger only a few weeks' dead, being threatened with eviction from the family home, to be separated and thrown into institutions. Davis concluded his castigation of Miller by writing:

> No Negro man would be permitted to take charge of a white man's estate, to the exclusion of his wife, and no white man should be allowed to take charge of the affairs of a dead colored man's estate, to the exclusion of his wife.

Willie Mae's legal team did its job. On New Year's Eve they were granted a temporary injunction which prevented Miller from acting as trustee to Verna Lee's fund. As far as the team could, it cast doubt on the validity of the Miller will. A notice was filed that Miller's will, should it be proven in New York, was invalid because it must have been made when Flowers was under the control and dominance of his manager – which, given the evidence against Miller in his treatment of Willie Mae, could be suggested was within his behaviour pattern. The notice also highlighted the fact that the supposed will was made in New York where neither man was an official permanent resident. Judge E. D. Thomas appointed two temporary trustees to control the trust fund, lawyers Hewitt W. Chambers and Thomas W. Holmes.

Negotiations went on for a few weeks until, on 26 January 1928, Walk Miller accepted defeat and resigned as trustee of the fund for Verna Lee, with Chambers and Holmes given full authority to administer it. This, again, would appear to suggest there was no New York will. In return Willie Mae, through her attorney, H. A. Allen, withdrew her claims against Miller over his behaviour. 'Miller,' said the *Atlanta Independent*, 'withdraws entirely from any connection with the administration of the estate'.

Eight months later Walk Miller was dead.

CHAPTER 3

A Black Man in Georgia

The birth date of Theodore Flowers has caused historians problems for many years. Nat Fleischer, the hugely respected founder of *Ring* magazine, went with 5 August 1895, though the evidence for that is hard to establish. In his 2004 book on the politics of black celebrity which centred on Flowers, Andrew M. Kaye agrees with Fleischer and dismisses the date of 11 February 1894 offered by Henry Grady Edney in the first book on the boxer published in 1928. Yet Edney, from Henderson, North Carolina, had the co-operation of Willie Mae Flowers in writing what is more an elegy than a biography. And surely, Tiger's wife would have known when he celebrated his birthday?

In the 1900 United States Government census, Theodore is listed as seven years old, born in February 1893. That information would have been provided by his parents, who would have had no reason to avoid the truth or create a fiction that he was born in February rather than August.

When Theodore signed for the First World War draft in 1917, he gave his date of birth as 13 February 1894, while his commemorative seat in Lincoln Cemetery, Atlanta, has the date as February 1897. He would not be the first man to take a year here or a couple there off his age, but whether the 13th or the 11th, it seems fairly clear that he, his parents and his wife put February as his month of birth, and given the details in the earliest available census after he was born, I would argue that 1893 is most likely to be the correct year. That makes him two-and-a-half years older than boxing records have suggested since Nat Fleischer's time.

Theodore – the name means Gift of God – was born in Camilla, Georgia, which is in the south-west corner of the state, about fifty miles from the borders with Florida and Alabama. His birth was either not registered, as was the case with so many children of poor, African-American parents, especially those born at home, or was lost in the system somewhere down the years. Camilla is a small town in the middle of cotton, peanut and pecan country. Theodore's father Aaron Flowers had been born across the state line in Alabama, while his mother Lula Hunter was from Georgia. There were no Hunters in the 1860 census for Mitchell County, which suggests her parents were not slaves of a family of that name in Camilla or the surrounding farmlands. Perhaps, as many did, they took a family name that had no connection with the slavery years, or perhaps they moved there after the Civil War brought what amounted to freedom.

Aaron and Lula were married in Camilla in December 1888, and their first son, Carl, was born in August 1890. Theodore was their second, or at least the second to survive. In 1899 Aaron, Lula, the two boys and their two sisters, four-year-old O.C. and the baby, Gertrude, moved 100 miles east across the state to the large coastal port of Brunswick. They set up home in a rented house at 505 B Street.

It is unclear exactly why they made the move. There had not been a lynching in Camilla since the first town elections in 1868 when a political rally led to a march of freedmen, who were in turn chased out of town, and seven of them hunted down and killed as an example to the rest to stay out of politics.

That said, nowhere in Georgia was risk-free for its black inhabitants in these years. Slavery had ended officially in 1865, followed by the period known as Reconstruction, but white and black people alike suffered their share of frustration and inadequacy. It is important to remind ourselves that as much as they understood the nature of their servitude, for slaves the plantation was their home, and what they knew. Booker T. Washington talked in his autobiography *Up From Slavery* of the day of emancipation. At first, he said, there was an outpouring of joy. Then after the tears, laughter and songs came a sober reflection on how they were going to cope. He used the phrase, 'the great responsibility of being free'. Very few African-American slaves could read or write, they knew nothing of the law beyond the moral code of right and wrong provided by the Bible but interpreted mostly by their masters. Suddenly they had to make their own plans for providing for themselves and their children.

Washington also remembered the great frustration of the white families who had relied for generations on the ability of slaves to do their menial tasks. They did not know how to do the practical, everyday things that slaves knew out of habit, and with the slaves gone, finding out, if indeed they possessed the drive, energy and commitment to find out, might be a process of trial and error. The plantations of the inherently lazy or incompetent fell fairly quickly into ruin.

The complex emotional ties cannot be underestimated. According to Washington some slaves felt an attachment to the family they had served, some of them for half a century and more. They had nursed, nurtured and looked after these white folk from infancy to the grave. There was a loyalty to what they knew, and if they considered their masters and mistresses to have been, in the circumstances, fair, then they cared about them. Washington remembered the sadness that the slaves on the plantation where he was born felt when one of the white slave owners was killed in the war, fighting for the side that would have kept them in slavery. These were times of psychological as well as physical turmoil.

Washington was mentored and encouraged by Samuel Chapman Armstrong at Hampton Institute, whose theory was that by its general state of demoralisation and lack of self-esteem, the condition of slavery had deprived African-Americans of the need to consider the rewards of hard work and to have ambitions of their own. This was a contentious generalisation, but whatever the basis of his theory, the result of it was that he was determined to drive his students towards these twin goals. In his 1986 introduction to the Penguin edition of Washington's autobiography, Louis R. Harlan wrote: 'Armstrong sought above all else to inculcate in his students the virtues of self-reliance, hard work and thrift.'

The line comes down through Washington and Tuskegee, where he developed these principles in his own students, to Willie Mae Spellars as she was when she was being taught there, and on to her husband Theodore Flowers.

It is possible that some lesser incident persuaded Aaron and Lula Flowers to move their young family out of the countryside to a bustling town, where there was a degree of safety in numbers. They might also have gone in search of better housing and more lucrative work. It is likely that the Flowers home in Camilla was a single room board shack. The best description of the one-room cabin comes from W. E. B. Du Bois in his book *Souls of Black Folk*:

> Light and ventilation are supplied by the single door and by the square hole in the wall with its wooden shutter. There is no glass, porch or ornamentation without. Within is a fireplace – black, smoky, usually unsteady with age. A bed or two, a table, a wooden chest, and a few chairs compose the furniture, while a stray show bill or a newspaper makes up the decoration for the walls.

Larger communities provided better homes, a higher level of companionship, churches within easier reach, and as poorly funded and staffed as they were, better schools. Jobs were low-paid and physically tough, but the work was regular and better than sharecropping. Black people settled into their own areas of towns, which in the larger cities were later, fashionably, referred to as ghettoes. It was natural for African-American people to want to be together, relatively safe assuming they managed to mind their own business, or not let their eyes rest on a white man's wife or daughter, or walk around too late at night.

Aaron Flowers found a job with the Georgia railroad, which by 1910 employed around 11,000 African-Americans. However, everything was relative. Du Bois also said: 'To be black in Georgia was to fall victim to white oppression, to live each day in the shadow of violence.'

After Reconstruction had come reaction and repression. Any black citizen found wandering around alone might be arrested and thrown into jail accused of anything from vagrancy – sometimes described as 'walking around in idleness' – to theft of a dog that might have been running alongside them, from illegal gambling to owing a local white man money. Without a chance to defend himself, a black man would be handed a prison term with the alternative of a fine that he could not pay. A landowner would then step in on cue to pay the fine, which was considered a loan to be repaid through labour. Before he knew it, the frustrated, bewildered convict would then be whisked off to a farm, plantation or mine, to work out his sentence in terrible, barbaric conditions, beyond the reach of his family. If the white man who had loaned him the money felt like selling him on as a contracted labourer, then no questions would be asked, and the man might simply disappear into one labour camp after another for years, if he survived that long. The length of his sentence meant nothing for the simple reason that pretty soon nobody other than the victim, or his powerless family, cared what it was. Men could be killed without trace, or might die of disease without even rudimentary medical help. Those who tried to escape were hunted down with dogs, brought back, tortured and sometimes murdered.

Punishments for alleged rule breaking were brutal. A man or boy might be bound to a stake by his hands and feet, tied into a foetal position so that he could barely move, and left for hours in the sun.

Thousands of black men and hundreds of black women were bought and sold by companies or landowners whose profits were swelled by labour that cost them only the most basic food and shelter. These people, so many of whom had committed no crime at all, slept in their rags in hovels, and were fed food enough to stay alive and no more.

In 1908, a survey revealed that 2,219 of Georgia's convicts held in prisons were black. Only 347 were white. So many more were in what amounted to enforced labour camps with no hope of release. How much they talked about it is open to question but Aaron and Lula Flowers, and their growing family, would have understood all of this.

In the same year President William Taft told a black audience in an Atlanta Methodist church: 'I have heard it said that your lot in the South is a hard one. I do not believe it. You are now in the South and you look reasonably happy.'

Their response was not recorded.

Later that day Taft spoke to black students at the Georgia State Industrial College in Savannah. He said, 'You have had your association with a moral race and your condition would not be what it is but for that association. And I want you to listen. The best friend the Southern Negro has is the Southern white man.'

In the summer of 1902, Lula Frazier was arrested and charged with adultery in Waycross, Georgia. The sheriff who pulled her in, Thomas J. McClellan, recommended a white lawyer, William F. Crawley. They were a team. In Lula's case they must have been frustrated when the town prosecutor refused to bring a case against her – on the grounds that the man she was accused of adultery with was Nathan Frazier, her husband. That small fact didn't stop McClellan and Crawley informing her in her cell that she had been found guilty and fined $50, upon which, a white farmer, Edward J. McRee, appeared, paid the fine and took her to his plantation, where she was kept for his pleasure. As well as being a landowner, McRee was a leading member of the county legislature. He expected to make the law and expected to have it upheld for his own benefit. Lula Frazier was lucky. Nine months later a new sheriff arrived in Waycross and her family was able to obtain her release. McRee, McClellan and Crawley were eventually brought to trial on multiple charges of peonage and handed down paltry fines. McRee for example, pleaded guilty on thirteen sample charges, technically faced a sixty-five year jail sentence and a $65,000 fine – and was, instead, fined $1,000. McClellan and Crawley had to pay $500 each.

Douglas A. Blackmon in his superb *Slavery by Another Name* also tells us that on a train in the south of the state, a white man passed through a black coach and flipped a burning cigarette on to the lap of a black woman. When her husband protested, the white man shot him dead. His body was put off the train at the next station. No effort was made to arrest the killer.

A Methodist minister, the Revd W. W. Willams, preached that African American women should try to resist the predatory sexual attacks of white landowners. For that, Williams was hauled out of his house, stripped and whipped in the street. On another day he might have been strung from a tree or burned alive.

Every so often an investigation would be held into the system known as peonage – the employment of criminals as cheap labour. In Atlanta in 1908, the harrowing ordeal of a fourteen-year-old boy, Daniel Long, was laid before a commission hearing. Daniel had been convicted of stealing a watch chain in Marietta, then sold to a turpentine camp in the south of the state. There he was whipped, sometimes seventy-five strokes twice a day, at the apparent whim of whoever was in charge of the labourers. When asked by the commission chairman, he removed his shirt and revealed the grotesque state of his back.

His mother described how she set off to find him, eventually traced him to the camp, only to be told he had been sold on to a farmer. Mrs Long said she was threatened with being murdered if she continued to search, and when she asked for more details of what had happened to him, was told by a white man, 'I don't know anything about the goddamn black son of a bitch. I beat hell out of him.'

She did go on and found Daniel lying in a hut at the farm, his clothes stiff with his blood and stuck to his wounds. The farmer either took pity or saw the point in not having the boy die on his land and let him leave with her. It is not recorded how she managed to get him home, but it was three months before she was sure that he would live.

Joel Hurt was one of the most powerful businessmen in Atlanta. He made his money from property and investments, including the city's Trust Company Bank. He also ran mines and steel furnaces in a place called Lookout Mountain near the state line with Tennessee. Now it has a golf club, a college and a road quaintly named Red Riding Hood Trail. Life in Hurt's mine was no fairytale. Hurt appeared before the hearings in Atlanta, smartly dressed and utterly relaxed. He remained that way even as stories of the abuse of African Americans in his employment were told in ever-more horrific detail. His son, George Hurt, explained to the investigation, without any hint of a sense of guilt, that a black man named Liddell had died, not from the effects of a severe whipping, but from a blood vessel burst in the act of struggling against the whipping. George Hurt offered the incredible opinion that the blood vessel was most likely weak because the man, 'was guilty of committing masturbation to such an extent than his mind had become affected'. Neither of the Hurts faced prosecution.

In 1921, when Tiger Flowers was establishing himself as a boxer and around the time he and his wife had their baby girl, a case of a white man murdering black employees did reach the courts, but this was an isolated triumph for the law. A white farmer, John S. Williams, was fifty-four years old, a father of twelve, and a pillar of his community. When he was under investigation for keeping labourers illegally on his plantation forty miles outside Atlanta, nothing was discovered. However, Williams panicked and killed eleven men, with the help of his black foreman, Clyde Manning, whom it was said dared not disobey him. When the bodies of the dead men surfaced in rivers in the area, Williams and Manning were arrested, and convicted of murder. Both were sentenced to life imprisonment and died in jail.

After the conviction and sentence, the Governor of Georgia, Hugh M. Dorsey, spoke out. 'In some counties the Negro is being driven out as though he were a wild beast. In others, he is being held as a slave. In others no Negroes remain.'

For this, he was heavily criticised in some sections of the white press. There were calls for his resignation – even for him to be impeached. He responded strongly: 'Since 1885, mobs in Georgia have shot, hanged, burned or drowned 415 Negroes, some of them women... in the last sixty days a mob has taken a helpless old Negro woman from her home and drowned her by night.'

Dorsey's outspoken opposition meant he was voted out at the next election.

Even when legitimately employed, the black man had few rights. In October 1905, a young worker, Willie Roberson, who was still a minor, earned $1 a day cleaning and greasing engines on the railroad. He was at his job, lying under a locomotive, when a driver moved it, crushing his legs. His mother sued for lost wages and injury compensation as he was too young to lodge a lawsuit, but in its defence the rail company said Roberson had been given ample time to finish the job and therefore was responsible, through his own negligence, for his own injuries.

The *Atlanta Constitution* belatedly reported a lynching in July 1919. Two months earlier two white men attempted to rape two black women in the black district of a township named Milan. A seventy-two-year-old man, Berry Washington, came to the aid of the women, who were daughters of a local widow. Washington, a member of the local African Methodist Episcopal church, shot dead one of the attackers, John Dowdy, and then gave himself up to the police. A white crowd gathered, took him out of the jail and hanged him. After being asked not to report it, to their shame newspaper editors agreed it was not in the public interest. It was only when the National Association for the Advancement of Colored People released the case to press in the north that it was reported in the south. No one was brought to trial for Washington's killing.

And, of course, there was the Ku Klux Klan. Once any initial euphoria at the coming of freedom was over, the black people of the Deep South must have known it was just the beginning of a struggle that would go on for generations. History shows us that revolutions provoke resistance and counter-revolution, and so it was when Confederate soldiers, having lost the war, feared the complete loss of their way of life. Many had lost their homes, and their families. And, of course, black people who had been theirs to do with as they pleased, or who were free but knew their place, such a short time before, were now, according to the law at least, to be given respect as full and proper members of society. The era that has become known as Reconstruction lasted only a dozen years before official attempts to carry through the constitution were abandoned in the South as impractical and unenforceable. It then became common for blacks to be barred from 'white' parks, from using the same drinking fountains, from using the same waiting rooms on stations, from 'white' railway coaches. There were even separate Bibles in courtrooms for black and white people to swear on. Black property owners were forced to sell up, cheaply, to white buyers, and move out of an area. In *The American Century* Harold Evans wrote that in 1896 in Louisiana there were 130,334 eligible black voters. Eight years later, only 1,342 were brave enough to register.

The Ku Klux Klan was formed in Tennessee at the end of the Civil War, but was initially a loosely connected set of individual groups of white supremacists, not a powerfully constituted organisation. Historian Elaine Frantz Parsons described it as a chaotic multitude of anti-black vigilante groups, disgruntled poor white farmers, wartime guerilla bands, displaced Democratic politicians, illegal whiskey distillers, coercive moral reformers, sadists, rapists, white workmen fearful of black competitors, employers trying to enforce labor discipline, common thieves, neighbors with decades-old grudges…

The looseness was the Klan's strength as it was hard to define, but also its weakness, and over time its members lost interest, got old, or were put off by the Congress Investigation into it in 1871. As it declined, other organisations replaced it: the White League in Louisiana, the Red Shirts in Mississippi and the Carolinas. And in many of the remote areas of Georgia, local white justice was the only justice available. And that was no justice at all.

The magnificent black journalist, Ida Wells, campaigned tirelessly from her base in Memphis, Tennessee, for basic rights for African-Americans, and for women. She was eventually driven out of the city. Her printing press was wrecked after she had condemned a lynch murder in her newspaper. If she had not been away on business, she might well have been lynched herself. She also believed that although some lynchings were random, or in reaction to a perceived crime, others were aimed at anyone who showed signs of developing a successful business, or had an interest in political improvement.

Postcards of lynchings were sold on the open market. One example, from Oklahoma, showed the burning of the body of a lynched man with the inscription, *Coon Cooking*. Another card that was posted carried a photograph of a charred corpse hanging from a tree with the message on the back, 'This is the barbecue we had last night'. They made postcards, too, from a photograph of the hanging body of Joseph Richardson of Leitchfield, Kentucky, who was taken from the jailhouse and killed on the public square at 1 a.m. on 26 September 1913. He had been arrested on suspicion of assaulting an eleven-year-old white girl, Ree Goff. It later transpired that all he was guilty of was stumbling into her while drunk.

In September 1918 a black farm worker, Sandy Reeves, was lynched because it was said he had assaulted the three-year-old daughter of his employer. It emerged that he had dropped a nickel while working, the little girl had picked it up, and he had taken it back, at which she burst into tears. That cost him his life.

In 1915 the Ku Klux Klan was reinvented by William J. Simmons at Stone Mountain, Georgia, at a meeting attended by members of the lynch mob who had murdered a Jewish businessman, Leo Frank, in Atlanta. Frank had been in prison for two years after being convicted, almost certainly erroneously, of the murder of one of his factory workers, Mary Phagan. Frank had originally been sentenced to death, but that had been commuted to life imprisonment by Governor John Slaton, who also happened to be a partner in the law firm that had defended Frank. The excuse for the mob murder of Frank was Slaton's apparent conflict of interest. One man who attended the lynching was Thomas Watson, a lawyer and politician, who had at one time supported the rights of black men to vote, but who had become reactionary enough to oppose not only black rights but those of Jews and Catholics. He approved of the reorganisation of the Ku Klux Klan and celebrated Frank's lynching in his newspaper, *The Jeffersonian*. Watson still has a statue in front of the Atlanta State Capitol building with an inscription that reads: 'A Champion of Right Who Never Faltered in the Cause'.

Eleven days after William Simmons and his new Klan cronies burned a cross on Stone Mountain, the white supremacist film *Birth of a Nation* by D. W. Griffith premiered in Atlanta. To mark the occasion members of the Klan rode on horseback up and down Peachtree Street. This movie was a spin-off from the books of Thomas Dixon. Whites had flocked to see the stage version of one of Dixon's novels, *The Clansman*, and his previous book, *The Leopard's Spots*, glorified lynching as a socially laudable method of dealing with the African-American 'menace'.

Incredibly, on 1 July 1916, the Klan received an official charter from the State of Georgia. That was the day that in France the Battle of the Somme began in all its horror. By the following year the United States had joined what it knew as The War in Europe. Black soldiers were shipped across the Atlantic to fight alongside whites. They were segregated in troop ships, in mess halls, sleeping quarters, and refused permission to attend social functions outside their units. They were segregated in everything but death. And when those that did come home returned to the South they were treated with contempt. Some were lynched for wearing the uniform. The *Savannah Tribune*, a newspaper aimed at African-American readers, protested even before the Armistice that the Negro was being induced, 'to die for a fiction called Democracy'.

By 1920, when Theodore Flowers was just starting out on his boxing career, the Ku Klux Klan's membership had risen to around four million. It claimed to base its philosophies on the Bible, on its allegiance to the Stars and Stripes and, incredibly, on the US Constitution. As it rose in power, it proved increasingly difficult to oppose. The progressive Governor of Oklahoma, J. C. 'Jack' Walton, blamed race riots in Tulsa on the Klan. The violence escalated until in September 1923 he declared martial law throughout the state. Walton was under a twenty-four hour guard by state troopers, and within two months was out of office, having been found guilty in what was considered a Klan payback of 'illegal collection of campaign funds, padding the public payroll, suspension of *habeas corpus* (the principle by which an accused person must be brought before a judge or into a court to be tried), excessive use of the pardon power, and general incompetence'.

The Klan's confidence in its ability to control the political destiny of, not only the South, but the United States as a whole, brought chaos to the National Democratic Convention of 1924, when it refused to sanction the selected candidate on the grounds that he was a Roman Catholic. In 1925, when Tiger Flowers travelled the country to fight on thirty-one separate occasions, from Savannah and Macon in Georgia, to Toledo and Canton in Ohio, from Boston to New York, from Chicago to St Paul, Minnesota, the Klan hit a chilling peak. In the first week of February, in Oklahoma City, Lucy Trigg-Davis, 'Imperial Lecturer of the Women of the Ku Klux Klan' advocated capital punishment for any white American who indulged in an inter-racial marriage.

On 8 August 1925, 40,000 Klan members marched in Washington DC, drawing a crowd of perhaps 200,000, to the foot of the Washington Monument, within sight of the White House. Rain cancelled their plans to burn an eighty-foot-high wooden cross.

On that day Theodore Flowers was in a county jail in Orange County, Florida. He had been arrested, charged with reckless driving and speeding near Orlando. He had said he was on his way, with a black friend named Allen, to see his mother, Lula, who was for some reason in St Petersburg. He had set out in his car the previous day and was driving on the South Dixie highway when he overtook a motorbike ridden by an off-duty white policeman, P. G. Bullock.

For a reason not explained, perhaps because they were driving fast or perhaps because he saw two black men riding in an expensive car, Officer Bullock accelerated and Flowers, not recognising that he was a traffic cop, put his foot down and got away. Bullock quickly enlisted the help of an on-duty colleague, M. E. Hancock, who joined in the pursuit and five miles later Bullock caught up with Flowers, who presumably thinking the incident was over, had slowed up again. When Bullock tried to overtake, Flowers swerved and forced him off the road. Bullock fell off his machine and suffered slight injuries. Then Hancock, who was in uniform, arrived and arrested the fighter without any apparent difficulty.

It was confirmed that Bullock was not in uniform and had no credentials with him to prove he was an officer of the law. The implication is obvious: Flowers simply did not know that the motorbike was being ridden by a policeman and sped off in order to avoid a confrontation with an apparently irate white man and then forced him off the road when the incident developed into something more aggressive. As soon as he recognised Hancock as a police officer, he did not resist arrest. He was held on a bond of $500. Presumably, once it was established who Flowers was, he either paid a fine or the charges were dropped, because a fortnight later he was in Boston, boxing again, but the incident highlights the kind of pressure a black man faced, particularly if he rose above his station and, the Lord forbid, bought himself a nice car.

J. Edgar Hoover, the head of the Federal Bureau of Investigation, was more interested in pursuing supposed Communists than doing anything more than making an occasional show of clamping down on the Klan. In 1933 the White House was given information that Hoover was actually a Klan member, which was rapidly denied. Whether or not that was ever true, Hoover would remain in power at the FBI for fifty years and his record in investigating crimes against black Americans was dismal. He did so when forced to out of expediency, or by political circumstance but not out of a sense of justice. By contrast, according to Anthony Summers' ground-breaking *The Secret Life of J. Edgar Hoover*, he kept the politically active singer Paul Robeson under surveillance for thirty years and did the same to Martin Luther King as the Civil Rights movement gathered force. Hoover planned a campaign to discredit King as, 'a fraud, a demagogue and a moral scoundrel'. Unknown to the Attorney General, Robert Kennedy, he had his agents wire-tap hotel rooms to discover details of King's sex life. It might be pointed out that heterosexual intercourse between consenting adults was not a crime – but the illegal bugging of hotel rooms most definitely was. The assistant director of the FBI, William Sullivan, dictated a memo following a meeting with Hoover outlining the process that would, if it were successful, ensure, 'Negroes will be left without a national leader of sufficiently compelling personality'.

As it was the Klan's political impetus in the 1920s burned out, thanks to the exposure of one of its leaders. On 24 November 1925 David C. Stephenson was sentenced to life imprisonment for the kidnap, assault and rape of an Indianapolis schoolteacher, Madge Oberholtzer.

As Grand Dragon of the Indiana Realm of the KKK, Stephenson had once declared, 'I am the law in Indiana.'

At the height of his power, it was believed that one in three males in the state was a Klan member. He referred to them as citizens of an invisible empire. That was about 250,000 men, all of whom paid $10 membership, $4 of which somehow found its way into Stephenson's pocket. He also collected a rake-off from the clothes members were required to wear at gatherings.

He came crashing down with his conviction for his terrible attack of Oberholtzer, a twenty-eight-year-old white woman who was involved in a programme to tackle illiteracy among the local African-American community. She swallowed poison and died eighteen days later but not before testifying against him.

As he had supported Indiana Governor Edward Jackson in his election, even after his conviction Stephenson was arrogant enough to believe he would be released with a pardon, or at the very least have his sentence cut to a minimum. When that did not happen, Stephenson published from his prison cell a list of public officials who were on the Klan payroll. Some were embarrassed into resigning, and the Mayor of Indianapolis, John Duvall, was sentenced to thirty days in jail for corruption.

Almost overnight Klan membership went into free fall, dropping from an estimated six million to around 120,000. There were still dangerous, embittered groups of vigilantes in the South who would remain active for generations, but as a political force, for the time being at least, it was dead.

African-American involvement in politics had endured a rocky ride. In 1895, the founder of Tuskegee Institute, Booker T. Washington, preached a message of gradual integration, advising black people to take a patient path forward through education and economic improvement rather than attempt to challenge the white race head-on. It became known, disparagingly, as his Atlanta Compromise Address.

W. E. B. Du Bois, then a professor at Morehouse College, said Washington's advice amounted to complete surrender. The two opposing voices perhaps encapsulated the dilemma that faced the African-American as the century drew to its close, and the truth was there was no immediate solution. Theodore Flowers was a subscriber to the Booker T. Washington view of change through example, but then, as far as we know, nobody in his immediate family was a victim of peonage or lynching. And it was natural that while some people would want to talk about the horrors that existed, others would want to avoid and ignore them as tragedies that happened to someone else. Joe Louis, for example, remembered his childhood on a sharecroppers' farm in Alabama as one that did not directly confront the race situation.

> My folks seemed to get along with the white people in the area. Maybe it was because, 'you got your place and I got mine'. Probably we never crossed the line to cause the angers and hurts and lynchings that took place all over the South.

Similarly, the lightweight champion Ike Williams was born in Brunswick in 1923 and spent the first nine years of his life there before his family moved north to Trenton, New Jersey. He did not remember it as a particularly stressful time. He told Peter Heller for his book *In This Corner: 42 World Champions Tell Their Stories* in 1971, 'I would say there was less racial trouble [in Georgia] then than now because Negroes knew their place then. There was no such thing as mixing with whites.'

In 1901 President Theodore Roosevelt did not appear to anticipate the extent of the hostility that he would provoke when he invited Booker T. Washington to dinner in the White House. Allen Candler, the Governor of Georgia, said: 'No Southerner can respect any white man who would eat with a Negro.'

James Vardman, who would be voted in as Governor of Mississippi the following year, said the White House was now, 'saturated with the odor of the nigger'.

In 1902 in Atlanta W. E. B. Du Bois led a delegation of African-Americans into the new Carnegie Library to ask that black people be allowed to use it as well as whites. Their request was denied. The library chairman asked Du Bois, 'Do you not think that allowing whites and Negroes to use this library would be fatal to its usefulness?' They were promised that a separate library would be provided... and it was, almost twenty years later, in 1921.

The great light-heavyweight champion Archie Moore, who was born to a teenaged mother in Mississippi in 1916 and raised by his aunt and uncle in St Louis, Missouri, told a story that serves as an example of the everyday fear that permeated the black homes of the South in the 1920s. He described in his autobiography how, when he was a boy, he went back to Mississippi with his aunt and sister for a summer holiday. He told of sitting on an old horse, being led by his sister and their cousin along a country road, when a white boy hit the animal with a stick to make it rear up. Moore was thrown off, somehow avoided being trampled, and in his anger grabbed the boy, shook him and shouted at him. The boy ran off, Moore trudged back with the horse, his cousin and sister having taken off ahead of him.

> When I arrived there was a great commotion and my auntie took me inside and implored me never to hit a white person. I replied I hadn't hit him and explained I might have fallen under the animal or perhaps my sister might have been trampled. Auntie didn't care about that, seeing we were both unharmed. She was emphatic. She wanted me to promise. My aunt then said we would have to leave. Regardless of whether I promised or not, we would have to leave. When I asked why, I was told it was because I had hit a white boy and it would only cause trouble for the relatives who lived there if I stayed. Young as I was, I said that if I had to leave Mississippi for such a reason I would never return. I was then eight years old and I have never been back.

There were some dissenting voices. A judge in Georgia, Emory Speer, in opposing the forced labour system said:

> What hope can the respectable Negro have, what incentives to better effort or better life, if he, his wife, his daughter, or his sons, may in a moment be snatched from his humble home and be sold into peonage. Let us for a moment put ourselves in his place, and imagine our furious indignation or hopeless despair if our loved ones, or ourselves, could be subjected to such a condition of involuntary servitude.

Few in the Deep South took any notice.

And it was out of all of this that Theodore 'Tiger' Flowers rose to become the middleweight champion of the world.

CHAPTER 4

The Birth of the Tiger

Theodore Flowers' memories of Camilla were simple enough, according to Henry Grady Edney's quasi-romantic vision. Life was a homely joy among the fields, and he was surrounded by good, honest, Christian folk. It may be that neither Edney nor Willie Mae wanted to go into unhappy areas of the past, or perhaps, as Joe Louis did, he felt his family never 'crossed the line' and so never antagonised the white people around them. Then again, he was only six years old when Aaron and Lula took the family to Brunswick. If there had been minor problems or worries, or perhaps more significant difficulties, it's possible he would not have been aware of them. When they arrived in their new home, Theodore was sent to the Risley School in Albany Street, Brunswick. He stayed there for six years, to the age of twelve, when he left to earn a living. That would have been 1905. He had already been working in the school holidays to help supplement the family income by running deliveries in a grocery and a meat market. His pay, which would remain the same for many years, was around $1 a day.

About this time he also felt himself ready to make the commitment to become a member of his local Baptist church, where full-immersion baptism would have been the practice. Baptists do not christen infants, but prefer to wait until a person is old enough to choose the spiritual path he or she themselves wishes to take.

He had played the usual boyhood games – marbles, baseball, wrestling, and fishing on the River Turtle, or in shady, slow moving, estuary waters. Again, the vision provided for us by Edney, with the help of Willie Mae, is of an idyllic childhood played out to a backdrop of gentle, sunny, innocent days.

The fact that Aaron was a man of principle and truth is borne out by a civil court case in Brunswick in 1907. An African-American, Joe Mays, bought a return rail ticket in February from Savannah to Brunswick for a three-week stay in the town. On his way back, although his ticket was valid until the following week, the white conductor told him it was not. Mays asked him to look at the ticket again, but was verbally abused, grabbed by the collar and choked, punched twice in the face and shoved against a wall. The conductor claimed Mays, 'made a smart remark and reached for his pocket as if he were getting a weapon', and therefore he struck him in self defence. Aaron Flowers, described in court as a porter, testified for Mays – and therefore against his employer. That took courage.

When he was fifteen, in 1908, Theodore found himself a childhood sweetheart in Willie Mae Spellars, who was not quite twelve at the time. They just happened to like each other's company, though for her at least, it was love at first sight. Whether it was meeting Willie Mae, or just one of those 'Damascus Road' moments that change a man's way of life, we can only speculate, but at the end of 1909, with a whole new decade stretching out ahead, the sixteen-year-old Theodore took it upon himself to curtail his 'manly' habit of swearing.

> I was working in a garage… I was cleaning cars. Everybody was cussin' in the garage and I was too. Then sudden like, the bells began to ring and the whistles blew and I knew it was 1910 coming in. I stood right up then and I said, 'Flowers, you are going to stop cussin' from here on', and I did, but it sure was hard at first…

Willie Mae Spellars was born in July 1896, the year her parents, Lewis and Mamie, had married. She had brothers and sisters from her mother's first marriage, Arthur, Hattie and Pearl Adams. In the 1900 census, Lewis is listed as a day labourer, and Mamie was adding some no doubt much needed cash by taking in laundry. This was hard work that would have taken up much of her time. Mamie's age in 1900 was thirty-nine, and her eldest boy, Arthur, was seventeen, yet when she died of a stroke at Theodore and Willie Mae's home at 282 Parsons Street, Atlanta, in March 1925, she had lost ten years somewhere along the line. She was registered by Willie Mae as fifty-four at time of death, which is an illustration of how difficult it is to be precise in these matters. Mamie, sometimes spelled Mammie, was the daughter of Green Roundtree or Roundtrees and Mammie Brown, both born in Georgia. It's probable that they, and perhaps Willie Mae's mother herself, were born into slavery but if so Green was one of those who embraced his freedom and took seriously the responsibilities that came with it. He registered himself qualified to vote in Lowndes County, Georgia, on 11 July 1867. At the turn of the century Green was living in Cat Creek, near Valdosta, which is the main town in Lowndes County. He was aged seventy-five, widowed and said his father was born in South Carolina, his mother in Georgia. Lewis Spellars, Willie Mae's father, died some time in the first decade of the century, as by 1910 Mamie, her mother, was a widow – and still washing clothes and linen for a living.

Willie Mae was obviously bright and had a degree of independence and ambition, because she wanted to pursue an education to the point where, at the age of sixteen, in 1912, she was able to go to Tuskegee Institute to study under the great Booker T. Washington. According to Edney, and therefore on the basis of her own testimony to him, she was there for three years. Tuskegee taught African-American students in agricultural and industrial subjects as well as producing teachers, but it is not known what Willie Mae studied. She would have been one of around 500 young women on courses there at the time. Washington's wife, Margaret, took a great interest in the education of the women, many of whom were from poor backgrounds. Any suspicion that this was just a story put out to enhance Willie Mae's reputation is dispelled by the fact that Tuskegee professor Dr George Lake Imes was at her husband's funeral service in 1927 and by later documentation that she hosted a meeting of the Los Angeles Tuskegee club.

When Willie Mae returned to Brunswick at the age of nineteen, she married Theodore, who was twenty-two, in a quiet service conducted by the Revd M. A. Davis on 22 November 1915. They could not afford the church fee, so Theodore arranged to pay with 75 cents down and the rest in installments. In terms of finances they really did have nothing.

During Willie Mae's time at Tuskegee, Theodore had tried his luck, briefly, in the North, as an increasing number of African-Americans did at that time because of the lack of opportunities and dangers in the Deep South. The 1915 directory for Philadelphia shows he was living at 925 North 45th Street. He may have been attempting to earn some better money only to find it didn't work out, or perhaps it was a short-term project, as he knew Willie Mae would be coming home later in the year and they would marry.

Theodore, like any twenty-three-year-old man with a new wife to provide for and a home to build, wanted better.

Willie Mae said, in Edney's book: 'It seemed that Theodore and I could never have a comfortable home on the small pittance which he was making…'

And then one day – a beautiful spring day in 1916, as Willie Mae recalled – it all changed. It is not recorded exactly how Flowers met Rufus Cameron, but Cameron was invited to their home for lunch – and the rest, as they say, is history.

Cameron, known as Rufe, earned a modest living as a professional boxer and treated them to tales of his travels. Originally from Rusk in the Texan countryside, about 160 miles north of Houston, he had left the farm where his family worked as sharecroppers, had found his way to Los Angeles, and had learned his trade as a boxer.

By 1916 he was twenty-nine years old, and boxing had taken him to San Francisco, over the Mexican border from El Paso to Juarez, to Missouri and Idaho, and dozens of small towns along the trail. At one point he had been promising. One reporter had said, 'He has the grace of a panther and can hit like a mule.' In truth, though, Cameron was just one more nearly man in a cynical, cut throat business where success and failure walk side by side. A better black heavyweight, Jeff Clark, so clever they called him the Fighting Ghost, knocked out Cameron in thirteen rounds in Juarez in 1913, and the following year outpointed him over fifteen rounds in Clark's home town of Joplin, Missouri. Cameron had fought well, but coming second counted for nothing. He would never make it.

Flowers was enthralled, however, and asked Cameron to teach him how to box, and the big man, perhaps with nothing better to do that day, gave him his first lesson.

Willie Mae remembered: 'Theodore was delighted. He liked boxing. He knew from that first try-out that he could learn, and that he would learn.'

How long Cameron stuck around we don't know, but he stayed long enough to work with him on the basics and to drum into him what was required, in training as well as fighting.

Willie Mae said her husband was up early each morning to run miles before breakfast, to punch the bag he had set up in the back yard and to skip and jump. One of the neighbours, believing he had lost his mind, suggested to the new Mrs Flowers that she may have to consider finding him a place in a hospital for the insane. Another called him 'Tiger', no doubt with more than a hint of mockery – and the name stuck. When he began to box in real fights, he decided Tiger had a better ring to it than Theodore.

In the story of Flowers' death, published in *The Brunswick Pilot* of Friday, 18 November 1927, the unnamed writer refers to his boxing career having begun, 'some twelve years ago under the management of Lee Bailey, colored boxing promoter of the famous L. Street Park'. Today there are two parks on L. Street. One is named Miller, which has a stadium that was built on it in 1952, and the other is Orange, which looks too small to be the venue. My guess is that the arena would have been the Miller Park, with the bouts probably in the open air. The results of these shows have been lost, although boxing had been taking place in Brunswick since the 1890s. A 'sparring match between two Negro pugilists' took place at Dart's Hall on 26 March 1895, for example. Given that Edney and Willie Mae are specific about the arrival of Rufus Cameron in the spring following the marriage, Tiger's fighting on the promotions of Lee Bailey almost certainly began in 1916.

Flowers still liked to fish and enjoyed quiet, rural places, perhaps in some kind of flashback to his early years around Camilla. Although he left school at twelve, he could read and write well enough, and enjoyed, as well as his Bible, works like *The Scrap Book* by Elbert Hubbard, which included quotations from William Blake, Izaak Walton and Oscar Wilde. One he marked was by Donald G. Mitchell:

I thank Heaven, every Summer's day of my life, that my lot was humbly cast within the hearing of romping brooks, and beneath the shadow of oaks. And from all the tramp and bustle of the world, into which fortune has led me in these latter years of my life, I delight to steal away for days and for weeks together, and bathe my spirit in the freedom of the old woods, and to grow young again, lying upon the brook side and counting the white clouds that sail along the sky, softly and tranquilly, even as holy memories go stealing over the vault of life. I like to steep my soul in a sea of quiet, with nothing floating past me, as I lie moored to my thoughts, but the perfume of flowers, and soaring birds, and shadows of clouds.

Perhaps this offers us another clue to Flowers' ability to keep his own company without the need of conversation as he toured the country later in his fighting days. He had a sense of an inner peace, whatever the world threw at him, and this would have provided him, when necessary, with a defence against prejudice and oppression. The maxim offered by men like Bishop Randall Carter, who would speak at his funeral service, that a man could conquer prejudice and hatred by carrying himself in gentleness and quiet, by an unassuming confidence that demonstrated those with black skin were as refined and cultured as anyone else, would have bolstered his sense of resilience. It was the same message that would be carried through to the non-violent protests of the Civil Rights movements in the 1950s and 1960s, and is echoed by the words of the mother of Elizabeth Eckford, who attempted to attend the Central High School in Little Rock, Arkansas, in 1957, one of the first group of African-American students to do so. Elizabeth was warned, if she should be subjected to any abuse from white people, 'Pretend not to hear them. Or better yet, be nice, and put them to shame.' Just a fifteen-year-old girl, Elizabeth was not strong enough to carry out her mother's instructions. She tried, but as a white mob of men and women, some only young teenagers like herself, walked alongside and behind her screaming, 'Get back to Africa, nigger', she sat down at a bus stop in tears. A white journalist from the north who was covering the story bent down and told her gently, 'Don't let them see you cry'. Tiger Flowers, and so many others like him, needed, as they went wherever life took them, that 'sea of quiet' which Donald Mitchell described.

Another passage Theodore liked was Oscar Wilde's thoughts on solitude in De Profundis.

Society, as we have constituted it, will have no place for me, has none to offer: but Nature, whose sweet rains fall on unjust and just alike, will have clefts in the rocks where I may hide, and sweet valleys in whose silence I may weep undisturbed. She will hang the night with stars so that I may walk abroad in the darkness without stumbling, and send the wind over my footprints so that none may track me to my hurt; she will cleanse me in great waters, and with bitter herbs make me whole.

Theodore Flowers learned, with the help of men like Mitchell, Wilde and Bishop Carter, and of course from his parents, and from, more than all of them, his Bible, how to be in this world but not necessarily of it. Edney tells us that Tiger saw his Christian life as a duty and responsibility, and that after growing too old to attend the Sunday school, he took his turn in teaching there. His Bible was a living, breathing way of life.

> His favourite pastime was reading the Bible and getting from its pages the teachings and lessons for living a life which would be suitable to die by... He loved his Master. He believed in Him. He believed that all he was or all that he aspired to be could be attained only through Him.

When he was well into his boxing career he gave a rare clue about how he went out of his way to stay out of difficulties. He knew what challenging a white man, especially one purporting to be a representative of the law, might lead to. He told a reporter in Boston in 1925:

> Once a white sheriff was going to start trouble when he found us (me) swimming in the river. I swam and was carried by the current four miles down the river and swam four miles back. Sure was a good workout just to keep out of a fuss.

It is true that most black people got through their lives without being physically harmed. However, to survive under oppression, to be wary or afraid of those in control, and to be forced by experience to identify those people as threats instead of public servants and equals, is to be denied the right to thrive or live in its fullest sense.

By 1917, the trickle of African-Americans leaving the South to find work and more security in the Northern cities had become a mass exodus. In his inaugural address on 1 July 1917, the Governor of Georgia, Hugh M. Dorsey, said 50,000 blacks had left the state in the twelve months just ending. Generations had lived and died without a chance of bettering themselves. Now there was an energy, a new determination, a sense of resistance and change. It's also an inescapable fact that opportunities in the North also offered a relief from the haunting shadow of the lynch mob, or white-capping, where black people were driven out of a particular house or district, or of suddenly finding themselves trapped in the peonage system, working in misery in a mine or on a remote plantation. Eventually, the flood of men travelling north was so significant that white employers in Georgia worked to attempt to prevent it, sometimes by intimidation, occasionally by force.

Theodore, for the second time, decided to try his luck in Philadelphia. By early 1917 he and Willie Mae were living in a room in a modern, three-storey house at 1233 Pine Street. He had a job with the Keystone Construction Company, which was involved in the building of the city subway system. 1233 Pine Street still exists, just along from Dirty Frank's Bar and across a bit from the Last Drop Coffee House. This was the red light area in the 1970s and 1980s, and the centre of the 'gay bath-house culture', but is now a more fashionable district, popular with students. 1233 Pine Street was built in 1900.

There is no record of Flowers boxing in Philadelphia or surrounding areas, although Willie Mae appears to have spent some of her time while he was out at work attempting to obtain him fights. Edney claims she actually managed to stage some fights for her husband. If she did, they were extremely low-key, off the radar of sports writers. Nat Fleischer, in his series of books written under the general title Black Dynamite, claims Flowers trained at a gym run by the old light-heavyweight champion Philadelphia Jack O'Brien. Ed Sullivan of the New York Graphic said that in 1917 O'Brien's gym was no more than a marquee, in which he staged bouts and paid anyone a few dollars to put on a few rounds of entertainment, much in the way boxing booths worked on fairgrounds in Britain. Sullivan said Flowers' ring experience in Philadelphia consisted of a few of these unofficial battles. Another version, cited by modern Ring editor Nigel Collins in his book Boxing Babylon is that after the United States had entered the war on 6 April 1917, Flowers sparred or boxed at a Liberty Loan rally staged or hosted by O'Brien. He looked so good that the old champion recommended he try boxing for a living. Nothing more came of it at the time. Edney says he trained with O'Brien in his lunchtime breaks and at the local YMCA in the evening.

He also switched from working on the subway to a job in the Hog Island shipyards, helping the war effort. Years later his manager, Walk Miller, with his publicists' flair for exaggeration, would convert this into actual war service in the US Army, but although he had signed the draft papers to make himself eligible, there is no evidence that he was ever called out of his essential job in Philadelphia. By November 1918, the war was over.

Theodore and Willie Mae went back to Brunswick. Maybe work had dried up, maybe they were homesick, or their families in Georgia needed them; perhaps they just could not settle in a city that big, or given their faith, felt that God was leading them back to the South. Perhaps and maybe is all we have.

According to the Morehouse Tiger, the yearbook named in his honour from the Atlanta college of which he was a benefactor, Flowers had worked in the shipyards of Brunswick even before he married Willie Mae in November 1915. If so, that was only a brief period of time because Edney does not refer to it at all, and we know that in 1915 he had been in Philadelphia. It is likely that, as this was a tribute written after his death, the dates are mixed up, and that Flowers found work in the shipyards upon his return to Brunswick at some point towards the end of 1918 or the beginning of 1919. It may be the truth, or it might have been Willie Mae's earnest desire to push the positives through Edney's elegy, but Edney claims that in only a brief time Theodore had risen to become a first class boilermaker. Details are hard to pin down, but at the time of the 1920 census, Flowers was working as a boilermaker, not in the shipyard, but in an oil refinery in Brunswick. This was almost certainly the Atlantic Refining Company, which had opened its Brunswick plant in 1919 on a site of around eighty acres bordering Turtle River and the saltmarshes, two or three miles from where Theodore and Willie Mae were living at 1913 Amherst Street. His mother Lula, his brother Carl and his wife Bessie, and sisters O.C., Gertrude and Verdean, as well as another brother, Uly Smith, all lived at no. 1912. Aaron Flowers, on the day the census was taken at least, was not there.

Theodore Flowers was ambitious, in spite of his love of quiet places and solitude, and had been dabbling in boxing since he met Rufus Cameron in 1916.

Pa Stribling, the father of light-heavyweight contender William 'Young' Stribling from Macon, told a story that Tiger was working as a stevedore – a general term for dockworker – in Brunswick when he developed a reputation for his boxing ability in impromptu lunch break sparring sessions. According to Stribling, one thing led to another – workmates brought in better and better opposition from the outside, but the result was always the same. Flowers beat them all.

'Brunswick businessmen began to realise that in the quiet polite little Negro they had something,' said Stribling in a 1939 interview with the Atlanta Constitution.

There are several professional fights listed for Flowers in 1918, but none so far has either date or place. According to Edney, one of these was against a local heavyweight so big that Tiger's friends and acquaintances had worried for him when the match was made. He won, and picked up a payday of $64 that was the equivalent of several weeks' work in the oil refinery or shipyard. It is quite possible that 1918 was actually 1919, but we have to wait for the arrival of any specific evidence to be sure.

His mother, Lula, did not approve of his fighting, as she felt it did not sit properly with the rest of his life as a Christian. However, he had no problem justifying it, by citing the words of Psalm 144:

Blessed be the Lord, my strength, which teacheth my hands to war and my fingers to fight.

The importance of the opinion of his family, or particularly his mother, is illustrated by the fact that at the height of his fame, he still wanted Lula's approval. 'I wish mother would look at things differently,' he was quoted as saying by the British writer James Butler. 'I never strike an opponent in anger, no matter how badly I am punished, although I always do my best to win.'

He also believed God expected men to be ambitious, to work towards a better quality of life. Back in *Hubbard's Scrap Book* Edney tells us he referred again and again to a passage written by Orison Swett Marden.

> People little realize that their desires are their perpetual prayers – not head prayers, but heart prayers, and that they are granted. Most people do not half realize how sacred a thing legitimate ambition is. What is this eternal urge within us, which is trying to push us on, up and up? It is the urge, the push in the great force within us, which is perpetually persuading us to do our best.

And so Tiger Flowers continued treating boxing as a legitimate ambition, continued learning and pushing on and up until the day Billy Hooper took a train into his life.

Hooper had a menial job in the downtown gym in Atlanta which a small time manager, Walker, known as Walk, Miller, ran near the junction of Forsyth and Hunter Streets (later renamed after Martin Luther King). Hooper had been boxing on and off for the best part of ten years and was a seasoned, tough professional who was probably aware that he was past the time where his career might go anywhere. Aside from that, he was black, and everybody knew opportunities for black fighters happened so rarely it wasn't worth the dream.

An unnamed promoter, who might or might not have been Lee Bailey in Brunswick, had made Miller an offer for Hooper, or according to Pa Stribling, the best man he had at middleweight or above, to box Flowers for $75. There was only one rail ticket sent so Hooper, who knew what he was doing anyway, went by himself. The fight with Flowers was on a Friday night, and Miller had him down to box on one of his own shows in Atlanta on the Monday, so told him to be back in good time.

Monday arrived, but Hooper didn't. It was the end of the week before he showed his face in the gym. Miller recalled his shock when he set eyes on him. 'Both his eyes were closed and his face looked like a piece of chopped meat.'

Miller thought he had been in a wreck of some kind, then when Hooper told him it had happened in the fight with Flowers, the manager believed there had been some kind of set-up – that the man from Brunswick was not who was advertised, or was way too big. Hooper said, no, there hadn't been a train wreck, there was no set-up and Flowers was just a local middleweight, as they had been told. It was just that he was so good Hooper had no choice but to take the pain as best he could for the full twenty rounds.

It is likely that this happened on 17 March 1920, when Flowers ignored or overcame the pain from his right wrist, which was allegedly fractured in the fifth, to hammer Hooper over the full distance to win a decision. It is said, but not proven, he switched to boxing southpaw, winging away with his left hand, with the right hanging by his side. Whether or not he boxed left-handed before this fight, he remained a southpaw for the rest of his career.

Flowers had obviously learned from experience and moulded his style to fit his strengths. He was immensely fit and strong, with the stamina to keep up a work rate others could not match, throwing punch after punch from unpredictable angles. This had the effect of keeping an opponent occupied with defence. Most fighters who concentrate on throwing as many punches as possible tend to sacrifice some power because they don't wait long enough to plant their feet on the canvas and pick their punches with any kind of economy. In fact, some say he tended to slap and cuff as he whirled away non-stop. Whatever the truth of that, by 1920 he had become a serious handful for anybody around his weight in his area of Georgia.

Miller offered to make a rematch between Hooper and Flowers in Atlanta but, at that point at least, Hooper did not want to know. He shook his head and told him to find someone else for the job.

The following week Miller travelled to Brunswick. Flowers was, in spite of his victory, by no means convinced that a full-time professional career was for him. 'I found him a bashful sort of lad, who wasn't sure he approved of fighting,' said Miller.

However, no doubt after talking it through with his family, and having the encouragement of Willie Mae to help him make up his mind, he decided to give it a try. Miller signed him to a three-year contract and he turned up in Atlanta with a small Bible his mother had given him. According to Jimmy Jones, Bill Hooper worked his corner and helped with his training for some time after his arrival. Tiger, like Hooper, earned his keep by doing the menial tasks that kept the gym in order.

Miller did succeed in matching them again, in Atlanta on 27 September 1920, and again Flowers won on points, this time over ten rounds. There is no evidence yet of the claimed eleventh round knockout scored by Flowers in another fight, earlier, and in Brunswick, against Hooper. It is likely that they boxed just twice, both fights going the distance. Hearsay evidence is notoriously unreliable, obviously, and my instinct is to suggest that somehow the eleventh round knockout has been confused with the first points win.

By forsaking lowly-paid, honest labour for the sometimes lonely, often uncertain, and immeasurably corrupt world of professional boxing, Theodore Flowers had taken an enormous, and enormously brave, gamble. But again, ambition to provide for a family drove a man then, just as it does now, even against the kind of odds Flowers, and his wife, knew he was facing.

CHAPTER 5

'We are in the Midst of a Growing Menace'

Boxing so often reflects life. Black fighters knew the best they could hope for was to be tolerated and patronised.

Back in the crossover days when some fights were conducted with bare knuckles and some with gloves, Peter Jackson, like Tiger Flowers, prided himself on his manners and fair behaviour. He was an exceptional talent, a heavyweight so good that he fought the future champion of the world, James J. Corbett, known as Gentleman Jim, to a marathon sixty-one-round, three-hour draw in San Francisco in 1891. Corbett said, in his autobiography, *The Roar of the Crowd*:

> That night I thought Peter Jackson was a great fighter. Six months later, still being tired from that fight, I thought him a great one. And today, after thirty-three years as I sit on the fifteenth floor of a New York sky-scraper writing this, I still maintain he was the greatest fighter I have ever seen.

Jackson was born in the Virgin Islands, began boxing in Australia and arrived in the United States in 1888, when he was already twenty-seven. He was a 6 foot 1 inch, 196 lb natural athlete who knocked out another black fighter, George Godfrey, to establish himself. He could never get an opportunity to box for the world championship, which at first was in the hands of John L. Sullivan and then Corbett, who knocked out Sullivan in the twenty-first round in 1892. It was not a colour line. It was a colour wall, impenetrable, towering above the business – and particularly the heavyweight end of it.

Corbett said his decision to take on Jackson caused great consternation even in his own family.

> It was a great blow to my father when he heard the news. He did not like the idea of my fighting a colored man. You see, when he had first come to America he had landed at New Orleans, where mixed bouts are disliked more than in any other place in the country, and he had inherited this prejudice to the full. So he wouldn't speak to me for months.

After they had fought each other to an exhausted standstill, Corbett sr. pushed his way into his son's dressing room and, ignoring the official result, proudly declared, 'You whipped the nigger!'

Corbett said he and Jackson both went to a bathhouse to ease their bruised bodies, and, as tired as they were, exchanged compliments.

John L. Sullivan, the boisterous, blustering Irish-American world heavyweight champion from Boston, Massachusetts, had no intention of boxing Jackson, and was honest enough to say so. The usual reason accepted for his refusal to countenance the idea was that he did not approve of giving a black man a shot at the world championship, which is true, but equally plausible is that he was well aware of the possibility that he could lose. And for that kind of a risk, he would want more money than any promoter could afford to pay him. He was as racist as the next white man of his time, but Sullivan also knew the value of the title he held and saw no reason in selling it cheaply.

In the end poverty broke Jackson's health and he returned to Australia when mortally sick with tuberculosis. He died in 1901, aged around forty.

In 1895 when Jackson's physical decline was becoming apparent, Charles Dana, editor of the *New York Sun*, wrote of the emergence of the black athlete as a threat to the sporting order.

> We are in the midst of a growing menace. The black man is rapidly forging to the front ranks in athletics, especially in the field of fisticuffs. We are in the midst of a black rise against white supremacy. Just at present we are safe from the humiliation of having a black man world's (heavyweight) champion but we had a pretty narrow escape. What almost happened a few months ago may happen sooner than we anticipate unless the white man perks up and follows the narrow path in his training. Less than a year ago Peter Jackson could have whipped the world – Corbett, Fitzsimmons, Choynski, Joe Goddard, Frank P. Slavin, Peter Maher or Charley Mitchell – but today he is a human wreck and thus the white race is saved from having at the head of pugilism a Negro.
>
> But the menace is still with us. There are two Negroes in the ring today who can thrash any white man breathing in their respective classes.

Dana was referring to the world featherweight champion, George Dixon, and the man he considered the uncrowned lightweight champion, Joe Walcott, who would win the welterweight title six years later.

Unlike some of his contemporaries, Dana did not doubt the courage of black fighters, instead citing an inferiority complex that at certain times, in certain individuals would surface. This was an intelligent analysis, though only partially true. Some black fighters must simply have got tired of trying when so much was loaded against them. Dana believed that recent improvements in education and the inspiration provided by those who were successful had increased the confidence of the African-American and therefore had increased the probability that he would fulfil his potential in the ring as well as out. His article carried the prejudice he might have been expected to employ but dug beneath the surface well enough. He believed he was making an accurate assessment of social circumstances.

James J. Jeffries, who held the heavyweight title from 1899 until he retired as undefeated champion in 1905, was quite happy to make his reputation at the expense of black fighters. Hank Griffin, Jeffries' first professional opponent, was a good black boxer who also worked as a sparring partner for Bob Fitzsimmons, Jeffries' predecessor as champion. Jeffries also knocked out the ailing Peter Jackson in 1898 and immediately before he challenged Fitzsimmons in 1899, he beat the capable African-American, Bob Armstrong, over ten rounds. He also fought what amounted to an exhibition over four rounds against Griffin when he was champion and he avoided Jack Johnson, when the clever Texan emerged as an eligible contender.

In 1904 interviews with the San Francisco Bulletin and San Francisco Post, Jeffries was quoted as saying of Johnson, 'What's he ever done? He has a shady record aside from being shady in colour.'

And to Johnson's manager of the moment, Tim McGrath, who had put Johnson's name forward as a challenger, he said, 'Well, you might as well forget that, because I'll never fight a nigger.'

Again, in another conversation, Jeffries said, 'Jack Johnson is a fair fighter, but he is black, and for that reason I will never fight him. If I were not the champion I would as soon meet a Negro as any other man, but the title will never go to a black man if I can help it.'

Johnson, never one to say nothing and smile sweetly, told a writer from the Police Gazette that Jeffries' way of thinking was 'bosh' and 'ridiculous'.

Marvin Hart, the Louisville heavyweight who earned recognition as champion when Jeffries retired, did fight Johnson on the way up and was awarded an arguable twenty-round points decision over him in San Francisco in March 1905. When Hart won the vacant title four months later, by stopping the light-heavyweight Jack Root in twelve rounds, a return with Johnson would have been an obvious match to make. Hart, however, would have none of it.

The previous year he had turned down a fight in Philadelphia because no white opponent could be found. 'I do know that colored men are on the fighting map,' he said. 'There are plenty of them around there about my weight but I wouldn't dare go back to Louisville if ever I got in the ring with one of them.'

He changed his mind when he saw Johnson as a stepping-stone to a world championship fight and then, having been awarded the decision he needed, said he would never box a black fighter again. When the great but tiny Joe Walcott issued a public challenge to him, he rejected it, not because Walcott was so small the match would have looked ridiculous, and he himself might have looked bad, but because as 'a Southern gentleman' it would have been wrong to take the fight.

The English writer, B. Bennison, reflected on the Johnson of 1908, and at the same time betrayed his own racial insensitivities, in his book *Giants on Parade*, written more than a quarter of a century later:

> Johnson, those days, was a normal Negro, and he was in good hands. He had not taken to strut and pose. A ten-pound note would have been as a small fortune to him then. He had not acquired a fleet of high-speed motor cars. He was just a great, big laughing coon.

Johnson hounded Hart's successor, the Canadian Tommy Burns, until in Rushcutters Bay, just outside Sydney, Australia, on Boxing Day 1908, Burns gave him his chance. He made the most of it, winning a one-sided fight that the police eventually called off as 'no longer an exhibition' in the fourteenth round, but it was a victory that was felt for generations.

'No event in forty years has given more satisfaction to the colored people of this country than has the signal victory of Jack Johnson,' was the verdict in the *Richmond Planet*.

It set off the 'White Hope' campaign and culminated in Jeffries coming out of retirement to 'restore the championship to the white race' in Reno, Nevada, on 4 July 1910.

The Johnson-Jeffries fight was huge news across the world. In Brunswick, Georgia, the seventeen-year-old Tiger Flowers would have been well aware of it.

An African-American undertaker from just up the coast in Savannah bought a return train ticket to Reno, intending to bet every cent he had on Johnson. Buttons with Johnson's photograph on them were popular in the black communities. Before the fight Jeffries told reporters:

> I'll lick this black man so badly that he'll never want to see a boxing glove again. I've had to do a lot of training to put myself in shape and I've had to give up a lot of pleasure. It's no fun for a man of my inclinations to have to deny himself everything, to knuckle down and work his blamed head off just on account of a coon.

A band played in the specially constructed arena to entertain the predominantly white crowd as they waited for the fight to begin and as the atmosphere built up. One of the jolly little ragtime numbers on their listed repertoire was called *All Coons Look Alike To Me*.

To enable his congregation to hear news of how the fight was progressing, Bishop Henry McNeal Turner of the Atlanta African Methodist Episcopal

Church installed an Associated Press wire service in his pulpit, and had the round-by-round action read out to his congregation, who must have been excited by what they heard, for Johnson handed out a one-sided boxing lesson to the old, deluded champion, who discovered to his amazement that he just didn't have it any more. The fight was eventually waved off by the promoter who doubled as referee, Tex Rickard, in the fifteenth round with Jeffries on the floor, hurt and exhausted.

Johnson's victory set off demonstrations of exuberance and recrimination, leading to lynchings, maimings and assaults across the country that left nineteen dead and 251 seriously injured. One wire service soberly reported, 'Most of the casualties were Negroes.'

At a construction camp near the small settlement of Uvalda, Georgia, halfway between Brunswick and Macon, white men shot three black workers dead and wounded five more. The chairman of the Atlanta Police Board said, 'We don't want Jack Johnson down in this part of the country... if he's wise, he will not come to Atlanta.'

No promoter in the United States wanted any part of him. Even in Britain, where no great objection had been raised when Sam Langford, the black Canadian, had knocked out British heavyweight Iron Hague in London in 1909, a proposed world title fight between Johnson and the new English star, Bombardier Billy Wells, was called off by the Home Secretary, Winston Churchill. It was to have been staged at Earls Court in October 1911, but ostensibly under pressure from the powerful non-conformist religious lobby, the Government acted to prevent it happening with only a week to spare. The arguments against the fight were ridiculously thin, one centred on the fight contract itself, another, set out by the Baptist Union in a letter to *The Times*, was a sanctimonious piece of clap-trap about 'doing the Negro race a disservice' by allowing them to take part in such unwholesome activities. A third came from the representatives of the elitist National Sporting Club, at whose Covent Garden headquarters the Langford-Hague fight had taken place. The NSC was an institution run by and for the benefit of aristocratic sporting gentlemen and assorted social climbers, and not for the ordinary boxing public.

George Swinton, an old soldier who had served the Viceroy of India and who was by then a member of the London County Council, which was the Government licensing authority involved, objected to the fight on the grounds that it would be staged, not behind the closed doors of the NSC, but in a public arena where ordinary people might be susceptible enough to be demoralised, or somehow morally tainted by it.

It was two years to the day of the Jeffries extravaganza that Johnson next managed to defend his title, against the undeserving 'Fireman' Jim Flynn in the Wild West town of Las Vegas, New Mexico (not to be confused with the modern Las Vegas in Nevada). It had been the stamping ground of Wyatt Earp, Doc Holliday and the Doc's girlfriend Big Nose Kate, of Billy The Kid and Jesse James. No doubt there were those who would have enjoyed seeing Johnson robbed in the boxing ring, but the fight was governed fairly. Flynn was way out of his depth and was disqualified in round nine for repeated, deliberate butting.

When the free-living Johnson was charged with taking a white girlfriend across a state line, he was found to be in contravention of the new Mann Act, introduced in 1910, to combat the interstate transportation of women for immoral purposes. It was designed as an attempt to curb prostitution, particularly that involving under-age girls, but the prosecution of Johnson was the first time anyone had bothered to apply it. Johnson had driven across a state line with a white, adult girlfriend, Lucille Cameron, who had indeed worked as a prostitute. Cameron refused to give evidence and the charge was dropped. However, when he did it again with another white woman, Belle Schreiber, the authorities managed to get a prosecution. Schreiber co-operated with the law-enforcers and Johnson was sentenced to a year and a day. By then, he had fled the country, first to Canada and then on to Europe.

A week before Christmas 1913, Johnson gave the black fighter, Battling Jim Johnson, a title shot over ten rounds in Paris, but it was not a major fight. Jack wasn't anything like fit, at thirty-five was already declining, and had to settle for a draw. Jim Johnson was the last black man to challenge for the heavyweight crown until Joe Louis fought James J. Braddock in 1935.

Jack eventually lost his title to the big Kansas farm boy Jess Willard in twenty-six rounds in Havana, Cuba, in 1915 and for the next two decades the white race closed itself around the championship.

Although Johnson's behaviour exasperated and annoyed some African-Americans who felt he should have been more sensitive to the task of setting an example, to others he was a hero. Eddie Futch, one of the great trainers of the last century, was born in Hillboro, Mississippi, in 1911 and recalled when interviewed in his eighties by the American writer Scoop Malinowski that he met Johnson several times. 'The first time when I was eight years old. Then, after I started boxing, he came to the gym where I was working. He was very cordial. He was a great defensive fighter with a good punch, very clever.'

For boxers like Rufus Cameron, who first taught Tiger Flowers the rudiments of the art, life was made more difficult by Johnson in that any dreams Rufus had of reaching the top and earning a fortune were destroyed before they had begun. However, as Cameron had proved, if a black man were good enough, tough enough and determined enough he could earn a better living in the short term than sharecropping, day labouring or even the railroad could provide.

Theodore Flowers also knew that he was not a heavyweight – and that there had been black champions in other weight divisions – although even when he was at the top, in the mid-1920s, there were still those who would not box him because of the colour of his skin.

A month before the Tiger's death the new light-heavyweight champion Tommy Loughran, who was born and raised in Philadelphia, refused to fight him in public. He said when he began boxing he was given permission to do so by his father on condition he never fought a black fighter. 'I gave the promise,' said Loughran. He said he had no personal objection to Flowers, but if they boxed it would have to be in a gymnasium with only newspapermen present as witnesses. In other words, it would have to be an event not worth anybody's time.

George Dixon, from Halifax, Nova Scotia, whom promoters liked to call Little Chocolate, had been the first black world champion while still in his teens. When he won a featherweight title defence against Jack Skelly, a white American, in the confines of the new Olympic Club arena in New Orleans in 1892, local newspapers were uneasy. This was the second of a three-day world championship festival that culminated in John L. Sullivan losing his heavyweight title to James J. Corbett, so that attracted most attention, but the significance of the appearance of Dixon as a world champion, fighting a white man, was not lost on the reporter from the *New Orleans Times-Democrat*, who declared it 'a mistake to match a Negro and a white man, a mistake to bring the races together on any terms of equality, even in the prize ring'. A Chicago writer observed the disquiet of the Louisiana fans as Dixon dominated the fight and knocked Skelly out in round eight. 'The sight was repugnant to some of the men from the South... the idea of sitting quietly by and seeing a colored boy pommel a white lad grates on Southerners.' In deference to Dixon's status as a world champion, the audience was mixed for the first time for a major fight in New Orleans, with blacks having their own section – that would not happen again in the city for many years. The *New Orleans Times-Democrat* concluded: 'The white race of the South will destroy itself if it tolerates equality of any kind. Negroes have their legal rights; they should have no more. Now let us have no more Negro fights here.'

Dixon and a companion were allowed back into the arena the following night to watch Corbett beat Sullivan. They were the only black people there. The Skelly fight was Dixon's first and last in the Deep South.

The mixed race issue was addressed again in Mississippi in 1897. One of Jack Johnson's biographers, Randy Roberts, recalled the reaction to a fight between a black boxer, Joe Green, and an opponent described as 'The Swede', which was stopped by a man named Henry Long, described by the *New Orleans Daily Picayune* as a 'loyal Southerner', who told the reporter:

> The idea of niggers fighting white men, why, if that darned scoundrel would beat that white boy the niggers would never stop gloating over it, and as it is we have enough trouble with them.

Joe Walcott, known as the Barbados Demon though born in what is now Guyana, had a phenomenal career spread over two decades, and claimed the world welterweight title for several years from 1901. Walcott fought out of Boston, and another early welterweight champion, who fought as Dixie Kid, was actually from Los Angeles. Joe Gans the lightweight champion known as The Old Master, boxed twice in Louisville, Kentucky, and once defended his title in Hot Springs, Arkansas, but mostly kept to his home state of Maryland, the Northern states or the west coast.

There was uproar in European sporting circles in 1921 when the French hero Georges Carpentier lost his world light-heavyweight title in unsavoury circumstances against a challenger from Senegal, known as Battling Siki. As the fight was being filmed, Carpentier agreed to put on a show for the cameras and his team made an agreement with Siki that guaranteed a knockout victory for the champion. In other words, the African agreed to take a dive. Consequently, Carpentier did not pay too much attention to training. Unfortunately for him, he upset Siki by hurting him. Siki promptly disregarded the script and charged Carpentier repeatedly, eventually knocking him out in the sixth round. When the referee declared Carpentier the winner on a foul – he decided Siki had tripped him rather than landed a legal blow – the public demonstration was so great the verdict had to be changed. Siki was announced champion.

Tex Rickard wired Siki an offer to defend his championship for $100,000 in Canada or Argentina, where there was no serious opposition to mixed race contests. He knew the United States would not accept that. In the *Los Angeles Times*, De Witt Van Court wrote that Siki could not make the impression he had made in Europe. 'The color line is too strongly drawn here and he will never be given the freedom of cafés and attention he had been accustomed to receiving in France.'

Another plan to have Siki defend in London against a white Englishman, Joe Beckett, was rejected by the Home Office. *The Times* called it a wise decision and opposed mixed fights in principle.

> To allow them to take place on English soil would, in these days, be an act of suicidal folly, and the action of the Home Office in this particular case would meet, we are convinced, with the warm approval of the general public.

Siki instead lost the light-heavyweight championship to Mike McTigue in Dublin on St Patrick's night, 17 March 1923. The decision is generally regarded as unfair but Siki was considered expendable and McTigue was Irish, from County Clare, though he fought out of New York. Afterwards he said, within the hearing of English sports writer Norman Hurst, 'I can always beat niggers.'

Siki did try his luck in the United States but was never likely to get another world title shot. Twice attempts were made to match him with Tiger Flowers, once in Atlanta, once by Tex Rickard at Madison Square Garden early in 1925. Siki told a writer from the *Chicago Defender*, 'I don't like fight colored man. Can't get big money.'

Siki, like Jack Johnson, saw no reason to play anyone's game but his own but in doing so helped and ultimately harmed no one but himself. He was murdered in Hell's Kitchen in December 1925, as he walked back to the small rented home he shared with his wife Lilian at 361 West 42nd Street.

The years did not soften the British opinion of him. At the end of the 1930s, B. Bennison, in his book *Giants on Parade*, wrote, 'Very properly, London's door was shut against him.' Bennison soberly recorded that Siki was killed, adding 'by whom nobody knew, nobody cared. A more monstrous Negro in the guise of a fighter I cannot recall'.

Even if an African-American, or black race boxer from another nation, reached the top, the long-term prospects of financial security were not good. Jack Johnson's retirement was long, but he was not wealthy. In spite of fighting in world championship contests for ten years Dixon died, penniless, of tuberculosis before his fortieth birthday. When Walcott retired he operated an elevator in a Boston hotel, was a handyman at Madison Square Garden and scraped by until his death at fifty-two when he was run over by a car in Ohio.

The prejudicial stereotype of the African-American fighter was that he was thick skulled, blessed with terrific physical strength, of inferior ring intelligence, lazy, cowardly and vulnerable to body punching. When Johnson challenged Tommy Burns for the heavyweight title in 1908, he invited Burns to hit him in the body to make a point. Burns had declared pre-fight that Johnson had a yellow streak running the length of his back.

The stigma attached to Johnson and his six and a half years as world champion left a generation of quality heavyweights in the boxing wilderness. Harry Wills, Sam Langford, Larry Gains, George Godfrey, Joe Jeannette, Sam McVey (also spelled McVea) and Bill Tate all might well have had their chance, along with others, but were excluded because of the colour of their skin.

Dempsey's employment of black sparring partners – in particular Bill Tate, but also Lee Anderson, Jamaica Kid and Panama Joe Gans, was considered outrageous by the *Baton Rouge State Times* in Louisiana, 'Every thinking white man knows the importance of absolute separation of the races in everything approaching social contact.'

As late as January 1925, in the supposedly enlightened state of California, the Commission voted to bar mixed fights. The decision was overturned on appeal the following week but the incident illustrates the breadth of resistance to allowing the black man an opening.

Wills came closest to getting his title opportunity. The New York Commission went so far as to order Dempsey to defend his title against him. However, Tex Rickard, who had promoted the Johnson-Jeffries contest in Reno in 1910 was Dempsey's promoter, and was disinclined to take on the heavyweight race issue again. Even within the three-man commission there was opposition to the fight from William Muldoon, the veteran former wrestler who had been around since John L. Sullivan's time. Muldoon hid behind the excuse of saying Wills needed to box an eliminator with Gene Tunney, but Tunney knew the truth.

He was opposed to a mixed match for the heavyweight championship. He remembered the after-effects of the Johnson-Jeffries fight. Rickard was guided by Muldoon.

Even so Dempsey was refused a licence in New York for a Tunney fight after a contract was produced showing that he had signed to box Wills in 1925. As they waited outside the commission door at the Flatiron building in Manhattan Dempsey, who usually remained polite about any prospective challenger, led his guard slip. Tunney recalled him saying, 'Wills will never get a chance at the heavyweight championship. I'll fix him.'

Dempsey, Rickard and Tunney eventually defied the New York Commission and moved their fight outside the Commission's jurisdiction. Their first fight in 1926 was in Philadelphia, the rematch a year later in Chicago. Harry Wills was just one of the worst of boxing's multitude of hard luck stories.

Thirty-five years later Dempsey said in his ghost-written autobiography *Massacre In The Sun*:

Wills was mostly a victim of bigotry. He was gypped out of his crack at the title because people with a lot of money tied up in the boxing game thought that a fight against me, if it went wrong, might kill the business... Harry's dead now. He died without ever knowing how he would have come out.

When Theodore 'Tiger' Flowers travelled to Atlanta in 1920, set on taking his boxing career as far as it would go, he was a man of Georgia as well as just one more black prize-fighter, and so would have been acutely aware of the size of the task he had taken on.

On the inside of boxing, the evidence is that a boxer is a boxer, whatever the skin colour. Black boxers were routinely a part of Jack Dempsey's training camps, in spite of his personal views about their rights to fight for titles. The great trainer Ray Arcel, who was young in the 1920s and 1930s, remembers being in Stillman's Gym in New York when pretty much everybody was broke and hungry but the black fighters would have it especially bad because of the lack of opportunities. Trainers, he said, would go out of their way to find them sparring jobs.

Trainers, too, would have the job of travelling with a fighter to prepare them and look after them when the job was done. That brought its own difficulties if the trainer was white and the fighter black. Finding an eating house or a restaurant that would at least tolerate them both was very difficult in some towns.

Paul Gallico, the *New York Daily News* boxing writer, who launched his career with a piece about sparring with Dempsey, would eventually turn away from sports altogether and write books like *The Snow Goose* and *The Poseidon Adventure*. When he saw Flowers box, Gallico was in his late twenties and still curious about boxing and still, no doubt, forming his own opinions away from the stereotypes which he had been served through his formative years. He made the naïve, ludicrous mistake of comparing African-American fighters to children, and referred to all those who managed and promoted them as unscrupulous exploiters. However, Gallico had the courage to speak out against the prejudices he witnessed. He was to write of the plight of the black American boxer as follows:

> ... he climbs into the arena to face such burning hatreds, and deep-rooted aversions, as would chill the ordinary white man. He must perform in an atmosphere of crackling hostility... The cries that come drifting over the ropes to him are laden with venom.
>
> He hears that he is yellow; he hears raucous pleas to his white opponent to hit him in the belly because he cannot take it down there; he hears that he is dirty...
>
> Often the referee curries favour with the mob by hampering him and giving the white man the breaks. If he is hit low and complains it is the releasing of a spring that touches off a storm of abuse and insults. 'Yellow, yellow, yellow!' rings in his ears. If he launches an attack on his opponent's body angry voices beat down upon him and warn him to 'keep 'em up, you...' and the rest is better unwritten...
>
> ... The men in the game will never give him a square deal... If they cannot seduce the honesty of the colored fighter, then they will defeat him in other ways. The odds he faces are almost insurmountable.

This is what the twenty-seven-year-old Tiger Flowers faced when he sat on the train as it pulled out of Brunswick station. What did he feel, what did he think as, out of the windows, the houses and streets he had known were replaced by fields, villages and small towns until eventually the city-scape of Atlanta came into view?

CHAPTER 6

'I Believe God Meant Me To Be What I Am'

Theodore and Willie Mae Flowers moved to Atlanta in search of a better life in 1920 and their daughter, Verna Lee, was born on 9 September 1921. It is possible, given a solitary reference in the aftermath of Theodore's death, that Verna Lee was adopted but the family story was that she was delivered by a local midwife and her birth was never registered. The reference to her being adopted was on 26 January 1928 in the *Atlanta Constitution*, when the initial litigation over the Flowers estate involving Willie Mae and Walk Miller was settled, 'Verna Lee Flowers, adopted daughter of the dead pugilist …'. However, public records were uneven, and the Flowers family in 1921 were not wealthy. In the 1930 census, taken on 11/12 April, her age was given as eight, which means she was born between 13 April 1921 and 12 April 1922 – and as I later discovered that she celebrated her birthday on 9 September, it would have been 1921.

By then Aaron and Lula Flowers' family had grown up. Their eldest child, Carl, married Bessie Anderson in 1919, and in June 1920, Theodore's little sister, O.C., married C. G. Williams. Both weddings took place in Brunswick.

It was in December 1923 that Theodore and Willie Mae joined Atlanta's Butler Street CME Church. It is not known at what point Theodore had switched denominations from Baptist to Methodist but not long after joining Butler Street, he became a member of the steward board. Some of the Christians who worshipped there apparently questioned, as had his mother, if his determination to box for a living sat properly with his membership of the Church. However, he convinced them. It was said that his argument was plain and simple. 'I am a professional pugilist,' he said. 'I believe God meant me to be what I am.'

The churches were a particularly important focal point for the Southern black communities. At Butler Street a part of the outreach work was the provision of meals for the homeless. When he became world middleweight champion and hit it rich, Flowers gave $1,200 to buy new chairs and make repairs and improvements to the building. He was conscious of the Biblical requirement to pay a tithe, a tenth of one's earnings, to help the church.

He also gave to Morehouse and to other black educational institutions in Atlanta.

The Colored, later Christian, Methodist Episcopal Church, to which Theodore and Willie Mae belonged, was more aligned to the Booker T. Washington ideas of gradual integration, of change by example, while the African Methodist Episcopal Church was more radical, more demonstrative and less interested in integration.

Under Walk Miller, Tiger boxed where and when he could in obscure, unreported fights on small, low-budget promotions. In the gym he trained hard but also cleaned up, washed towels, sometimes the kit of more established fighters. He learned the business from the bottom up. Officially, he was a porter and earned big city wages – all of $15 a week, three times what he had earned in the early days of his marriage in Brunswick. And then there was money from fighting. The exact dates, and sometimes the places, of his early career contests are perhaps impossible to pin down now. We know he had some under Lee Bailey in Brunswick, and Miller promoted small local shows for pin money that drew his regular clientele, but attracted minimal publicity.

On 30 June 1921, Miller wrote to Chicago promoter Harold Walsh, telling him the game was slow in Atlanta 'due to the hot weather and no outdoor place to stage shows'. Miller promised to remember Walsh's stable of boxers when he did promote again and was optimistic that the picture would brighten up. 'I am just running occasionally here with cheap talent and will not try and stage any real good shows until later in the year.'

The letter to Walsh carried a letter heading advertising 'Walk Miller's Stable of Boxers' and stating that Miller could provide 'A Good Boxer In Every Class'. The letter also promised, 'Our Boys Stay In Condition And Ready To Fight'. It was a habit Miller stuck with right up to the time he had his New York office. Then his selling point was that he managed only 'Fighters Who Fight'.

In spite of his letter to Walsh, Miller did stage a big show in August 1921, which drew a good-sized crowd at the Atlanta Auditorium, between a sixteen-year-old man-child named W. L. – known as Young – Stribling and Freddie Boorde, who claimed to be the featherweight champion of the South. Miller provided a belt for the winner, and Stribling, from Macon, won on points. Miller would promote Stribling several times, and when he reached world class, would manage him for a year.

The names of Flowers' early opponents might be recognised by a few diehard record hunters, but few others would be interested. However, men like Henry Williams, Battling Mims, Battling Hazel, Rough House Baker, Tiger Moore and Sailor Darden all had their own stories to tell. Tiger beat all of them and more. They were all black fighters operating on promotions where it was unthinkable to have black and white box each other.

Sometimes African-American boxers would more or less tour the small town circuit, fighting each other time after time to keep the paydays coming in. Even world-class men like the heavyweights Sam Langford, Joe Jeannette, Sam McVey and Harry Wills had to fight each other repeatedly, when proper sporting logic would have offered them all chances at the world championship itself. It's the way it was. Clay Moyle's meticulous biography of Langford carries the great man's most accurate fight record to date. Moyle has seventeen fights between Langford and Wills, fifteen between Langford and McVey, fourteen between Langford and Jeannette. Good black fighters were employed in seemingly ever-decreasing circles until they were worn out.

Nevertheless, they were entitled to dream.

And Willie Mae, through Edney, said her husband was, 'ambitious to the core. Indeed, he considered ambition a virtue. He felt that every man should aspire to the greatest heights possible.'

He was careful to negotiate the path he had chosen, however, without attempting to provoke trouble. He was only too well aware of the suddenness with which an African-American man's life could change in Georgia.

He was once quoted by the British writer, James Butler, as saying, 'I am a Negro man who knows his place.' He might, or might not, have said it at all, or might have said it with a heavy sense of irony that Butler did not identify, might have said it as a cold statement of fact, a blunt assessment of the social situation to an outsider from another country. Or it's equally possible that his publicity-conscious manager, Walk Miller, might have said it for him, without his knowledge.

Miller was white, a fact that gave him more room for manoeuvre in the business than could have been afforded Lee Bailey, the African-American who had promoted Tiger in Brunswick. Bailey, incidentally, did not make boxing pay. By 1930 he was working as a house carpenter.

Walker Valentine Miller was born in Bath, just outside Augusta, Georgia, on 9 September 1889, which made him Flowers' senior by less than four years. Perhaps it was the proximity in their ages that enabled their relationship to develop. They were young men together, filled with energy, ready to shake up the world, or at least their small piece of it. Miller was one of eight children and fighting his way up the financial ladder took persistence and considerable front. He had both in abundance. Miller was a born hustler, but had travelled too – in 1908, while a teenager, he had been a cyclist, appearing in Chicago, New York and, according to his syndicated obituary, Europe. He returned to Atlanta, supposedly, to set up an athletics club and his gym. Like Flowers he remained a man of the South, keeping his home in Atlanta even while he was based in New York in his peak years.

Three of Walk's brothers died while still young men. Perhaps losing Mark to tuberculosis in 1908 at the age of twenty-three, John at twenty-seven in

1918, and Royal at thirty-six, again to consumption, in 1923, made him realise how fragile a hold we have on our lives. Perhaps his need to hustle, and to act selfishly, was given focus by the untimely deaths of his brothers.

When the draft registration call came in 1917 Walk was living in Newark, New Jersey, and working as a mechanic. Three years later he was in Atlanta, running a pool hall, which could have hidden all manner of possibilities, and was living with a twenty-year-old Spanish-speaking wife, Annette. At one point he also had a job as a streetcar conductor. In the end he was just one more small guy who wanted so badly to be big time.

Jimmy Jones wrote the 1969 biography of Young Stribling, known as the Georgia Peach, who fought for the light-heavyweight and heavyweight world titles before dying as a result of a motorbike crash at the age of twenty-eight. Jones planned to write a book about Tiger Flowers, too, but as far as I know nothing came of it. Jones, who lived in Macon, Georgia, knew Miller and Flowers. It would have been a good read.

In *Ring* magazine in May 1975 Jones described Miller as a 'quiet, soft-spoken man until he was riled – and then he could be mercurial and raucous'. Jones said the impression the world had of Flowers – deeply religious, and a man of few words – was accurate.

If ever there was a model and modest gentleman in the boxing business, it was Flowers. He was studiously polite and courteous to everyone, including his opponents, and so far as it is known, did not have an enemy in a profession where enmity, and even infamy were common.

Jones said from the early part of his career Flowers attributed whatever success he had in the ring to God and carried his small Bible with him wherever he went.

If circumstances had ever allowed Flowers to box the bigger, heavier Stribling – and it was a fight that would have sold out major arenas in Georgia – the Tiger might have needed divine intervention to have had even an outside chance of winning. Stribling didn't go rushing to box black fighters and Flowers, it was said, understood the risk of boxing Stribling, so it was an academic point, but an illustration of how things were came when Stribling fought the light-heavyweight champion of the world, the Irishman from New York, Mike McTigue, in Columbus, Georgia, in October 1923.

When McTigue arrived with his Jewish manager Joe Jacobs, a longstanding injury to his right thumb was apparently bothering him. In spite of taking along with them a referee they trusted named J. Harry Ertle, McTigue grew uneasy about the atmosphere as he trained at a local military base, Camp Benning. He was used to boxing away from home from time to time, but he became acutely aware that boxing Stribling in Georgia was another matter.

Beyond the Stribling fight, McTigue was negotiating a far bigger payday against the hugely popular Frenchman, Georges Carpentier, and viewed with increasing distaste the idea that he should lose that because of any undue problems he might face in Stribling. McTigue waited until the day before the fight, then said he had broken his suspect thumb in last-minute sparring. He arrived at the office of the promoter, Major J. Paul Jones, in Columbus with his hand in a plaster cast. Understandably, Jones and his associates were not amused, and were not pacified by McTigue's assurance that he would return to fight Stribling when his thumb had healed. Free and frank discussions continued late into the night before, with nothing resolved, McTigue retired to a hotel room to get some sleep. He had not been there long when two lawmen burst in, waving guns at him. A mob was gathering outside as he was taken to Major Jones' office.

In front of McTigue, Jones grabbed Joe Jacobs and marched him to a window with a gun at his head.

'See those trees out yonder?' he said. 'Just name the one you and your fighter would like to hang from. There is one tree apiece and plenty of rope.'

Jacobs, allegedly, said: 'If you hang me, there will be some guys down here from New York that will blow this dump off the map.'

Meanwhile, a gun was being pressed into the stomach of McTigue. Broken thumb or not, he agreed to box.

Getting a reliable account of the fight is obviously difficult, and Jimmy Jones was just one who believed it was a one-sided win for Stribling, but it appears McTigue boxed mostly one-handed, using his boxing skills as Stribling waded in. Both men liked to hold and spoil – to the point where Stribling was known to some cynics as Willie the Clutch as well as the King of the Canebrakes. At the end of ten dull rounds Ertle, half of whose fee was being paid by McTigue, pointed perfunctorily to both corners, indicating a draw.

Promoter Jones was having none of that, jumped into the ring and demanded Stribling be given the verdict as the crowd bayed and whistled, remonstrated and jostled. Ertle, who was city marshal of Jersey City, New Jersey, and who had refereed the fight between Jack Dempsey and Georges Carpentier before 80,000 people at Boyle's Thirty Acres, was used to pressure, but this was something else. He refused to change his decision and left the ring, only to be forced back at gunpoint. Again, he refused to give the fight to Stribling. This time a gentleman from Mississippi, known as Captain Bob Roper, who did some fighting himself, spat in his face. Roper was a wild, unpredictable man who once tried (unsuccessfully) to spook world middleweight champion Harry Greb by draping a live snake around his neck, which was revealed when he took off his robe before the first bell.

Local newspapermen had been called into the ring by Major Jones and asked for their opinion as to who had won. As they had to live in the town it was not a surprise that they considered Stribling the winner. The ring announcer declared Stribling the light-heavyweight champion of the world and the news went out over the wires, while troops came into the arena, bayonets at the ready to break up the mêlée and send everyone in the rough direction of home. They led Ertle, McTigue and Jacobs to comparative safety, and got them out of town on a train. On the way back to New York, Ertle signed a statement confirming that his verdict was a draw and that he had not changed it even under threat.

If that was the kind of hospitality afforded a white world champion, it was obvious what Flowers would have been risking had he fought Stribling. Tex Rickard was to say Tiger would never box Stribling because he knew what the situation would be if, by some freak occurrence, he was given a fair shake of it and he won.

CHAPTER 7

'The Lord Will Sustain Me'

Tiger Flowers' boxing career has only really been documented from the autumn of 1920, when he was winning ten-round decisions over Billy Hooper and Battling Mims in the Atlanta Auditorium. Mims, from Milledgeville, the old capital of Georgia, is thought to have boxed Flowers a total of seven times – and lost the lot. Mims was tougher than Chihuahua Kid Brown from Augusta, whom Flowers knocked out in eight rounds at the Business Men's Athletic Club in Atlanta on 2 May 1921, and again, some say, only three days later inside two. Flowers also beat an obscure Canadian named Jim Fain at the same venue on 23 May 1921, this time in four rounds, when the referee was listed as one J. Walkington Miller – which sounds as if Walk was having a bit of fun. These were small, relatively obscure contests for pin money but boxing was popular and drew plenty of customers. Tiger also knocked out Whitey Black in one round, Battling Troupe in four, outpointed Battling Mims again and then took a trip to the Pekin Theatre in Savannah to knock over another obscure opponent, Jack Moore, in a couple of rounds.

The progress was checked all too soon, when he lost to a smaller but vastly more experienced fighter whose ring name was Panama Joe Gans before 4,000 fans, at the Atlanta Auditorium on 6 August 1921. It was the biggest crowd a fight had drawn in Atlanta for many years and obviously the biggest fight of Flowers' career up to that point.

Born in Barbados as Cyril Quinton, Gans was younger than Tiger, who was already twenty-eight, but knew too much, had seen too much. Quinton had lived for a time in Panama, hence the nickname, and had taken the ring name of the great lightweight champion from Baltimore, Joe Gans, in order to sell himself. Panama Joe had already got the better of Jeff Smith, who had once claimed the world middleweight title, and had won recognition as the 'colored world middleweight champion' when he had outpointed George Robinson at Madison Square Garden, New York, on 8 October 1920

The Flowers–Gans fight was delayed a week when Tiger was injured in training. Maybe he had recovered, maybe not.

Lorenzo 'Fuzzy' Woodruff, boxing writer for the Atlanta Constitution, believed that at that time Gans was one of the best welterweights in the world, who had a 'left jab that was lightning in its rapidity' and who punched 'with the accuracy of a rifle and the kick of a Tennessee mule'.

His footwork is reminiscent of the great Negro warrior from whom he takes his name, the Old Master (Joe Gans). He shifts with the speed and ferocity of Ketchel ... he does everything that is in the book for a fighter to do.

In his corner before the opening bell Flowers was not his usual carefree, smiling self, but seemed pre-occupied and serious as if he knew he might be in over his head.

Flowers won the first by a shade, on work rate, but from the second took first a boxing lesson and then a beating. He was almost down in the third, his nose bled and his eyes were puffy by the fourth, he was knocked down momentarily in round five and increasingly bloodied when he was dropped twice in the sixth, the last time by a right uppercut to the pit of the stomach and he went down to be counted out on his back by the referee, Pa Stribling.

Woodruff said the crowd got value for money, something which fans around the country would become accustomed to when they turned up to watch Flowers fight.

Though Tiger was outclassed he was not outgamed and it was just a few seconds before the knockout that he was showing an ability to hit and hit hard and find the spot too.

Woodruff suggested there was no shame for a man on the way up to lose to Panama Joe. 'Candidly, Gans is the best piece of boxing machinery that Atlanta has had the privilege of watching in many and many a day.'

Flowers regrouped on Miller's promotions and out of town. He beat Kid Williams, Chihuahua Kid Brown, William 'Battling' Gahee (twice) and Whitey Black for the second time. One of his wins over Gahee, on Miller's show at the Forsyth Street Arena, Atlanta on 17 October, was previewed in the local paper. Gahee, it was said, had impressed observers of his workouts at the Businessmen's Club. He was clever and, for a big man, fast. The report, however, shows Flowers won a hard fight. Woodruff wrote, in his eccentric style that to us now would be utterly unacceptable:

Flowers, fighting like a demon possessed, won a decision from the Memphis darkey but it wasn't until the very last ten seconds of the last round that Tiger was not in deadly peril of having his own kinky head removed. If it was a scrap, gentlemen, that's what it was, a scrap.

Gahee is a dangerous man for anybody to meet. He is a fine fighter and knows a lot but he did not know enough to solve Flowers' freakishness.

Woodruff felt the fact that Gahee was 'a bit fat' made it impossible for him to stay with the pace the Tiger set. Again, it cannot be stressed enough that although barely anyone today knows of their existence these were good, tough fighters who learned their trade.

Ten days before Christmas 1921, in what seems now a crazy piece of matchmaking, Miller put Flowers back in with Gans, who beat him again, this time in five rounds. It was as if, as far as Flowers was concerned, Miller had no interest in building a career, no particular vision of a future beyond Atlanta, or at least the South, and that his interest was in drawing a crowd and making short-term money.

True, when Theodore brought the Christmas presents home for Willie Mae and little Verna Lee, he would have known he could afford them, but he must also have been wondering, at the back of his mind, if a man as small as Panama Joe Gans could knock him out twice, what were his realistic chances of making it in the middleweight division. And for how much longer could he afford to plough so much effort into boxing for a living? Edney said Willie Mae was behind him, giving him confidence and encouragement all the way, and as Christmas 1921 moved into New Year 1922, he would have needed her encouragement more than ever. His philosophy, that overcoming trials and obstacles was the lot of man, was of course Biblical. However much he was knocked down, it was his duty as a Christian to get back up and carry on.

Enjoyment, he many times said, depends upon one's temperament. We create, to a marked degree, our own happiness and overcome that which is destined to cast a shadow over us.

Flowers took another hit when Kid Norfolk knocked him out with a right hand only thirty seconds into the third round before his own fans in the Atlanta Auditorium on 30 January 1922. Again, he was badly overmatched against a heavyweight who was good enough to beat Jack Dempsey's main sparring partner, Bill Tate, and Jeff 'Fighting Ghost' Clark. In addition to that Norfolk, an African-American from Virginia whose real name was William Ward, had only six months before hung in tough in a fierce fight with rising middleweight Harry Greb in Pittsburgh. Norfolk outweighed Greb by seventeen-and-a-half pounds and was said to have thumbed and gouged repeatedly in the clinches, which permanently damaged the sight in one of Greb's eyes. Not that Greb complained. He just thumbed him back and got on with the job of winning, which the newspapers felt he did, even though officially it was a no-decision contest. By matching Flowers against Norfolk AKA Ward at that stage of his career, Miller was either naïve, ignorant or lacking in care. Or all three. Edney said Flowers found solace in the Scriptures during the difficult days:

> … his favourite pastime was reading the Bible and getting from its pages the teachings and lessons for living a life which would be suitable to die by … he loved his master, he believed in Him. He believed that all he was or all that he aspired to be, could only be attained through Him.

No Decisions bouts littered the records of fighters from 1911 onwards in an attempt to counter the arguments of those who considered boxing to be illegal. The logic was that if boxing contests were declared exhibitions, there could be no winner unless there was a knockout, which according to the spirit of the law was officially an accident. It was nonsense, but boxing survived legally in some American states because of it. Promoters and those interested in the order and structure of the sport took to canvassing opinion among newspapermen at ringside in order to find the winner. This could only work reasonably well in major contests in major cities as local reporters were quite likely to write in favour of a local fighter, given that they had a living to earn and had to make that by maintaining some kind of relationship with the promoter and/or the boxer involved. At a higher level, there were more reporters from further afield, whose judgment was unlikely to be clouded by issues of 'friendship'. Even so, newspaper reporting of world championships could not always be relied on, which means the efforts of modern historians to work out who actually won these contests based on newspaper reports, while certainly of significant value, are to some extent flawed. Evidence for this is provided by Al Buck's column in *Ring* in April 1949, when he wrote:

> The Associated Press paid little attention to fights out of town in the No Decision years. The managers usually made their own decisions, wiring the results to the New York newspapers. Frequently their thrilling stories of ten round battles were written long before the men entered the ring. More often than not they were filed before the fight was over.

Lest Buck's claim should be considered overly cynical, he pointed out that it was not uncommon for sports editors to receive two completely contrasting reports of fights – one filed by the manager of one boxer, and one by the manager of the other. Buck quoted the old-time manager, 'Dumb' Dan Morgan, who managed the welterweight champion Jack Britton. Morgan was talking about a fight between Britton and Mike O'Dowd, one-time middleweight champion. Morgan worked out that there was only one public 'phone in the arena and four in the nearby streets. He explained:

> First I put Abe Yager in the 'phone in the club. Next I hired four fellows and put them in the 'phones in the neighborhood. I had Paddy Mullins, O'Dowd's manager, shut out, and in the papers next day Britton was declared the winner. We had a lot of fun in those No Decision days.

Stories have persisted of 'brown envelopes' being handed to journalists, which helped persuade them to write in a particular way. Certainly writers were courted by promoters to the point of being installed in all-expenses-paid hotels. Nat Fleischer admitted in 1954 that, while editor of the supposedly neutral, objective *Ring* magazine, he had worked as a publicist for the leading promoter of the 1920s, Tex Rickard, and for the company that took care of business, based at Madison Square Garden, after Rickard's death. Fleischer said that in Miami for the Jack Sharkey–Young Stribling heavyweight fight in February 1929, the company had spent more than $100,000 on publicity – and that writers had consumed $32,000 worth of liquor, in spite of Prohibition.

> We had 448 newspapermen in camp and most of them lived in the three hotels we had leased… at the expense of the Garden. Their board, food and drinks were all on the house.

It was the way it worked. No doubt Miller did his share of lobbying and 'fictionalising' reports of fights when they were away from Atlanta – but he also knew that he and Flowers were battling against the tide of prejudiced opinion. It's easy to see how difficult it was for an unfavoured fighter to break through, especially, a black man from the South, whom nobody would have thought twice about.

Maybe, even as early as 1922, Walk Miller knew he had to take chances to get Flowers noticed, which is why he put him in with Panama Joe Gans and Kid Norfolk when it should have been fairly obvious that he was not ready for such company. Or maybe Miller was learning, too, and at that point beneath his friendliness and charm just didn't worry too much if his men were knocked out as long as the crowd enjoyed the show. For his part, Flowers demonstrated throughout his career that he feared nobody. It is pretty likely that after these defeats he dusted himself down, mentally as well as physically, and waited for the next job, the next payday.

After Flowers had lost so decisively to Kid Norfolk, when Miller had an offer for him to have some fights in Mexico, they were not in a position to say no. Tiger's career was going nowhere, and so three weeks after the Norfolk knockout, he was back in the ring in, of all places, Juarez, the teeming Mexican city on the other side of the Rio Grande to El Paso, Texas. Juarez was a party town. A promoter called S. G. Gonzalez was staging weekly shows in the Garden Arena. Prohibition was in force in Texas but across the bridge in Juarez, Americans could play all they liked at joints like the Central Café, which Gonzalez owned, Harry Mitchell's, Big Kid's, Joe Miller's Castle and the Ritz Sidewalk Café. The placed buzzed. If Americans missed the midnight curfew, which was when the border post closed, they had the inconvenience of having to stay over in Juarez and party all night long. The Roaring Twenties indeed.

It was the perfect place for Flowers to make a fresh start. All that the people who watched him fight there cared about was today. Yesterday didn't matter because it had gone. Tomorrow would take care of itself. If Flowers had been knocked out in the past (and most of the 'shiny, happy people' would not have known that anyway) so what? All that mattered to the playboys and girls of Juarez was how he looked, how he fought, how dramatic and colourful he was. It was probably in Juarez that the natural showman beneath Flowers' passive personality began to emerge, with Miller's help, of course. He would go on to wear a long ring gown with a gaudy tiger's head emblazoned across it. Always popular amongst his own, he would learn how to come alive in a ring and make people of all races want to watch him again and again. In Mexico there was a far more relaxed attitude to those from other cultures. The political mood was rarely stable for long but during one of its more tolerant periods, in the summer of 1919, the former world heavyweight champion Jack Johnson, who was living there, took out an advertisement in a magazine named *Gale's*, that read:

> Colored People: You are lynched, tortured, mobbed, persecuted and discriminated against in the 'boasted' land of liberty; own a home in Mexico, where one is as good as another, and it is not your color that counts, but simply you.

Flowers' first opponent in Juarez was a scrapper named Gorilla Jones from Alexandria, Louisiana. It was scheduled for fifteen rounds for a spurious title named the South West Middleweight Championship. Flowers showed no ill-effects from the Norfolk knockout or the 1,400-mile train ride from Georgia.

'Tiger Flowers has arrived,' wrote J. H. Murray in Juarez. 'The bounding bengal from the forests of Georgia cleaned up on the middleweight Tarzan of the Mexican border and the Southwest, when he thumped 'Fighting Gorilla' Jones into submission in the ninth round.'

This fight has sometimes been recorded as a fourth round knockout but Murray was specific: 'Jones' seconds threw up the sponge in the ninth round, after Flowers had floored Jones eight times, the bell ending the fifth round saving Jones from a clean knockout.'

Jones, said Murray, was down in the first round and looked up at Flowers, astonished, while referee Paul Murdock counted. Jones tried to fight his way into it, but, 'the Tiger was always there and there always, swaying, slashing,

slashing and swaying to grimly pound Jones to the floor for knockdown after knockdown. Right now the Tiger is the fistic sensation of the border.'

Not surprisingly, Flowers stayed on. He drew over fifteen with Jim Barry, a black heavyweight from Sacramento who won as many as he lost in his long career. They fought well enough to have a rematch three weeks later, and this time Flowers made light of the weight disparity to win in five. A would-be journalist named Myron Townsend was gushing in his praise. 'No homo sapiens of flesh and blood could have possibly withstood the Tiger's fierce onslaught for more than a few rounds.'

Townsend was attentive enough to provide some detail. He said referee Carl J. Studer, later if not then a friend of Walk Miller's, refused to allow them any rest time on the inside and prevented any clinching by prising them apart. That would have suited Flowers, as it allowed him to move in and away again without having the inconvenience of Barry using his weight to lean on him for any length of time. Flowers' volleys of punches from a crouching stance at close range, and then his long range boxing, were too much for Barry, who collapsed in the fifth from a left hand to the stomach and right to the jaw. He struggled to get up, but his legs quivered and he sank back down.

> After seconds had carried Barry to his corner, he threw up his supper and writhed in agony when he was trying to recover his senses… He came here with the reputation of being an iron man but Flowers quickly put him in the melting pot and the metal in him ran red…

Townsend did not understand the boxing scene enough to put Flowers' performances into full perspective – beating the likes of Gorilla Jones and Jim Barry did not make the Tiger anything like a world class middleweight – but in his favour he was bold enough to take on the issue of race and predict that he might have the character to beat the system.

> If Flowers wasn't of African lineage he would already be recognized as one of the world's greatest and he may yet rise above race color and previous condition of servitude, for he is quite a gentlemanly fellow and knows his modest pedestal in his niche of the hall of fame. Possibly he may be another George Dixon or Joe Gans or Joe Walcott, who will fight his way to the top, despite racial handicaps.

Townsend also identified Flowers' ability to entertain and excite, though his claims of genius were premature.

> His boxing style is nothing more than brilliant. In his fighting methods and in his ring personality he's original and unique. He's a genius in attack. His delivery astounds spectators.

In between the Barry fights, Tiger knocked out old rival Chihuahua Kid Brown in the first round. Boxing in Juarez was good, profitable work. He could send regular money home to Willie Mae in Atlanta and begin to invest.

Boxing in the early 1920s was uncompromising, sometimes brutal. There was nothing in the way of established safety regulations, nobody seemed to think too much of the cost of being in too many hard fights or of being knocked out. There was no apparent interest in the possibility that boxing could lead to either acute or chronic brain damage. A man could be knocked out as many days in a row as he chose if he was crazy enough to keep on climbing into the ring. Flowers would have thought little of it, but it is impossible to ignore now that he boxed Lee Anderson for the 'colored light-heavyweight title' in Juarez on 9 May 1922, and was knocked out in the seventh round. Only one week later he was back, winning a fifteen-round decision over Frankie Murphy, another Atlanta boxer who had travelled across the border. They were fighters working a circuit, entertaining and earning as often as they could. And if they fought hurt, still bruised or cut, or even slightly concussed, from their previous job, well, who worried about it? Sometimes managers looked after fighters thoughtfully, given the norms of the time, but others were little more than purveyors of meat.

Just as with Panama Joe Gans and Kid Norfolk, there was no disgrace in the Flowers of that time losing to an experienced light-heavyweight as good as Lee Anderson, who was talented enough to have fought the fading great Sam Langford half-a-dozen times in the past eighteen months.

Nat Fleischer did not share the stereotypical views of so many of his contemporaries about black boxers lacking heart or being vulnerable to body punches, or being in any way less intelligent in the ring than white fighters. Fleischer wrote in his ground breaking, five-volume *Black Dynamite*, 'Stocky Lee Anderson was one of the toughest Negro fighters of his time. Not a clever boxer, he was aggressive, rugged, dead game and a good hitter...'

Fleischer was under the impression that Anderson was from Arizona, although others suggest he may have been a Georgia native. He stood around 5 foot 9 inches, and scaled around 175 lbs. In 1921 he had been one of Jack Dempsey's sparring partners when the world heavyweight champion made an exhibition tour of the country. Fleischer wrote:

> This was a good indication of Lee's durability under fire, for Dempsey seldom pulled his punches, even in workouts, and a fighter had to have an ample supply of ruggedness and ability to stand up before him.

After at least seven fights in three months in Juarez, Tiger Flowers returned to Atlanta, perhaps because his story there had run its course, perhaps because he missed home and felt he had been away from his family long enough.

Sam Langford, the next fighter to play a part in the Flowers story, remains one of the greatest boxers in the history of the business. He was a descendent of a slave who fled north during the American War of Independence and settled in Nova Scotia. Langford was short – around 5 foot 7 inches – yet had the ability and power to become a contender anywhere from middleweight to heavyweight. The trouble was that he was too good for his own good, he lacked the right connections – and of course he was black. He fought Jack Johnson in 1906, conceded nearly 30 lbs but climbed off the floor in round six to last the full fifteen round distance. Johnson held the 'colored' heavyweight title at the time, but conquered the divide between the races when he defeated Tommy Burns in Australia on Boxing Day, 1908. A rematch between Langford and Johnson in 1909 or 1910 would have been an important fight in terms of the state of the heavyweight division, but commercially it had little attraction. Consequently, Johnson had no interest in it. The boxing world, anyway, was consumed by the search for a 'White Hope' rather than in wasting time on another black man. In 1912 Langford had to sit aside as Fireman Jim Flynn, whom he had knocked out twice, fought Johnson for the title.

Langford would willingly have fought for the middleweight championship, and claimed it at one point, but was kept at a distance there as well. The closest he got was a relatively meaningless six round no decision contest with world champion Stanley Ketchel in April 1910. When Ketchel was shot dead later that year, four contenders were named to sort out a successor. Langford was not included.

He beat most of the great fighters of his day – and his day lasted a very long time. By the early 1920s he was losing his sight but knew of no other way of making a living. Even with blurred vision, he had far too much ring craft and power for most of the young pretenders who attempted to use him as a stepping-stone.

When he was matched with Flowers at the Ponce De Leon Ballpark in Atlanta in a rain-delayed fight on 5 June 1922, the half-blind, thirty-nine-year-old Langford had already spent the first half of the year, as he had most other years, on the road looking for work. He had stopped off in Ashland, Kentucky; in Memphis, Tennessee; in Dayton, Ohio; in Nashville and Indianapolis. He arrived in Atlanta less than two weeks after a ten round bout in Chicago, and a further two weeks later would be boxing in Jack Johnson's home city of Galveston, Texas.

The wooden Ponce De Leon Ballpark, north east of downtown across the road from a funfair, was the home of the Atlanta Crackers minor league baseball team. Fifteen months later it would burn down, but when Flowers fought Langford there it held around 8,000 people in the stands and, obviously, more on the pitch. It was an ambitious venue for a promoter to stage a fight between an ancient contender and a local hopeful who had made encouraging progress in Mexico, but whom Atlanta fans would remember as vulnerable. Before the fight Bill Hooper, working the Flowers corner after boxing Roughhouse Ware on the undercard, warned Tiger that if he let Langford get his big punch on target he was coming out of there 'feet first'.

Flowers made a typical start, blazing forward, throwing streams of punches, some solid and some of which looked as if they were slaps – that is, delivered with the inside of the glove, or with the glove open. The crowd got behind him, yelling and cheering, as he dominated the first round. Langford looked old and slow. At one point Langford poked out his jaw and laughed as if to taunt Flowers about a lack of power after punches had crashed against his head. Boxers have a way of lying in the ring, of double bluffing. Was Langford really hurt, or just trying to lure Flowers into making mistakes? Whatever the truth of that, Langford finished round one with a bruised eye. Cliff Wheatley, for the *Atlanta Constitution*, thought Flowers had thrown about one hundred punches in the first three minutes.

> At the end of the opening stanza... it seemed that Langford wouldn't be able to land a solid punch all night and it was very plain that he had no way of preventing Flowers from landing whenever he wanted to.

However, all was not as it seemed. It was said that Langford told his cornerman between rounds, 'This boy's making mistakes and if he goes on making them, we're going home early.'

At the start of round two Langford came forward but still Flowers peppered him with a barrage of around twenty punches before they clinched. Then, on the inside, perhaps when Flowers was not only still but in focus, Langford landed some body punches and, as they parted, smashed in a short right to the jaw. Flowers probably neither saw nor felt it. He crashed back, his legs and senses all over the place. He tried to get up, but was still crouching, his gloves touching the canvas when referee John Glenn completed the count. According to Wheatley's ringside observation, Flowers 'saw nothing and heard little until approximately a minute later when his seconds finally brought him back to life.'

At that moment it must have seemed as if Flowers was heading for the boxing scrapheap.

Wheatley wrote that while Langford's 'legs aren't at all what they used to be and his waistline is several inches larger than his chest, "Tham" still knows how to chop and he is still a master in timing'.

After the fight an Atlanta doctor told Langford he was risking permanent blindness by carrying on boxing. He didn't stop until 1926, when at the age of forty-three, in Drumright, an oilfield town in Oklahoma, he was beaten in one round by a local trier named Brad Simmons. Langford just could not see any more. In 1944, the *New York Herald Tribune* carried an article named 'The Forgotten Man' by sportswriter Al Laney. He had found Langford living in a shabby third floor hotel room on 139th Street in Harlem, just a block away from where Flowers had a home in his peak years. Old Sam was blind, and spent his days listening to the radio.

If Tiger Flowers felt like doing something else for a living after Langford had knocked him out, effectively humiliated him in front of his own people, it did not show. A month later he was in Memphis – to fight Kid Norfolk, who had knocked him out at the start of the year. This time, against most expectations, Tiger did better and earned himself an eight round draw.

Later in that month of July 1922, however, he lost in the second round to Jamaica Kid in Covington, Kentucky. The Kid was a quick middleweight from New York City, supposedly born in British Honduras [now Belize], who would be a good sparring partner to top class fighters but no more than that. Of all Flowers' inside-distance defeats this was probably the worst. As entertaining as he was, he just didn't seem to have either the defensive skill or the punch resistance to go any further.

Four weeks later he had taken some kind of refuge over the border in Juarez, where not too many would have known about his defeats by Langford and Jamaica Kid, and more would have remembered his exciting, largely successful stay earlier in the year. In Mexico they did not bother themselves about any moral, social or political implications of mixed race bouts.

Andy Palmer, an Italian from Arizona whose real name was thought to be Andrea Palermo, was a useful opponent, but on 22 August 1922, Flowers outworked him over fifteen rounds for a decision in front of several thousand fans. Hy Scheider of the *El Paso Times* wrote:

> Flowers won so far off by himself that it looked like a one-man fight. And it was a solitary slamming session from the sixth round to the finish… Palmer put on his poorest exhibition. He was soggy in the seventh round. He was sluggish in the eighth and he froze up steadily from then on to the finish. The further they went, the further away the Negro galloped on points against his white opponent…
>
> In a nutshell, Palmer was surprised by Flowers and his willingness to mix at all times and the crowd was disappointed in Palmer's poor showing. So was Palmer.

When timekeeper John McIntosh rang the bell at the end Palmer ignored referee Carl J. Studer, turned on his heels and walked to his corner, where he sank down heavily on his stool, his head in his hands. When his trainer spoke to him, Palmer got up and left the ring. Hy Scheider scored the fight 11-2-2 in rounds to Flowers, with just the first and sixth to Palmer.

The *El Paso* writer said the money from this fight would enable Flowers to telegraph payment on 'the last of the little farms he has taken over in Georgia'. What these farms were is unclear but there is a photograph in the Edney biography of Flowers of him standing in an orchard, captioned 'Gathering peaches on one of his numerous farms'. It is probable that as early as 1922 Flowers was in the process of buying land that would be worked by black tenant farmers in order to secure his family's income. Information may still come to light but I was unable to discover where the land Flowers is said to have bought lay.

Sometime later, Myron Townsend, who had given Tiger such glowing reports in his first stay in Juarez, wrote in the *El Paso Herald* that Palmer was asked back by promoter S. G. Gonzalez and cabled back the reply, 'I will accept your terms. Will fight anybody but Tiger Flowers.'

Townsend also said a light heavyweight from New Orleans, 'Happy' Littleton, said the same thing to Gonzalez. Townsend may have had his suspicions over the veracity of the telegrams, as he wrote that they were 'so near alike that they could have been worded by the same man'.

After the worst defeat of Flowers' career had come the best win. He was already twenty-nine years old, but at last was attracting crowds and he moved on from Juarez to Memphis and then on to the Coliseum Arena in New Orleans as 1922 drew to a close where, on 13 December, he stopped another Palmer, Eddie this time, at the end of the tenth round. The fight drew 3,000 fans, who saw Palmer badly beaten before he quit.

Flowers left New Orleans immediately and took the train back to Juarez – a little matter of 980 miles – where three days before Christmas he won a wild fight with Frank Carbone of Brooklyn on a tenth round disqualification. According to Nat Fleischer, writing many years later, Carbone was brought in especially 'by a bunch of gambling sharp-shooters'. This was by far the most groundbreaking win of Tiger's career to that point, one that suddenly took him on to a fresh level.

Walk Miller's contact for the Juarez fights was Nick Sollitto, who had moved there from Brooklyn to make a fortune from the good times. Sollitto, who was referred to erroneously in the *El Paso Times* as Flowers' manager, had known Frank Carbone for years. Flowers, as he had already proved, didn't care who he fought. Carbone was sturdy, strong, tempestuous – and not untalented. It was not unreasonable to believe that he could do what the likes of Lee Anderson, Panama Joe Gans and the Jamaica Kid had done; knock Flowers out.

They went toe-to-toe from the first bell. The opening round was punch for punch in the centre of the ring for the whole three minutes. As the relentless pace went on, the more it suited Flowers. Carbone couldn't hurt him and began to fade. One story said it was Flowers who began the butting in round ten, but that made no sense. He was winning the fight anyway. More likely is Fleischer's version that Carbone, knowing he was losing, butted Flowers repeatedly and the tame referee, Curley Joe Morgan, imported from Cleveland for the gambling sting, did nothing about it. Eventually Carbone butted Flowers hard enough to drop him, then landed another punch as the Tiger sat on the canvas. It really does seem from this distance that, for whatever reason, Carbone wanted out of the fight. Maybe there was a counter sting going on, or perhaps Frank was just at the end of his tether physically and emotionally. The referee hesitated, not sure whether to follow orders or to pay more attention to the mob of fans who had paid to see a fair fight and who were gathering with a considerable degree of menace at ringside. Eventually S. G. Gonzalez told the referee, Morgan, to make a decision, and he disqualified Carbone. The fans were still angry and the police, some in plain clothes, had to dive in amongst the crowd to escort Carbone from the arena. They did not do much of a job. One version is that someone in the crowd hit Carbone over the head with the butt of a gun, while Fleischer insists Carbone did not understand that he was being taken to safety by the police and laid into them, which provoked one of the lawmen to crack him on the skull with his gun. Fleischer, in a rare show of wit, said Carbone was knocked into 'a transportable commodity' and was so deeply unconscious that he had to be taken straight to the local hospital. As the police carried him along the road, they saw that all he had on was one boxing boot, one glove and a bit of hand-wrap dangling from the other fist. The rest had been torn off by the angry customers. Fleischer wrote:

> Throughout the entire riot, the coolest person in the arena was probably Tiger Flowers. When the row started, he retired to his corner, donned his bathrobe and sat there at his ease, watching the progress of hostilities. Nobody molested him.

The El Paso Times, which carried the message across its front page 'The Sun Is Shining For You In El Paso', said Flowers was now the biggest drawing card in the area.

Perhaps Christmas and New Year at home, or maybe some effects of the Carbone fight at the end of a tough year, delayed Tiger's return to the ring until 21 February 1923, just after he had turned thirty. Then he boxed two relatively low key eight round fights, points wins over 'Fighting' Bob Lawson, and his early career rival Battling Mims, in Nashville. Lawson was a black light-heavyweight known as The Alabama Bear, but who lived for a time in Atlanta, and knew Flowers from Walk Miller's gym. They had posed together for a portrait in 1920, wearing suits and ties. Flowers stayed on in Nashville to knock out 'Evansville' Jack Ray on 19 March.

A month later, on 20 April 1923, Flowers was in Toledo, Ohio, the town south of Detroit made famous four years before when Jack Dempsey won the world heavyweight title there from Jess Willard. Flowers was no doubt anxious to prove himself a little more than he usually was – the opponent Miller had found for him was Jamaica Kid, who had stopped him in two rounds in a shocking result the previous year. This time they went twelve rounds to a no decision. The newspaper verdict, from writers who would have had no obvious bias either way, was that Flowers had won easily. *Toledo Times* sports writer Lou Klewer was impressed.

> Coming with the speed of a whirling tropical hurricane, Tiger Flowers, the Dixie Demon, tore into Jamaica Kid in the twelve-round final of the colored boxing show at the Coliseum last night and decisively defeated the former sparring partner of Jack Dempsey. Jamaica Kid never had a chance. Flowers hit him with every punch known to the boxing world, and created a few wallops on the spur of the moment.

The Jamaica Kid did well to get through to the final bell. After absorbing an accidental low blow in the fourth, after which he was given five minutes to recover, he was put down on his knees in the eighth and floored again for a count of five with a hard left to the head in round eleven. The local fans jeered him when he was repeatedly warned for hitting on the back of the head by local referee Ollie Pecord, the Toledo referee who had worked the brutally one-sided Dempsey-Willard heavyweight title fight in 1919. Pecord incidentally, had been a professional baseball player and then a prizefighter himself in the 1890s. Klewer reported that after the show a number of people called promoter Ed Harris to ask for Flowers to be brought back.

Flowers' three-year contract with Miller had expired in March and neither man had rushed to renew it. However, the Tiger was attracting attention now for his performances on the 'black circuit' and for the win over Carbone. Miller put out a story published in the *Atlanta Constitution* on 3 May 1923 that a promoter in Juarez, presumably S. G. Gonzalez, had offered Flowers a signing-on fee of $1,000 plus a 200-acre ranch, while a well-known but unnamed manager in Toledo had offered him large sums of cash to sign for him, and another businessman in Atlanta had tempted him, without success, with a $2,500 signing-on bonus. However, according to this story, Flowers had told Walk, 'I don't like having these gentlemen worrying me about a contract, as I want to fight for you as long as we both live or I am able to box.'

At another time the offer to take his family to Mexico, where African-American people were welcomed, might have been attractive but there was still too much work to be done, too many ambitions left unfulfilled.

Accordingly, a new contract was drawn up. It bound Flowers to Miller for life and was, according to the *Atlanta Constitution*, proof of the fighter's greatest asset, his strong, loyal character. That may have been so. Flowers may have trusted Miller with his life. Or it might have been a case of 'better the devil you know'...

Perhaps the reality of what he had just signed hit Flowers hard and fast, and perhaps not, but it was no time at all before Miller over-stretched him again. Maybe the fact that he had improved enough to iron out his record by dominating Jamaica Kid persuaded Miller to gamble – or maybe Walk just didn't see the point in turning down paydays. Flowers was basically working the circuit, fighting whoever was available. A rematch with Kid Norfolk wasn't the wisest move Miller might have made, but then good judges felt Norfolk was declining and Flowers improving. Perhaps the decisive issue was that the job, in Springfield, Ohio, on 8 May 1923 was for the 'colored light-heavyweight title' and therefore meant it was worth a little more money. Norfolk had knocked out Flowers in three rounds in Atlanta, but to be fair to Miller they had drawn a return over eight in Memphis. However, Flowers boxed around the 160 lb mark and Norfolk was a natural light heavyweight (175 lbs) who was used to taking on heavyweights. With the light-heavyweight title on the line over twelve rounds, Norfolk was more likely to make sure he was in top shape. And yet again, just as Flowers seemed to have turned a corner in his career, he fell apart. Norfolk knocked him out, referee Matt Hinkel completing the count after only two minutes fifty seconds of the first round.

Not that Tiger had time to dwell on it. Only seven days later he was back over the border in Juarez, where he showed no ill-effects as he pounded out a fifteen round points win over an obscure but durable enough Sailor Tom King.

And only ten days after that, Walk Miller rolled him out in Toledo against Panama Joe Gans for the 'colored middleweight championship'. It was a punishing schedule, the kind of which no modern-day boxer would contemplate, but it seems to have had no impact on him. He ignored his previous defeats by Gans and steamed into him, and there was nothing Gans could do to keep him off. Gans even tried to hit him low to slow him down, and butted him, to the point where Ollie Pecord, the referee, offered Flowers a disqualification victory on three separate occasions. This was a common practice in those days. Few would have thought it unsporting of Flowers to have accepted the offer, but he didn't make the decisions, Walk Miller did, and Miller was confident Tiger could win the championship by knockout, and so declined. Gans was durable enough to cope, however, and lasted the distance to keep his dubious championship on the 'No Decision' rule. By common consent Panama had lost every round which illustrated amply the nonsense of the situation. Flowers drew national media attention for that performance, a fact that was referred to in a preview of his next fight, at the Bijou Ring Arena in Nashville against none other than his first teacher, the heavyweight Rufus Cameron. An unnamed local reporter said Flowers had already convinced Nashville fans of his quality, and was popular among African-American audiences wherever he went because of his whirlwind style. 'He is in big demand in all parts of the country and is drawing record houses for colored fights.'

Ad Thatcher, the Toledo promoter who had staged that great Dempsey-Willard fight in 1919, said he would bet $5,000 that Flowers could beat new world champion Harry Greb.

Flowers conceded 38 lbs to Cameron but fought his typical all-action battle and at the end of ten rounds was a clear points winner. It was a tough night, though, and Cameron must have tested his resolve, for Henry Grady Edney refers to something Flowers said in the fight. It is not known at what point it happened, but according to Edney he had need to tell himself, 'The Lord will sustain me.' The *Atlanta Constitution* writer was in no doubt, however, about Flowers' superiority. 'He took every round... and twice had the big fellow down for the count of nine. The bell saved him (Cameron) in the fifth round.'

Twice in July 1923 Flowers beat James 'Tut' Jackson over twelve rounds, at the Atlanta Auditorium and again in Springfield, Ohio. Jackson was a decent young heavyweight from Ohio, so it is not out of the question that they agreed to box in Flowers' home city first, then for the return to be in Jackson's territory. Jackson stood about 6 foot 1½ inches and scaled somewhere around 192 lb, neither of which appeared to bother Flowers in the slightest. They were travelling the same bizarre, bruising journey and, as always for any of these men, work was work. Jackson, like Flowers, had been thrown in deep. In what must have been a traumatic week in November 1922, 'Tut' had been knocked out by Sam Langford, again by former contender Carl Morris, and then by Jack Dempsey's main sparring partner, Big Bill Tate.

The *Atlanta Constitution* preview of the first fight refers to Tiger as 'the uncrowned colored middleweight champion of the world', a reference to his dominant performance against Gans. The local writer also declared that over the past year he had won the middleweight and light-heavyweight championships of Mexico, the light-heavyweight championship of Australia. He and Jackson topped the bill with Rufus Cameron matched against Kid Brown in the preceding bout, with two other ten-round contests between white boxers held earlier in the evening.

> Special arrangements have been made to take care of the crowd, separate entrances having been provided for colored patrons on the Gilmer Street side of the auditorium. Special box offices handle the tickets to the colored sections.

Walk Miller had been thumping the tub, announcing that the fee he was paying Jackson was the highest guarantee ever paid for a fighter in Atlanta.

Several 'out of city' newspapers sent writers to report from ringside. Advance ticket sales had been so good that Miller worried about ticket scalps buying them and carrying out their parasitic business of selling them on at inflated prices. The Atlanta police busied themselves outside the arena making sure ticket touts were not in evidence.

The fight is recorded in most sources as a twelve-round points win for Flowers, but the *Atlanta Constitution* recorded that Miller altered it effectively to a No Decision contest when the boxers were in the ring before the first bell. The local writer was annoyed. There was, apparently, no hint of the alteration in status until Miller announced himself that if the fight went the distance there would be no decision, that it would be accepted as a draw.

> A last minute arrangement through which the Tiger Flowers-Tut Jackson bout was turned into a no decision affair last night at the Auditorium robbed the former of as clean-cut a verdict as we have seen earned in an Atlanta arena in some years, as Flowers lashed his much heavier opponent around the ring through every one of the twelve rounds the struggle stretched.

He declared it 'manifestly unfair' to Flowers, whose ambition was to go as far as he could in boxing. Miller's reason seems flimsy. Jackson had come in ten pounds above the agreed weight of 175 lb at the ceremony at 3 p.m. on the day of the fight, but why that in itself worried the promoter is unclear. He showed no compunction at all in putting Flowers in against heavyweights on other occasions.

Flowers made the weight difference work for him, using as the writer put it 'his dazzling speed and condition and queer boxing style' to dominate the fight. The best round was the eighth when he sent Jackson reeling back into the ropes with a right hand.

Morgan Blake, in the *Atlanta Journal*, said Jackson took a severe pasting. Afterwards Billy Palmer, Jackson's manager, called Flowers wonderful and the 'fastest piece of fighting machinery I ever saw'.

In the rematch in Ohio according to Ralph E. Quick of the *Springfield Sun,* 'the Georgia cyclone hit Jackson with everything but the ring posts' in the opening round – and then kept up his work rate as Jackson boxed with increasing caution, apparently intent on curling up in a defensive shell and seeing the torture through'.

Before July was out, Flowers had taken another newspaper No Decision 'verdict' over a modestly talented opponent boxing under the name of Whitey Black at the Danceland club, which was mostly known as a music venue, at the intersection of Forest and Woodward on Detroit's West side. A local writer, Lloyd Northard, was miffed that Flowers appeared to carry Black for the full ten rounds. Black was an obscure figure, but Tiger had beaten him twice before, once inside a round, and did not appear to try too hard to hurt him this time. It appears that pre-fight there had been speculation that this was not a good match and that matchmaker Walter Langlois and both managers had to assure everyone that the fight was for real and would be competitive. Once the bell rang, though, it seemed as if Tiger wasn't exactly exerting himself.

> Flowers had Black ready for the finishing punch in every round from the third to the tenth, but his alleged tiger tendencies never asserted themselves... While Flowers' intention was to be charitable to Black, it looked to many that it would have been much more merciful to have knocked him out earlier in the match instead of lacing him the way he did. 'Lady Luck', or some person overflowing with the milk of human kindness, came to Black's rescue in the fourth round. A hard right over the heart dropped Black to one knee, and he stayed down for the count of eight. As he came to his feet, scarcely able to stand, the lights suddenly went out, plunging the place in darkness. It was at least three minutes before the lights were turned on again and Black had regained some of his strength.

There was a story, possibly apocryphal, of a fight somewhere in Ohio (the incident does not fit his acknowledged record, so it's impossible for the time being to pin it down) when Flowers was warned off winning against a white opponent. This account was attributed to an old trainer named Harry Wyle in Muhammad Ali's notoriously unreliable autobiography from the 1970s, *The Greatest, My Own Story*. Wyle tells of the time Flowers was paid a visit by town deputies, who warned him that if he won he would not leave town alive. He refused to throw the fight, speaking softly and civilly, as they attempted to provoke him. He knocked out his opponent in the third round, was booed from the hall, and as the deputies closed in on him, he escaped by climbing out of a restroom window, still in his boxing gear, and got out of town on a freight train. The inference was that if he had not had the brains and luck to flee so promptly, he could well have been lynched. Maybe it happened, maybe it did not, but given the situation it would not have been a surprise to discover Wyle was telling the truth.

It is always pertinent to remind ourselves just how difficult it was for an African-American to do a job that entailed travelling because of the places he could not go to, the restaurants he could not use, the hotels he could not sleep in. It seems as if Flowers and Miller avoided talking about the situation, perhaps because as men of Georgia they understood it and accepted it. Flowers was never a man to create a fuss but the likelihood is that if he was in pain or hurt after the fight, it would not have been Miller who looked after him, who applied the compresses, but a black trainer or second, who remained in the background.

By August 1923, America had a little more to concern itself with than boxing. The government was in turmoil. Warren Gamaliel Harding, the twenty-ninth President, died suddenly of a stroke in San Francisco at the age of fifty-seven. It was said Harding had struggled to control and comprehend the corruption that surrounded him. He once said, 'My God, this is a hell of a job. I have no trouble with my enemies...

 my goddamn friends, they're the ones that keep me walking the floors at nights.'

Nevertheless he thought nothing of inviting those same friends to the White House for nights of poker and bootleg whisky, and of smuggling his mistress, Nan Britton, into an anteroom for their mutual pleasure.

Even allowing for their natural conservatism, and traditional support of the Republican party, Theodore and Willie Mae, along with so many African-Americans, probably felt isolated by Harding's almost disinterested, procrastinating Government. Lawyer and Democrat William McAdoo said a Harding speech was an army of pompous phrases moving across the landscape in search of an idea. Alice Roosevelt Longworth, daughter of Theodore Roosevelt, said, 'Harding was not a bad man. He was just a slob.'

Vice-president Calvin Coolidge took the oath as Harding's replacement. Within a fortnight he had witnessed a massive step forward in the conditions endured by workers in the United States steel industry. The old creed of working men as hard as possible for as long as an employer felt it justified was outlawed. From 13 August 1923, eight hours constituted a day's work.

However, the Flowers family, while acknowledging the value in the sentiment, probably considered Coolidge's capitalist creed bordering on the blasphemous. 'The man who builds a factory,' said Coolidge, 'builds a temple, and the man who works there, worships there.'

Flowers was constantly on the move. The death of an incompetent president and a change in the working practice of ordinary men may well have been a talking point for him, but he had his own job to do. It brought its own problems on the road because of the need to find accommodation where he was accepted, the part of town where he was safe to walk or do his roadwork, the gym that would welcome him. It was still a problem even in major cities in the fifties and sixties, let alone in some of the smaller, out of the way towns. Sometimes it must have been a relief for Flowers to box at home but that never lasted long.

When he did get a break in order to box at the Coliseum in Atlanta, on the Labor Day holiday weekend of 4 September 1923, he confirmed his superiority over Jamaica Kid, described in a preview by the local *Constitution* as 'one of the ring's most rugged fighters'. Ed Danforth from the same newspaper marvelled at the Jamaica Kid's ability to withstand the punishment Flowers laid on him, and saw why Dempsey had employed him as a sparring partner.

How it went the distance remains a mystery to the ring patrons, for during each of the dozen sessions Flowers jabbed, slammed, hooked, punched, crossed, uppercut, boxed and fought practically without return. Jamaica Kid weathered it all. Nothing but a hardy human stamina kept him alive.

Today the fight would probably have been stopped as too one-sided to have any further point, which is why of course, modern fighters often have a higher percentage of inside-the-distance wins on their record. Such sensitivities did not bother the sporting men of the 1920s. Danforth did not worry that Flowers had failed to knock out a so-thoroughly beaten man, instead considering his form a revelation. Danforth had probably seen Flowers as he was gaining experience, had probably seen him knocked out along the way, and maybe had never really considered him as a potential top class operator. Now, he revelled in what he had seen.

His speed was dazzling. His style remains a mystery from gong to gong. One minute he was orthodox. The next session he was slamming backhanded swings [not then illegal in Georgia rings] and coming in with a left that traveled from nowhere, always to the point of Jamaica Kid's iron chin.

Miller had talked optimistically of taking Flowers to Cuba but chose Mexico instead. Only thirteen days later, on 17 September 1923 the elation of Tiger's impressive performance against Jamaica Kid was followed by crushing disappointment as he lost a match in strange circumstances. He retired after five rounds against the ancient, white heavyweight contender Fireman Jim Flynn in Mexico City, where Flynn had been based for several months. Whether the journey or the altitude got to Flowers, or he just wasn't himself for some reason not easily identifiable or some darker forces were at hand, we cannot know, but it was not like the Tiger to pull out meekly because of a damaged hand, which was the reason given. It was said he broke his hand in the second round, but he had won all five of the completed rounds and wasn't in any apparent trouble from anything the cumbersome Flynn was doing. He was out of the ring for ten weeks afterwards to let the hand heal, but unless it was an unusually severe break that would not in itself have forced him to stop boxing for that long. Perhaps it was his mind that had to heal as well as the hand. Maybe is all we have but it is possible there was pressure brought to bear on him – the fight was only two days after martial law was declared in Oklahoma because of the rising level of Ku Klux Klan-inspired racial violence. However strong a man is, sometimes he is simply not strong enough. Perhaps, for once, Flowers had no choice but to forfeit a win he was surely capable of achieving. After all, Flynn was a washed-up forty-four year old, who a generation before had unsuccessfully challenged both Tommy Burns and Jack Johnson for the world heavyweight title. Fireman Jim was strong, but fighting someone of Flynn's bulk would not normally give Flowers a second thought. Sometimes there are results that simply defy logic and this is one of them.

Flowers did not box again until 27 November 1923, when, back at home at the Atlanta Auditorium, Miller put him in with the capable veteran African American, George Robinson, who had fought somewhere around a hundred fights. Perhaps Tiger was still out of sorts and perhaps the hand was still troubling him. Again, we cannot be sure why he fought badly, but the official result was a draw.

He knocked out his old friend, Rufus Cameron, in the fourth round, in Albany, New York, on 6 December and back at the Atlanta Auditorium, three days after Christmas 1923, he outpointed Clarence 'Sailor' Darden over twelve rounds. Darden, from Virginia but at this time based in Boston, was another black boxer he had beaten in his early days. The fight was eagerly anticipated locally in that it drew previews in the *Atlanta Constitution* for four days. Darden, training in a room above the Tudor Theater, 'proved himself to be clever and shifty afoot, experienced and rugged'. Flowers worked out at 2 p.m. every day at Miller's premises, by now on Marietta Street. The theory ran that Darden's slick style might give Flowers problems, but in the end Darden, as capable as he was, couldn't keep the Tiger away. Local writer Henry Allen called the beating Darden received as 'a whirlwind whipping'. He said that for once Flowers began slowly but gradually increased his pace from the third and hit Darden at will in the sixth, eighth and ninth. Darden managed a rally in round eleven, then toughed it out to the final bell. 'Darden was in a bad way at the finish. His face was swelled until it has assumed proportions twice its normal size, his eyes were badly bruised and his nose was bleeding profusely.'

The New Year 1924 would have brought with it the same kind of uncertainty in the Flowers household that had blown in with 1923. Theodore was earning but it wasn't a fortune and he was now past his thirtieth birthday, with a toddler to provide for as well as a wife. The plan appears to have been to cram as many fights into as short a time as was workable.

On 23 January he was in Nashville, Tennessee, knocking out an obscure fighter named Herbert Moore. Most of the few fights of Moore's that have been found by record compilers were in Atlanta, and it's possible he also 'belonged' to Walk Miller. Flowers knocked him out in the second round.

Afterwards the Tiger travelled southwest, through Memphis and Dallas, almost 950 miles to San Antonio. There, eight days after the Moore workout, he easily defeated Sam 'Sonny' Goodrich, who had made his name in the city by defeating the elderly, half-blind Sam Langford the previous month. Goodrich, from California, found the improving Flowers too good and too fast, and went down on points after twelve rounds.

From San Antonio, it was back the way he had come and then north to Toledo, Ohio, a total of 1,500 miles for a fight with Bob Lawson, the black light heavyweight they called The Alabama Bear, and who was his friend, before 2,000 fans at the Coliseum. Lawson was usually tough and durable, but Flowers, who had already outpointed him in an eight rounder in Nashville, was far too accomplished. Referee Ollie Pecord stopped what had become a slaughter when Lawson was down for the third time in round ten, having also been knocked down in the ninth. Lawson, according to one report by Claud Griswold, was:

> … dizzy from blows he had taken and exhausted by defensive efforts that were practically futile. He [Lawson] seemed to have all the physical advantages of strength, reach, build… but he was decisively out-smarted by the Tiger. Lawson's opponent won by nimble wit or quicker brain. Flowers was nothing less than greased lightning… In and out he darted, first making his man ridiculous with wild misses and then driving him into a shell with stinging jabs, hooks and crosses to the face and body. Flowers took every round by a decisive margin.

When Pecord stopped it Lawson, said Griswold, was 'drunk from punishment. He was weak, tired, exhausted and discouraged.'

Flowers stayed in Ohio for his next two fights. He beat another old opponent, Battling Gahee, over twelve rounds in Barberton, just south of Akron, on 25 February. Gahee was originally from Memphis but after serving in the First World War had moved to Toledo, Ohio. As had several others who boxed the Tiger, Gahee had been employed as one of Jack Dempsey's sparring partners.

Flowers then travelled one hundred miles to Fremont, and spent time working out in the town ahead of another meeting with Jamaica Kid on 3 March. He had already beaten Gahee three times, and this was his fourth fight, at least, with Jamaica Kid. These were paydays, no more, no less, for men working the rounds and as far as anyone could tell, they led nowhere, so were entities in themselves valued purely for the entertainment they provided in the moment. In Fremont one of Flowers' training sessions was covered by a local reporter Albert O'Farrell, who called himself Colonel. He introduced the Tiger to the readers of the *Fremont News* as 'a typical Southern colored man and a polished gentleman who has rubbed elbows with the world to a great extent during his three years of travel over the pugilistic map'. O'Farrell said about 150 people witnessed the workout at the Fremont Athletic Club and he himself was impressed by what he saw. He said Flowers had a physique great sculptors would have loved to use. O'Farrell's piece is full of hyperbole and mixed metaphor, with diving seals, a snake's tongue, automatic weapons and Valentino's head all muddled up. On a calmer note, the Colonel found Tiger was relentless and tireless in a sparring session with an assistant trainer at the gym, Babe Silverwood, who was also boxing at that time, without too much success, as a middleweight. After the workout, Flowers took himself off to the Jewel Theatre to see a silent movie starring George O'Hara. It was a serial called *Fighting Blood*, in which O'Hara played a boxer. O'Hara was a committed fight fan, who also boxed as an amateur lightweight. Flowers trained again the next day before what O'Farrell called a record crowd, presumably meaning for a gym session at the Athletic Club. As to the fight itself, Flowers was improving, the Jamaica Kid wasn't, and although on paper it was a ten round No Decision exhibition, it was one-sided. Flowers dropped the Kid three times and handed him a steady beating.

Somewhere in this spell of activity, Flowers pulled out of a match with George Robinson because of infected eyes. If the problem existed at all it must have been nuisance value and no more. He boxed three times in the month when he was supposed to have been suffering badly, and three times more the next month.

After Flowers had dealt with the Jamaica Kid in Fremont, he was back on the road, on that trek south to Nashville, where Walk Miller was cynical enough, no make that cruel enough, to put Fighting Bob Lawson back in with the Tiger again. This time, on 19 March 1924, Lawson lasted into the sixth against his old friend, then was knocked down and counted out.

Theodore Flowers was treading the path which so many other talented black fighters had trod before. It must have seemed, in spite of what we can identify as his remarkable optimism, borne, of course, out of his faith, that he was moving around on a giant wheel turned relentlessly by Miller. And as thrifty as he was, as successful as he was at providing in the short term for his folks in Georgia, ambition is about more than pure financial gain. After learning the business, after all the improvements have been made and a man is as good and fit as he can be, if he has any self-worth or pride at all, he has to find out how good he is. This is why the routine, systematic thwarting of the ambitions of generations of black fighters has been so cruel, so demoralising, so inhibiting.

CHAPTER 8

The House That Tex Built and Men Who Wouldn't Have Killed a Cockroach

New York City was the powerhouse of professional boxing in the 1920s, just as it was the great social engine of America. Its commission was organised, it had Madison Square Garden as the most glamorous cathedral of the sport, and it had Tex Rickard, the most successful promoter in boxing history.

The sport had been made illegal in New York State in 1881. Taking part in a prizefight was a crime punishable by a fine and imprisonment for up to three years.

In 1894, the authorities decided the organisation of boxing was moving forward sufficiently for it to be permitted as exhibitions in athletic clubs before a members-only audience. It became obvious fairly quickly that this could not be policed, or at least not consistently. Occasionally, the law-enforcers would descend on an establishment that was not conforming to the rules but the 'Boxing Club' culture burst into life. Bill Brown ran one on 23rd Street, Jim Buckley had the Sharkey arena on Broadway and 66th, Billy Newman had two, the New York Polo Club and the Longacre, while Billy Gibson ran the Fairmont. Others were the Empire, Lenox, Union Park, Puritan and Greenpoint. Of course there was also the old Madison Square Garden for hire to anyone enterprising enough to run a club, even for one night only.

On 25 September 1896 the Horton Law was passed, confirming the existing situation but allowing longer and so bigger fights, beginning on that very day with a twenty-round battle between the great George Dixon and Tommy White at the Broadway Athletic Club.

The first heavyweight championship fight in New York took place in 1899 when James J. Jeffries knocked out Bob Fitzsimmons in the eleventh round before a crowd of 9,000 at the Greater New York Athletic Club on Coney Island, the holiday playground at the southern edge of Brooklyn. Jeffries also outpointed Tom Sharkey there in the last heavyweight championship of the nineteenth century and scored his famous twenty-third round knockout of Gentleman Jim Corbett in the same hall in 1900.

However, the Horton Law could not prevent corruption or the suspicion of it. Joe Gans fought into the twenty-third round against George 'Elbows'

McFadden before folding but some expressed a doubt about the credibility of the ending. Joe Choynski's fourth round KO defeat by Kid McCoy in January 1900 was considered open to doubt, and Peter Maher knocked out a ringer named Mike Morrissey, who claimed to be the Irish champion but who turned out to be a truck driver who had never boxed. He was flattened by the first punch. James J. Corbett's fifth round body shot 'knockout' of middleweight Kid McCoy in August 1900 had the fans screaming, 'Fake!'

Theodore Roosevelt, then Governor of New York State, repealed the Horton Law, condemning boxing to short exhibitions again, and New York City fell out of favour when San Francisco and Los Angeles became popular in the early years of the new century.

Another change of heart came when the Frawley Law was passed on 29 August 1911, which allowed Madison Square Garden to become a somewhat unruly host to the business for the next six years. The Frawley Law put the governance of boxing in New York State into the token hands of an unpaid three-man commission, with a restriction on the length of bouts of ten rounds. There were to be no points decisions, since the contests were supposedly exhibitions. Gamblers got around that one by using the newspaper reports as evidence of victory... and in turn one or two of the writers appeared to come up with surprising readings of what had occurred! The commission was weak, and its volunteers had no incentive to control anything.

In 1915 the Frawley Law was superseded by the Malone Law, which allowed the commissioners to be paid $3,000 a year, but it added little beyond that. Heavyweight champion Jess Willard retained his title in a ten round no decision fight with Frank Moran in the Garden in 1916, but the next year, after a boxer named Stephen 'Young' McDonald died following a contest, the law was repealed and the sport thrown into uncertainty again.

Following assurances from boxing promoters, managers, newspapermen and influential members of the sporting community, the Walker Law legalised boxing once again on 24 May 1920. The result of that was that a stronger New York State Athletic Commission was formed. From 1 September 1920, it was the commission's job to control the way the sport was run, and it acted to restrict contests to fifteen rounds instead of ten, enabled decisions to be given by a properly appointed referee and two judges, increased the money available to the three commissioners to $5,000 a year and insisted that medical officers should be present to deal with any emergency. Suddenly boxing in New York was ready for a new era of prosperity and respectability.

Tex Rickard was quick to take advantage. He signed a ten-year lease and promoted a show at the Garden on 26th Street, near Madison Square, headlined by Johnny Dundee and Joe Welling on 17 September 1920. Welling won an upset fifteen-round decision – and so Rickard brought him back to face New York's own world lightweight champion, the great Benny Leonard. That went down well and the following month he staged Jack Dempsey's heavyweight championship fight against Bill Brennan, which Dempsey won in the twelfth round. These were just three of thirteen boxing shows Rickard put on at the Garden in the three-and-a-half months from mid-September to the end of the year. The least he took in gate receipts was $19,200 and the most $145,935 for Dempsey-Brennan. He had proved boxing, staged properly, was a viable business.

Rickard then pulled a masterstroke, another Leonard defence, against Richie Mitchell in January 1921, in aid of a charity patronised by society hostess Anne Morgan. The event attracted a new kind of clientele.

Rickard issued tickets with seat numbers, prices and dates, and he employed security staff to make sure a ticket holder got the seat he had paid for – and to keep out those who felt it their right to sit ringside without a ticket, to pick pockets, to help themselves to coats, to crack unsuspecting victims on the head if such a thing took their fancy, and to influence what was happening in the ring with varying degrees of subtlety. Under Rickard, Madison Square Garden became relatively respectable, a place where a man might take a lady without undue worry. Rickard made absolutely sure that Anne Morgan's society friends felt comfortable enough to want to come back.

George 'Tex' Rickard was made for the Roaring Twenties, and was made for New York. He was born poor and earned and lost fortunes, exuded sober respectability yet barely survived a scandalous court case. He was a lawman, a poker player, a gambling hall proprietor in Goldfield, Nevada, a prospector in the Yukon, a cattle rancher in Paraguay, and then a fight promoter responsible for five separate million-dollar gates, a man who changed the face of the sport as America itself was changing.

His personal life seemed enigmatic: was he married four times, as some sources say, to women named Marie, Leona, Edith Mae and finally the thirty-year younger Maxine, or was it only twice? Was one of his wives in reality the infamous, beautiful, enigmatic Etta Place, who ran with Butch Cassidy and the Sundance Kid, then seemed to disappear into thin air before they met their violent end? How fortunate was Rickard to be acquitted of criminal charges of assault and abduction – what would now be classed as paedophile sexual attacks – when he was at the height of his fame in March 1922?

The old descriptions suggest he was a grey-eyed, unemotional, combination of new age sophistication and country boy hospitality. Undoubtedly he was shrewd, some said devilishly so.

'I never seed anything like it,' was his recorded reaction to the sight of boxing fans pouring through his turnstiles. People seemed to like him. Even Doc Kearns, Jack Dempsey's manager, who resented the way Rickard undercut him to get complete control of the champion, bore him no lasting grudge. 'He was simply playing his cards the way he saw them,' said Kearns. 'Always the gambling man, spinning the wheel with somebody else's money riding on the line.'

Rickard operated in a city in the grip of gangsters making fortunes from Prohibition. It was where over the years men like Owney 'The Killer' Madden, Dutch Schulz, Frank Costello, Lepke Buchalter, Jacob Shapiro and Lucky Luciano got rich controlling the city's underbelly, and what they could of its legitimate business too. And on the New Jersey side of the Hudson River, by the mid-twenties Abner 'Longy' Zwillman ran his unblinking eye over what he perceived as his kingdom. Even as a teenager Zwillman ran the numbers racket and used armoured trucks to smuggle Canadian whiskey into New Jersey. He was also a charmer who enjoyed society and a veneer of respectability by giving generously to charity. He pressed flesh with the best of them. New York crime 'families' spilled over into Jersey. Men like Gaspare D'Amico and Gaetano 'Tommy' Reina had their areas of control.

Consequently, more than is usual in ordinary life, things were not what they sometimes seemed. Quite what link Rickard had with any or all of the above, if he had a link at all, is not known. Zwillman himself was too young – not quite seventeen – to have been of significance at the time of the first of Rickard's million-dollar gates, the great occasion when Jack Dempsey fought the glamorous Frenchman, Georges Carpentier in July 1921. If Rickard had to pay homage to any of the crime syndicates, or cut anyone in on the deal, no doubt he would have viewed the situation with pragmatic calm. He had partners in Charles Cochran and William Brady but both withdrew from the deal. Others who backed him were the circus boss John Ringling, rising ticket broker Mike Jacobs and John Pierpoint Morgan, the financier father of the aforementioned Anne. Dempsey, who had been smeared as a slacker in the First World War in a murky domestic court case involving his wife, defended his world heavyweight title against Georges Carpentier, whom Tex built up as a French war hero, to provide the age-old bad-guy, good-guy scenario. Carpentier was far too light to tackle Dempsey with any real chance of success but Rickard kept the public away from his training sessions and instead traded on his star quality as the fabulous, enigmatic Orchid Man from Europe. Carpentier appealed to women and attracted headlines and photographs in the society pages. Dempsey, the one-time hobo from a poor family in Colorado, whose first wife had worked as a prostitute, was the Frenchman's flip side. Yet Dempsey was American – and a ferocious fighter whose attacking style made him wildly exciting. The public were at the same time intrigued and confused. And so on fight day Rickard drew more than 80,000 paying customers to a wooden arena at a spot known as Boyle's Thirty Acres in Jersey City, just across the Hudson from Manhattan. The vast bowl had taken only two months to build. One writer looked at the crowd in the stadium and suggested it looked like a great honey pot surrounded by flies. Maybe, given the fact that he had bought the backing of the corrupt mayor of Jersey City, Frank Hague, Rickard did not have to cut in anybody else but one thing is certain. If one of the 'families' felt like preventing the occasion happening, the arena would never have been built. As it was, the event was an incredible success. Dempsey won easily in four rounds and the crowd of 80,183 paid $1,789,238 for their tickets, an average of $22.31 each (or $250 at today's prices).

In January 1922, Rickard's world imploded when three girls between the ages of eleven and fifteen accused him of enticing them into sexual acts with him. The fifty-two year-old entrepreneur had, they said, met them at Madison Square Garden's indoor swimming pool – and invited them to a luxury apartment at the Garden Tower on West 47th Street, where the assaults had taken place. Rickard, who shared his main home on Madison Avenue with his wife, turned himself in. He protested his innocence. The mud thickened when two more girls came forward, both claiming to be eleven years old, with stories that supported those of the others. There had to be at least a preliminary hearing – and, after listening to the initial outline of the case, magistrate George Simpson not only ruled there was sufficient evidence to proceed but that the girls' story 'bore the imprint of truth'. They could describe details of his apartment, including the bedroom.

A week later a sixth girl, who was to have testified as a witness, disappeared. It transpired that she had been abducted by a fighter, Nathan Pond, and taken to a farm, where he had bribed her not to testify. Pond was arrested and charged. Another witness, a grown man this time, who was involved in the leasing of the apartment, left town without a forwarding address.

Rickard's defence was helped when two employees of the Society for the Prevention of Cruelty to Children asked to meet him in a bar in Hell's Kitchen, the gang-infested streets on the West Side between 34th and 42nd. They tried to shake him down for $50,000, claiming they could get the case dropped. Rickard was not stupid enough to swallow that, instead using it as proof somebody was out to frame him. The men lost their jobs but was the incident real or bluff, or double-bluff? The boundaries were blurring. And if the whole thing was a set-up, who was behind it? And why?

At the trial Rickard's legal team blackened the character of the girls, referred to their precociousness in sexual matters, cast doubt not only on their stories but on their ages, and revealed a list of arrests for each of these children or adolescents of the streets; begging, theft, robbery, the forging of cheques. Cases like this, before the advent of forensic evidence, were so often about who a jury wanted to believe, about whose character made them more likely to be telling the truth, and it's quite probable that the all-male jury would always prefer to believe Rickard, or a man in his position, over a group of poor, ill-educated female children street-wise before their time who were likely to make middle-class America uncomfortable about their very existence. Rickard might have been guilty, might have been innocent, might have been framed by anyone who wanted him out of the picture. We'll never know, but an hour and a half was all it took for the jury to find him not guilty.

Rickard's clientele from the social elite disappeared back to their cocktail parties. There were fights, but no big fights, until September 1923, when the heat had died down sufficiently for another Jack Dempsey 'occasion'. After the enormous success of the Carpentier extravaganza in July 1921, Rickard saw no point in confining Dempsey's defence against the raw, powerful Argentine heavyweight Luis Firpo to the Garden. Instead, he hired the Polo Grounds, the stadium in Harlem between 155th Street and Eighth Avenue that was home to the New York Giants. The capacity had just been expanded to 55,000, but with the pitch area also available, the crowd swelled to 82,000. Those at ringside paid $50 (approximately $650 today) to watch three-minutes-and-fifty-seven seconds of mayhem that have gone down in boxing legend. Firpo's non-existent defence and fighting heart meant he was down nine times, but along the way he also had Dempsey down twice, once a touchdown, but once a crazy backwards pitch out of the ring on to the ringside newsmen's desks. The champ only just beat the count. Rickard's gate receipts once again topped $1 million. Boxing was huge again.

1923 was also the year Owen Vincent Madden, known to the world as Owney, walked through the gates out of Sing Sing prison after serving nine years of a twenty-stretch for killing a rival gangster Patsy Doyle back in 1914. Who should be sent to meet him as he stepped back to freedom but Joe Gould who, a dozen years later, would officially steer James J. Braddock to the heavyweight championship of the world. Gould managed Braddock from the start of his career in 1925… but who owned Gould?

Madden, born to Irish parents in Leeds, in the north of England, in 1891 and raised from the age of ten in Hell's Kitchen, had survived being shot before he was twenty-one. As he lay in hospital with eleven bullets in his body, he refused to name names. 'Nothing doing,' he told police in his Yorkshire accent. 'The boys'll get 'em. It's nobody's business but mine.' When he emerged from Sing Sing, he knew the world had changed, and he himself had matured, grown even more dangerous, because he understood the need for a veneer of respectability. He bought, or muscled in on, the Club De Luxe run by former heavyweight champion Jack Johnson at the corner of 644 Lenox Avenue and 142nd Street in Harlem. Johnson was a front for Budd Levy, who owned a string of pool halls and bowling rinks, establishments that were so often a cover for gambling dens and speak-easies. Madden refurbished the place and reopened it as the Cotton Club, an up-market night spot for well-heeled white customers who liked the thrill of going uptown to Harlem for an evening, or a long night. Madden brazenly ignored the Prohibition Law to the point where he served his own brand of beer, complete with his name printed on the labels. The police closed him down once, briefly; then left him alone. Head of the FBI, J. Edgar Hoover, was even photographed at a table there, enjoying the show. The great black performers who provided the entertainment had to go in and out of the building by the back door.

The poet Langston Hughes remembered the Cotton Club in his 1940 autobiography, *The Big Sea*:

> I was never there because the Cotton Club was a Jim Crow club for gangsters and monied whites ... Nor did ordinary Negroes like the growing influx of whites towards Harlem after sundown, flooding the little cabarets and bars where formerly only colored people laughed and sang...

Word had it that Madden was controlling New York bantamweight Charley 'Phil' Rosenberg well before his world championship victory over Eddie 'Cannonball' Martin at the Garden in March 1925. Officially, Rosenberg was managed by Harry 'Champ' Segal, who by the 1940s was involved with Frankie Carbo's fight-fixing mob, alongside Blinky Palermo, Eddie Coco and Felix Bocchacchio, who resurrected the career of Jersey Joe Walcott. No doubt Madden's tentacles were spread wide. Segal was from the Lower East Side. He was once charged with the murder of another dubious character, Harry Greenberg, in San Francisco but provided an alibi to show he was in Los Angeles at the time. Champ was quoted in his 1959 biography as saying that Madden and himself did not cement their professional relationship until 1929 and added with a sense of comic genius, 'He wouldn't even kill a cockroach. Once you've done time, your name is mud. You can't go to court about it. They can print anything they want.'

When Madden took a fifty per cent cut of his business, and then, allegedly, gave half of his own cut to his partner George 'Big Frenchy' La Mange, Segal appeared to accept the situation without complaint – in fact, more than that, he laid out the red carpet. They had an office on 47th Street. According to Segal's testimony they had bits of fighters like Battling Levinsky and Maxie Rosenbloom, James J. Braddock, middleweight contender KO Phil Kaplan, flyweight champion Pancho Villa and Leo Lomski. Later they were in on the steering of the Italian Primo Carnera to the heavyweight championship, which was a textbook exercise in the exploitation of a human being. In spite of his four world title fights, in spite of having more than sixty contests in the United States, before he was thirty Carnera was left friendless and virtually penniless in a hospital bed. He returned to Italy with nothing but memories as those who had owned him moved on to fresh pickings.

Levinsky, also known as Barney Lebrowitz and Barney Williams, fought from 1909 to 1922, and made a comeback from 1926-30, but as in those four years he boxed only once in the New York area, it is a fair guess that the 'boys' had their piece of him when he was hot, not when he was in his mid-to-late thirties and washed up. Madden was still in Sing Sing during Levinsky's first career, but it's not impossible that old loyalties ran deep enough to make him a silent partner.

Segal said they all worked with manager Joe 'Yussel' Jacobs, who managed light-heavyweight champion Mike McTigue and later on, Max Schmeling, the German who won the world title on a foul from Jack Sharkey in 1930. This gives credibility to Jacobs' angry, defiant outburst in Georgia, when the promoter of McTigue's fight with Young Stribling threatened to string them up from a tree. Jacobs said if that happened his friends in New York would come down and 'blow this dump off the map'. They also dealt with Joe Gould, Bill Duffy, who fronted nightclubs for them and got off a murder rap in 1926 because of lack of evidence, and Frank Churchill, who controlled Pancho Villa and was sometimes called the Father of Filipino boxing. He worked out of New York, then Chicago and finally settled on a ranch in California.

Segal, by the way, once threatened to sue New York sports columnist Joe Williams for describing him as a small-time hoodlum. He objected to the phrase small-time.

When Jack Delaney, then the former light-heavyweight champion, was matched with Jack Sharkey in New York in April 1928, his backers made a deal with racketeers for him to throw the fight. Delaney refused but was given the option of laying down voluntarily on the canvas or being forced to lay down in cement. He folded in less than a minute and never forgave himself. Sharkey himself always vehemently denied taking a dive when he was knocked out by Primo Carnera for the championship in 1933, but hardly anybody believed him. He said even his wife had her doubts.

Segal took Charley Rosenberg to meet Al Capone in Chicago, when they had a fight there. He was offered the introduction by Max Greenberg whom he described as a good friend. Greenberg was killed by Frankie Carbo in 1933, shot five times in the chest in his room at the Carteret Hotel in Elizabeth, New Jersey. According to Ray Arcel, who trained Rosenberg, Segal once threatened to kill him. Arcel called Madden who warned Segal off.

Max 'Boo Boo' Hoff worked out of Philadelphia, bootlegging and running an illegal gambling house above his pool hall. He also had a substantial string of fighters including a former middleweight champion, Jeff Smith. Hoff also famously tried to muscle in on the manager-boxer partnership between Billy Gibson and New York's world heavyweight champion Gene Tunney, who beat Jack Dempsey to win the title in 1926. Hoff claimed a signed contract and lodged a $350,000 lawsuit to take control of Tunney's career only to discover the signature on the document read Eugene Joseph Tunney. The champion declared it was not his signature. His name was James Joseph Tunney. Hoff's claim collapsed. Speculation remained as to whether Hoff had attempted to forge the champion's signature himself, or Tunney had duped him.

Tommy Loughran, the light-heavyweight champion out of Philadelphia, knew the hoods. 'They wanted to have a prize possession, like a fellow with a race horse or a baseball team.' It was about money, yes, but also about power, influence, social impact.

The great coach Ray Arcel was a man who never sought to get even, who preferred a low profile. He knew all the bad boys and was once hired by Owney Madden to train his fighters. Arcel's testimony concerning Madden is a reminder that everyone has a good side somewhere.

> Owney was a wonderful fellow. He paid his way. Everybody loved to watch Owney at the fights. They seemed to change his personality. He would stand up at the front, shadow boxing, throwing punches and shouting instructions. He used to get beside himself until somebody pulled him back into his seat. He just loved boxing.

Dutch Schulz, Owney Madden's equal in psychotic violence, or alternatively another maligned man who wouldn't harm a cockroach, ran the Embassy Club, which was frequented by Dempsey's manager Jack Kearns. Schulz also sold his beer to the Madison Square Garden management for their social parties.

Bill Brennan was a good heavyweight whom Dempsey knocked out in a title defence in the Garden in December 1920. Brennan ran a speak-easy on Broadway called the Tia Juana and on the night of 15 June 1924, someone walked in and shot him dead. Dempsey said acidly, 'I guess Bill bought the wrong beer.'

And it was into this glittering, wild, partying, menacing world that two men from the South, one white and one black, named Walker Valentine Miller and Theodore Flowers walked in search of boxing glory and financial security in the spring of 1924. It was the beginning of their great years, and it was the beginning of their end.

CHAPTER 9

Good Times in Harlem

Tiger Flowers' New York debut was at the Commonwealth Sporting Club at 14 East 135th Street in Harlem on 29 March 1924. It was not Madison Square Garden, but it was New York. The Commonwealth club used the premises of a casino, where fight fans could also spend their money. It was run by two white promoters, the McMahon brothers Edward and Roderick, also known as Jess. Back in 1915 they had been involved in the Jack Johnson–Jess Willard championship fight in Cuba, had independent wealth and went on to found a wrestling dynasty that still thrives today. Flowers and Miller would have known that if he flopped at the Commonwealth Sporting Club, it would be back to the small-town circuit. If he impressed, then the fight world would open up. He was matched with Lee Anderson, who had knocked him out in seven rounds for the 'colored' light-heavyweight title in Mexico almost two years earlier. At thirty-four, Anderson was still tough but not quite what he used to be. Flowers didn't flop. He won the twelve round decision and looked good doing it. The McMahons wanted him back.

While they were ironing out the details, Flowers fitted in a quick two round win over a black light-heavyweight named Dave Thornton, who at some point was his sparring partner, in Nashville. Then he boxed again at the Commonwealth Sporting Club on 19 April 1924. The McMahon brothers gave him a fight they thought would be well within his scope. His opponent, Jimmy Darcy, who was actually a Romanian immigrant Valeri Trambitas, born in Bucharest and fighting out of Oregon, had lost ten out of ten before breaking the bad run with a newspaper decision up in Maine the previous week. Darcy AKA Trambitas was only twenty-five but had battled his way through more than 100 fights with only middling success. He outweighed Flowers by nine pounds, 172 to 163, but it did not help him. Flowers was in control from first bell to last for his eleventh consecutive victory. It was a mixed fight black man against white – but that had been acceptable in New York since George 'Black Shadow' Godfrey had fought Jack Renault at the Pioneer Sporting Club at 155 East 24th Street the previous year. The Godfrey–Renault match was alleged to have been made only on the understanding that, should he find himself winning, Godfrey would carry the white man to the final bell. It is not beyond the bounds of possibility that Flowers fought Darcy under similar constraints. In Godfrey's case, it was irrelevant. Renault won on a knockout in round eleven.

Within days Tiger went home to Atlanta, no doubt with tales of the excitement of life in New York, for a fight at the Auditorium against George Robinson. With a local journalist, Fuzzy Woodruff, refereeing, Flowers put on a show for his home fans, winning over twelve rounds against a veteran who while still very tough-minded and durable was near the end of his career. Flowers was winning as he pleased and had almost closed Robinson's left eye when he ran into the path of a right hand and crashed down face-first, apparently out. In his excitement Robinson, as with the more famous Long Count issue in the 1927 heavyweight championship fight between Jack Dempsey and Gene Tunney, forgot that in the event of scoring a knockdown a boxer had to retire to the furthest neutral corner. If he did not do so the referee could elect not to begin, or could suspend, the count. Woodruff had to tell Robinson twice to go to a corner. Eventually he did but by then Flowers was recovering his senses and he beat the count. From the corner Walk Miller yelled to Flowers to move to his right where Robinson couldn't see him clearly enough to catch him again. The Tiger recovered then poured forward again and took over up to the final bell.

In the same article, Woodruff wrote of the city's new boxing hero:

> He has never smoked. He doesn't know the taste of alcohol. He is a family man with a growing family. He is frugal, putting all his money in Atlanta real estate and in the last year he has made plenty... folks here are proud of the Tiger. In his professional and personal life he has been a credit to Georgia and the South. That's a great deal to say for a colored boxer.

As if that acknowledgement from a white Atlanta journalist was not enough, then according to Woodruff, the former heavyweight champion James J. Corbett had called Flowers the best middleweight in the world, or in other words, the uncrowned champion.

There was little time to relax with Willie Mae and Verna Lee. Four days later he was back at the Commonwealth Sporting Club to provide more entertainment for the customers of the McMahon brothers, this time defeating Ted Jamieson in another twelve round contest. The schedule was relentless offering no time for sore hands, bruised ribs or cuts and grazes to heal. Most modern boxers need time off after every fight before returning to the gym. The world inhabited by Tiger Flowers and the multitude of men like him was a harsher place. By the time he fought and beat Ted Jamieson, Flowers had fought three long battles in the space of a fortnight, and had travelled from New York to Atlanta and back again. Jamieson, a Scottish-born immigrant from Milwaukee, Wisconsin, had won the US amateur light-heavyweight title in 1917. He was in good form, unbeaten for more than a year, and back in 1920 had knocked Harry Greb down in a ten round non-title, no decision fight in Grand Rapids, Michigan. This was a much tougher match for Flowers than the Darcy fight but the Tiger coped well, and won the decision.

That was impressive and eleven days later, Walk Miller and the McMahons had him boxing again at the 135th Street casino arena, this time against Willie Walker, a New York middleweight who had some ability but, just as Flowers had shown at times, a fragile chin. In the past year Walker had been knocked out by old Panama Joe Gans and an unbeaten black prospect named Larry Estridge. Walker could not keep the marauding Flowers out, and by the seventh the referee had seen enough. The fight was stopped.

It appears the clientele at the Commonwealth Sporting Club clamoured for more. On 14 June 1924 the Tiger was back for his fifth appearance there in two-and-a-half months, when he outscored Joe Lohman, a twenty-six-year-old light-heavyweight from a German family in Ohio, in another twelve round distance fight.

A writer in the New York Age called him the 'picturesque middleweight of Atlanta, Georgia' and said his victory was an easy one.

> Flowers outpointed his heavier opponent in every round and on several occasions during the fight had him groggy, but each time Lohman rallied and managed to escape the knockdown blow the Tiger attempted to land. This fight came as the climax to a good card of bouts which drew a capacity crowd to the local club.

However, on the same page of the paper another article referred to a forthcoming show at Yankee Stadium and described Panama Joe Gans and Larry Estridge as the two best 'colored' middleweights in the country. The Tiger had a way to go yet to convince everyone.

Almost thirty years later, *Ring* magazine stalwart Jersey Jones suggested 'no fighter, on his way to the peak of his division, had a tougher road to travel than Theodore (Tiger) Flowers.'

As the spring of 1924 moved into summer, he was making his name, in Harlem, if not yet in Madison Square Garden. In order to increase their 'political' weight, it is possible that Miller sold a piece of Flowers to the McMahons but there is no evidence to suggest that was the case. The brothers were wealthy and successful enough to run an independent establishment and I could find no links between them and organised (or disorganised) crime. Perhaps because Flowers was black, and therefore it would be assumed his potential was limited, the controllers of the New York boxing scene let the McMahons and Miller earn what they could of the small money without interference.

Less than a week after beating Lohman, he was back in Fremont, Ohio, in a ten round no-decision fight with his old rival from way back when, Battling Gahee. Tiger had the better of it, according to the papers. Gahee probably knew the score, knew Flowers was too good, but no doubt they put up a decent show for the customers. There was never the slightest suggestion that Flowers ever minded going over old ground. A payday was a payday, whenever it came, wherever it required him to be. He was seeing America, saving his money, providing for Willie Mae and Verna Lee with increasing success, and was coming to no apparent harm. Life for the Flowers family was suddenly good. The long years of learning his craft, of overcoming obstacles and disappointments, seemed to be on the verge of paying off.

He moved on northwest from Fremont through Toledo, Detroit and Lansing to Grand Rapids, Michigan, the home city of the great old middleweight champion Stanley Ketchel. He was lucky. He moved on from Ohio to Michigan twenty-four hours before a tornado struck, leaving seventy-five people dead and more than a thousand injured. In Grand Rapids, on 27 June 1924, Flowers and Jamaica Kid provided ten rounds of entertainment. Flowers won, as he was expected to do, and in another week he was back in Atlanta, a small matter of 640 miles away. At the Auditorium, making light of conceding 15 lbs, he beat Lee Anderson on an 11th round foul. A reporter from the Atlanta Constitution, George Congdon, described Flowers as 'a slashing, ripping, tearing fury'. Though Tiger knew Anderson well, it didn't stop him doing a number on the man who was still attempting to lay claim to a piece of the light-heavyweight title. Flowers, wrote Congdon, turned Anderson's face into a 'mis-shaped, gory mass'. Flowers was offered the fight on a foul – in round six referee Bill Kaliska actually raised his arm in victory following one of a string of breaches of the rules by Anderson – but he did not want to win that way if he could help it. By the eleventh, however, the fouls were hurting, and when offered the disqualification win again, it was accepted. On the evidence to hand, it seems that Anderson, as some outclassed fighters do, deliberately fouled out of the fight. Flowers had knocked him down in the ninth. Congdon wrote:

> Anderson will carry back to New York with him a story of losing on fouls that will sound much better than a yarn of being blinded in one eye, then in both and finally beaten to a pulp by Flowers; but the crowd that saw the slaughter, by its hissing and jeering of Anderson, gave him the well-earned title of champion fouler of the world.

Congdon also said Flowers seemed twice as fast as when he outpointed George Robinson in the same ring only three months earlier. It is likely that his success in New York had increased the Tiger's confidence, and had made him even more of a handful.

He appears to have taken a few days to enjoy being at home because it was eighteen days before he boxed next, this time 450 miles north in Covington, Kentucky, where he beat Jamaica Kid on a third round foul. Then he was on the move again: the Commonwealth Sporting Club in Harlem beckoned, and on 2 August 1924, he stopped Jack Townsend there in eleven rounds. Time to enjoy New York? Not a bit of it. Ten days on, he had travelled another 1,800 miles across to San Antonio, Texas, to fight Oscar Mortimer at a downtown arena known as the Soledad Roof. He was too good for Mortimer, a black 6 foot tall light heavyweight from Kansas who also fought as Hank Griffin, and won in six rounds. Mortimer was knocked down nine times before his seconds threw in the towel.

And then suddenly the breakthrough opportunity that no doubt Flowers and Walk Miller had been dreaming of was on the table. A fight with the cunning, one-off whirlwind that was the middleweight champion of the world – white, black and all shades in between – Harry Greb. The title would not be at stake because the match would be made over the 160 lbs limit but, only nine days after Flowers beat Mortimer in Texas, it was a fantastic chance to show what he could do against the very best. There was no doubt that he had improved almost beyond recognition in the past year or so, and the ten round match against Greb in the Legion Stadium in Fremont, Ohio, on Thursday 21 August 1924 would make the boxing world take real notice of him – if he could cope.

Greb was like Flowers in that he fought as often as he could, wherever the journey took him, whether in the best of shape or not. And unlike so many of the world's leading boxers, he didn't bother about the colour of a man's skin. It took the right kind of money to tempt him into defending his championship but a payday was a payday. By his standards he was taking life pretty easy by August 1924. His fight with Flowers was only his tenth of the year. His attitude to the business is well illustrated by the fact that in the thirteen months between his world championship defence against Ted Moore in Yankee Stadium in June 1924 and the next against Mickey Walker at the Polo Grounds in July 1925, Greb had twenty-three non-title fights, two of which were against future heavyweight champion Gene Tunney, with other men who were at some point in their careers world champions, like Jimmy Slattery, Tommy Loughran, Johnny Wilson and of course Flowers himself, also on the list. Greb was a fighter through and through, and remains in many people's pound-for-pound all-time top ten. He was the only man who ever beat Tunney, and he gave Jack Dempsey hell in sparring.

CHAPTER 10

The World Middleweight Title and the Human Windmill

The middleweight championship went back to the bare-knuckle era – and was the most celebrated prize in the sport after the heavyweight title. It had also produced more than its share of sensational personal stories among its champions. One of the first champions was Bob Fitzsimmons, who was born in Cornwall in England and raised in New Zealand – and who would eventually become the first man to win world championships in three weight divisions; first middleweight, then heavyweight and finally, when in his dotage, light-heavyweight. Another was the eccentric, depressive, dangerous Norman Selby, alias Charles Kid McCoy.

McCoy was a strange individual. A talented boxer, originally from Indiana, he had a reputation for unreliability and single-minded independence – not surprising in view of his upbringing. His father was a religious fanatic and both his mother and sister were psychologically disturbed. He ran away from home when he was a child and rode the rails, living alongside the lost men, the hobos, who made what they could of life by keeping on the move. The phrase 'the real McCoy' is said to have emanated from his ring career – as fans and critics were prone to wonder before a fight whether or not 'the real McCoy' would show up, or whether it would be his alter-ego, the half-interested, seemingly preoccupied individual who boxed, shall we say, well within his capabilities. It also sprung out of his behaviour when he pleaded with his predecessor Tommy Ryan for a shot at the championship. He said he was suffering from tuberculosis and needed the money. Ryan took pity, agreed to the fight, but barely trained – only to find a perfectly fit, immaculately prepared McCoy in front of him. McCoy knocked him out in round fifteen. McCoy lost only a handful of fights in a career that spanned more than twenty years. He had friends in the movie business, including Charlie Chaplin, and D. W. Griffith who was responsible for the white supremacist film *The Birth of a Nation*. McCoy was said to have married eight women, two of them twice, but in 1924 killed his married lover and served seven years in San Quentin jail for manslaughter. By 1940 he was working as a gardener in Detroit when he killed himself, explaining in a note that he could no longer stand the madness of the world.

Stanley Ketchel was another wild, some say crazy kid, who began life in Grand Rapids, Michigan, as Stanislaus Kiecal, the son of Polish immigrants. Like McCoy he left home to ride the rails as a boy, and had grown feral in the hobo jungles. He was only twenty-one when he won the middleweight championship by knocking out Jack 'Twin' Sullivan in the twentieth round in Colma, just outside San Francisco, in May 1908. He lost and regained the title to Billy Papke, a ruthless, relentless fighter from Illinois, and even had a shot at the great heavyweight champion Jack Johnson. Ketchel shocked an apparently complacent Johnson by flooring him in the twelfth round, but was then laid out cold by the champion's next attack. Legend has it that Ketchel's front teeth were found embedded in Johnson's glove. Even by the age of twenty-three Ketchel's lifestyle meant he was burning out, and he was recuperating from his excesses at a farm in Missouri in October 1910, only a month past his twenty-fourth birthday, when he was shot dead over his breakfast by a farmhand. Ketchel had, it seemed, been messing with the man's girlfriend.

Billy, or William Herman, Papke had been a miner in Illinois. He was a brooding, reticent character whose life also ended in tragedy. In 1936, aged fifty, he drank all day in Los Angeles, then drove to the home of his estranged wife, shot her dead and killed himself.

Les Darcy was an Australian hero, who claimed the world championship at the age of nineteen. He travelled to the United States to make his fortune, stowing away on a boat to avoid restrictions on men of his age leaving the country during World War One. When he arrived in America, he was heavily criticised by newspapermen there and at home, and he was unable to get a competitive fight. Even his exhibitions were jeered. Darcy became depressed, made plans to become an American citizen and to join the US Signal Corps, but fell ill in Memphis with a strain of the streptococcus virus and died in May 1917. He was still only twenty-one.

The middleweight championship of the world had brought more than its share of tragedy when Harry Greb won a fifteen-round decision over the latest holder, Johnny Wilson, at the New York Polo Grounds on 31 August 1923.

Edward Henry Greb was born in Pittsburgh, Pennsylvania, on 6 June 1894. He was one of the busiest boxers of his or any other day; in 1917, Greb fought thirty-seven times, in 1919 he topped that with an incredible forty-five. As I said, boxing in mixed race fights did not trouble him. He avoided or blocked nobody, whatever the colour of their skin. By the time he boxed Tiger Flowers in August 1924, he had packed seventeen fights into the previous twelve months, including five championship defences. What was unknown at the time was that this extraordinary athlete had suffered serious eye damage – probably to the retina – in a fight with Kid Norfolk in 1921, since when his vision in his right eye had deteriorated. His doctor later said that it was so

Above: Theodore Roosevelt was President of the United States for eight years (1901-09). When in his first year in office he provoked fury by inviting the African-American education pioneer Booker T. Washington to dinner. James Vardman, who would be voted in the following year as Governor of Mississippi, said the White House was now 'saturated with the odor of the nigger'.

Right: Booker T. Washington.

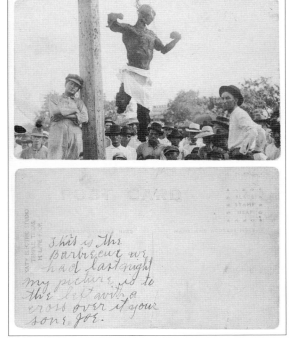

This is the Barbecue we had last night my picture is to the left with a cross over it your sons joe.

Left: Jesse Washington, a teenage African-American farmhand, was lynched in Waco, Texas, on 16 May 1916. He was accused of the rape and murder of his employer's white wife, Lucy Fryer.

Above: Clayton and Elmer Jackson, both 19, and Isaac McGhie, 20, were lynched in Duluth, Minnesota, for raping and robbing a white girl. A doctor's examination later found no evidence of rape or sexual assault.

Above: Jack Johnson, seen here at the wheel of one of his beloved fast cars, was heavyweight champion from 1908–15. His independent, defiant streak and the race riots that followed his epic 1910 victory over James J. Jeffries set the advancement of the black boxer back a generation.

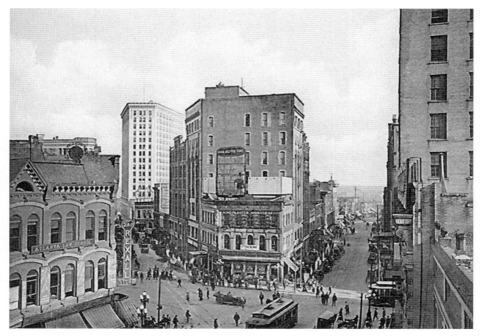

Downtown Atlanta as it looked around the time Tiger Flowers arrived in 1920, wondering what boxing might bring—and holding the small Bible his mother had given him.

Flowers fought in the left-handed southpaw stance, his right foot and glove forward.

The scars of life on the road are beginning to show this unusually poignant, serious study.

Pine Street, Philadelphia where Flowers lived with wife Willie Mae in 1917 when he worked on the building of the city subway and in the shipyards.

Battling Siki from Senegal won the world light-heavyweight title against the French idol Georges Carpentier in Paris, but then lost it to an Irishman, Mike McTigue, in Dublin on St Patrick's Night, 1923.

Siki, seen here walking in the Irish countryside with French boxer-writer Eugene Stuber, later twice turned down fights with Flowers. He was murdered in Hell's Kitchen, New York, in 1925.

The glamorous French war hero Georges Carpentier was eminently marketable.

Flowers was a tireless worker in the gym, perfecting his awkward, whirlwind style in hour after hour of work. His wife, Willie Mae, said he loved boxing from his very first lesson.

The decision the old champion Mike McTigue was given over him sparked outrage among fans and New York sports writers – and led directly to Flowers being granted a world middleweight title challenge against Harry Greb.

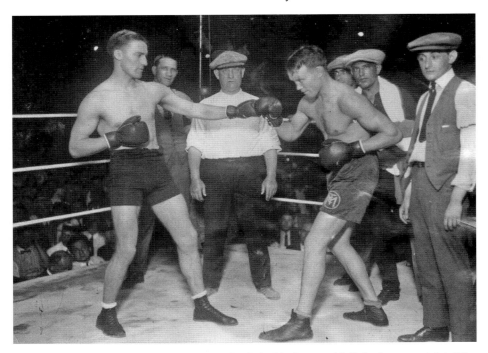

Tommy Loughran and Mike McTigue both held the world light-heavyweight title. Loughran refused to box Flowers because of the colour of his skin.

Above: Madison Square Garden, New York, the first great cathedral of boxing where the first of the great promoters, George 'Tex' Rickard, created a new clientele among wealthy socialites and made boxing a safe as well as exciting place to be seen in the early 1920s. Rickard was almost destroyed by an under-age sex scandal but survived to build another fortune.

Right: George 'Tex' Rickard.

The Jack Dempsey-Georges Carpentier fight in July 1921 at Jersey City was the first of Tex Rickard's famous 'Million Dollar Gates'.

Dempsey, unlike Flowers, was attracted to the bright lights. Here he struts his stuff with Hollywood pals Charlie Chaplin and Douglas Fairbanks. Not that the showbiz world would have opened its arms to a black boxer from the Deep South had Flowers wanted to be a part of it... Dempsey was to say after Harry Greb had lost to Flowers that he did not understand why Harry had given a black fighter a title shot.

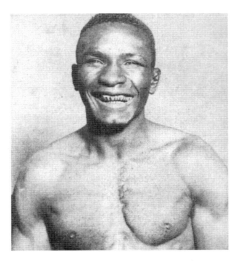

A gold-toothed Tiger Flowers took on Harry Greb in a non-title fight in Ohio in 1924.

Harry Greb, one of the best middleweights who ever lived.

Greb beat Mickey Walker in a 15-round classic in New York in 1925.

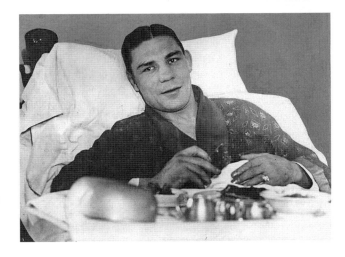

Greb recovers after a car crash when his sight was so poor he should not have been behind a wheel.

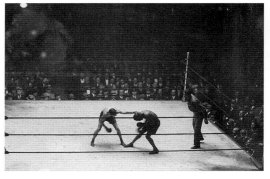

Harry Greb and Tiger Flowers fought through thirty close, tough rounds in 1926. Top left, Greb tries the old trick of holding Flowers' head in place for an uppercut.

Flowers won the middleweight title over 15 rounds at the Garden in February 1926. Old fighter Gunboat Smith refereed.

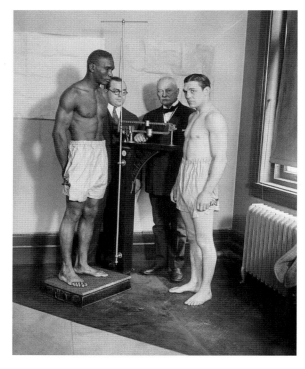

Flowers steps on to the scales and stares at Greb, who seems more interested in the camera.

Flowers and Greb trade punches in the second fight in August 1926. The Tiger's left is on its way as he darts inside Greb's lead.

Above: Flowers and Walker touch gloves at the start of the controversial title fight in Chicago. Flowers' manager, Walk Miller, is on the left. Referee Benny Yanger would never referee another fight in Chicago.

Mickey Walker (*top right*) and Jack 'Doc' Kearns (right in this photograph, seen with Tex Rickard) might as well have been on another planet to Flowers. They loved the night spots of New York—or whichever town they laid their heads.

An early photo of Owney 'The Killer' Madden, fourth from the right on this photo of Hell's Kitchen's Gopher Gang. In later life Madden loved boxing, loved to control fighters – and wouldn't have killed a cockroach, according to Champ Segal.

The Cotton Club in Harlem where Madden held court at the height of his fame. He sold his own label Prohibition beer and included FBI boss J Edgar Hoover among his customers.

A solemn Tiger Flowers poses with opponent Eddie Huffman and Georges Carpentier in Los Angeles in 1926.

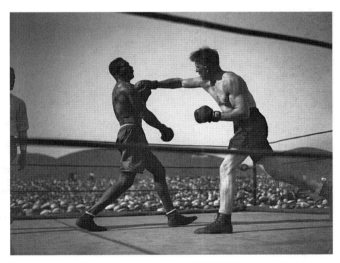

Huffman's one hope was his big right hand. He floored Flowers once but the Tiger got up and won the decision.

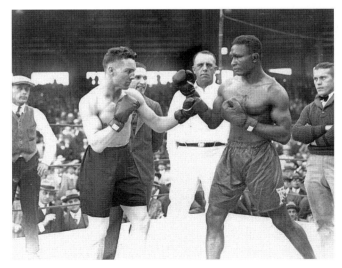

The lumps over Flowers' eyes are visible as he poses for his 1927 fight with Leo Lomski. The headaches and dizzy spells increased as the year wore on.

The body of the first African-American middleweight champion of the world is carried down the steps of his home on its final journey. His manager, Walk Miller, stands directly behind the casket.

SMILING MICKEY WALKER
WORLD'S WELTERWEIGHT CHAMPION

Mickey Walker would have had to box Flowers again had Tiger not died.

The scene inside the Atlanta city auditorium during the three-hour funeral and commemoration service when for a few brief moments Georgia set down its racial divide to pay homage to one of its greatest men.

A plot was donated to the Flowers family by the new Lincoln Cemetery and years on a seat in his honour was erected by his grave.

The people of Atlanta waited in long lines to pay their last respects at the Flowers home on Simpson Road.

THEODORE "TIGER" FLOWERS
(1895-1927)

Theodore "Tiger" Flowers was the first African-American boxer to win the world middleweight championship in 1926. Born in Camilla, Georgia in 1895, Flowers moved to Atlanta in 1920 where he began training seriously to be a professional boxer. Flowers lived at 1048 Simpson Road (now Joseph E. Boone Blvd.) in a 20 room Italian stucco mansion considered one of the most beautiful homes in the city. He died in 1927 at the age of thirty-two and was inducted into the Georgia Sports Hall of Fame in 1976 and elected to the International Boxing Hall of Fame in 1993. The home was demolished in 1962 for the construction of Fire Station No. 16, which housed the city's first African-American firefighters in 1963.

PRESENTED BY COUNCILMEMBER MICHAEL JULIAN BOND, POST 1 AT-LARGE
MMXIII

DEDICATED BY COUNCILMEMBER MICHAEL JULIAN BOND, POST 1 AT-LARGE
AND ATLANTA FIRE RESCUE DEPARTMENT CHIEF KELVIN COCHRAN
APRIL 1, 2013

The mansion was demolished in 1963 to make way for the first fire station for African-American firefighters.

severe that he was actually blind in the eye. For the last years of his career, his left eye was also a long way from perfect. He was a restless soul who loved what he did, and he ignored the damage for as long as he could, but even though he remained at the highest level to the end of his career his eyesight and age slowed him. Towards the end he said he felt it was time to go because he 'couldn't tell a dame from a priest unless I was close enough to smell her perfume'.

There is no fight footage of the man they called the Human Windmill, only a little bit of slow-motion shadow-boxing and playtime sparring with an elderly Philadelphia Jack O'Brien, both of which suggest that his style today would be dismissed as agricultural. However, styles change and you can't argue with the record – and the fact that as talented and classy a boxer as Gene Tunney held him in high regard. Greb was the only man to beat Tunney, over fifteen bloody, exhausting rounds for the American light-heavyweight title in 1922, four years before Tunney won the heavyweight championship against Jack Dempsey. Bill Brennan, the heavyweight who took Dempsey twelve rounds for the title, also fought Greb. He once said: 'You've got to be in perfect condition to fight that little bastard, but... if Dempsey was fightin' that buzzsaw... I would bet on Greb.'

Greb sparred with Dempsey for three days in New York City in July 1920 and drew crowds of around of 2,000 who paid 55 cents each for the privilege. On the third day Greb split Dempsey's left eye open with a right hand. They sparred again on 1 September 1920 in Benton Harbor, Michigan, and the young middleweight gave the world heavyweight champion another hard time of it, making him miss and punishing him. Again, they worked out for three days and the sessions were hard and uncompromising with Jack bleeding from the mouth.

Greb was not always the wild, devil-may-care operator his legend would have us believe, though certainly he had his moments. He took boxing very seriously indeed, trained hard when he was not fighting every week, did not by all accounts spar a great deal as he fought so often, but, like Flowers, forced his body through the pain and strain for as long as he was being paid. He had good reason, too. His wife, Mildred, was ill and needed care to be paid for, and they had a small daughter, Dorothy. When Mildred died early in 1923, Greb took four months off and then came back to beat Johnny Wilson for the title.

The Greb–Flowers fight, even without the championship at stake, drew huge interest. According to Dick Meade, in the *Toledo News-Bee*, Greb drew up the terms when he boxed Flowers. Greb knew how to protect his title. The No Decision rule was in place, and Meade reported that Greb insisted on the match being made above the middleweight limit – and also decided that the referee would be Ed Kennedy, a former fighter who had once boxed the great Joe Gans. Kennedy lived in Greb's home city of Pittsburgh. 'He absolutely refused to perform otherwise,' wrote Meade. Greb was not afraid of anyone, but neither was he stupid. If he was to risk his title, it was to be for far more money than was available in the comparative wilds of Fremont, Ohio. This was, after all, a man who had won his championship in the vast bowl of the Polo Grounds, New York. He knew his value, and the price of the crown he wore.

The promoter, Ray Bronson, a former professional fighter from Indianapolis, and Walk Miller, for Flowers, had no choice but to accept Greb's terms. Local worries were partly appeased when Kennedy received the backing of Harvey Boyle, head of the Pennsylvania Boxing Commission but Kennedy was well known to Greb and his manager Red Mason. He understood the way Greb sometimes fought on the edge of the rules. This was important insurance for Greb, who considered referees little more than interfering 'cops' who should, by and large, mind their own business. He didn't want a local, stickler-for-the-rules, jobsworth official disqualifying him.

Walk Miller ignored Greb's demands that Flowers not weigh in. Twenty-four hours before the fight the Tiger scaled 161½ lb, only 1½ lb above the championship limit, and planned to come in at around 159 lb on the night at the Legion Stadium, in front of the Ohio Commission representatives. This was in direct conflict of the champion's insistence on an overweight match. Miller was gambling high – on Greb going through with the fight and on Flowers perhaps forcing a rematch with the title at stake by making his point of boxing at middleweight, not above. Greb did not appear to bother to weigh in at all. Meade suggested he had made no attempt to come in anywhere near the limit and might have been as much as ten pounds above it. Against that a report published in the *Lima News* said Greb had weighed in during his physical examination by doctors and was 167 lb.

The crowd was swelled by around 1,000 fight fans, who had travelled from Toledo where Flowers was popular, by bus, car and train. A seat in the bleachers cost only $3.30, including 30 cents tax, and reports out of Fremont suggested the fight had drawn as much as $16,000 in advance ticket sales and was expected to hit $20,000 with the walk-up. However, Greb was on $6,000 or thirty per cent of the gate receipts, whichever was the larger, while Flowers, in order to get the fight, had to accept the short end of a few hundred dollars as a guarantee. A report in the *Afro-American* in February 1925 suggested the Tiger's eventual payday came close to $25,000, which may or may not have been a piece of Walk Miller spin. Whatever the source, it was almost certainly wildly off-mark. Another source, quoted in an International Boxing Research Organisation newsletter, says the total gate was $24,355, with Greb picking up $7,012.47 and Flowers $2,743.65. That's precise enough to assume some authority and sounds more likely. The *Toledo News-Bee* previewed the fight.

Tonight's encounter in the open air on the outskirts of Fremont is discussed as a struggle for the title, but is merely a No Decision contest and the only way the Southern darkey could hope to acquire the crown will be to knock the Pittsburgh flash a-kicking. Even then, it is doubtful if Greb will give up the honor, for he will contend the bout was arranged at catch-weights and in no sense a championship struggle. To make things all the more safe, Greb is going to have his own referee in the ring.

At least it was transparent. And for Flowers, it was the opportunity that mattered as much as victory. As long as he fought well, hard and took Greb the distance, in a reasonably close fight, his reputation would soar.

Greb had not boxed for six weeks, a rare break, since his one-sided but physically gruelling championship defence against the British boxer, Ted Moore, in front of 50,000 fans at Yankee Stadium, New York, on 26 June. In comparison to that great night – he had won on points over fifteen rounds, with Moore winning only a couple of them – this was a routine, mark-time type of payday. As he tended to keep himself in shape by fighting rather than extensive gym work, it is likely the champion was not in top condition. Joe Williams, recalling the fight only three months later in the *New York Evening Independent*, said somewhat sourly 'Greb, as usual, was in bad condition'. Flowers, as fit as he always seemed to have been, with no apparent injuries in spite of his hectic schedule, set his customary hot pace and Greb, maybe struggling a little with the southpaw stance, maybe just not sharp enough, needed all his cunning and ring craft to contain him and land the more accurate blows. It appears to have been a competitive, furiously quick fight, and one in which the Tiger did himself proud. Some writers felt he had much the better of it but the fight went the full ten rounds, which meant a No Decision.

Lewis W. Bryer from the *Columbus Citizen* felt about 11,000 fans watched in Bronson's new arena while Monroe Glatz of the *Fremont Daily News* estimated it at 12,000 and James W. Schlemmer of the *Akron Press* thought it was 14,000. Afterwards all three had Flowers winning a contest made controversial by the judgment calls of referee Kennedy. Schlemmer wrote:

> He didn't wallop him, or cut him to pieces, or get him groggy, or any of that, but Tiger Flowers piled up enough points in five of the ten rounds to make himself stand out clearly as the better man. And Tiger Flowers did that despite the fact that Harry Greb's very own, handpicked referee, Eddie Kennedy of Pittsburgh, was the third man in the ring.

Schlemmer was in no doubt of the shortcomings of the official.

> Kennedy was a farce... the crowd... even went so far as to hoot and hiss... The cards were stacked against the black man. The only way that Flowers

could have obtained Greb's title was through a knockout, and Eddie Kennedy, Greb's referee, couldn't have counted ten between last night and Christmas if Flowers had landed a lucky punch. Greb heeled and hit in the clinches. He didn't break clean – he didn't have to – for Flowers was the fighter being warned by the referee.

Bryer also criticised Kennedy for warning Flowers for a supposed low blow in the fourth, when it seemed it was a legitimate body punch that had made Greb go into a crouch.

George Pulford of the *Toledo Blade* was another writer who was disgusted by Kennedy's performance.

Greb said he was the best referee in Pennsylvania. If he is, preserve us from the dubs. Before the first round ended, Kennedy was the object of catcalls and words of advice from the multitude. Kennedy started picking on Flowers from the start, warning him about hitting low. Most of the time Kennedy spent hopping around like a rooster, waving his hands with the abandon of a waterfowl taking wing. He was in there to protect Greb, and until a storm of protest arose, he did nothing but nag Mr Flowers.

Schlemmer felt that beyond Greb's tactics before and during the fight, Flowers suffered because he was black. In a remarkably outspoken piece, the Ohio writer said:

... it's a hard task, this thing of trying to make 14,000 fans forget race, color and creed long enough to give a man a square deal. Tiger got a square deal from most of the fans, but in the opinion of this writer, press correspondents from 'away down East' and others who were prejudiced to the point of saying Greb won eight rounds of the fight, are deliberately lying to save the reputation of a world's champion who was licked by a better man, and a colored one. The fight was a dandy.

Schlemmer gave Greb only two rounds, the fifth and the tenth, so scoring it roughly the same way in terms of mathematics as Dick Meade, a second *Toledo News-Bee* journalist, but differing on the details. Meade scored the fifth and eighth to Greb. Boxing scoring has never been a precise art. Schlemmer also wrote:

Flowers gave Greb no target to shoot at. He was faster than Greb on his feet and carried the fight almost continually. Greb fought in an easy, rollicking, carefree style, but was plenty worried over the strange leaping antics of his opponent. As sure as black and white are different Flowers outpointed Greb Thursday night. Whether he could do it in a bout where Greb had a real chance of losing the title – that's a horse of a different stable.

Monroe Glatz, the Fremont paper's expert, saw it 7-2-1 in rounds to the Tiger. He gave Greb the fifth and eighth, with the second even and the rest to Flowers.

It was a slashing ten round battle, in which both boxers, fighting with an intensity of purpose seldom seen in the prize ring today, employed every known method of ring craft, cunning and generalship to gain their ends. Flowers pursued his adversary with the relentless fury of the jungle beast whose name he bears.

Glatz said Flowers was in trouble only once, in round eight, when Greb drove him to the ropes and showered him with a rain of blows to body and head. At one point he seemed as if he might be knocked out, but he found something within himself and rallied, taking the fight back to Greb in the closing seconds of the round.

Lewis W. Bryer scored 6-2-2 for Flowers, whom he said had handed the middleweight champion 'the licking of his life'.

Flowers carried the fight to the champion in each of the ten rounds. He made Greb back-pedal a score of miles during the thirty minutes they were in the ring. And whether it was long-range fighting or close-in bodywork, Flowers' superiority over the champion was marked. He made Greb miss hundreds of punches. A careful count of the number of times Greb landed clean punches to Flowers' head showed exactly six. Greb was holding on constantly, from the time Flowers uncorked his first Tiger Rush, in the first round, until the bout ended.

George Pulford felt Flowers was the better man on the night. He said Greb called on all his old tricks to contain Flowers in a fight where the pace was unrelenting.

Greb fought a foul battle, using his elbows, his head and resorting to his old trick of holding and hitting. This aroused the crowd and before the first round ended the boos began, mingled with cries of, 'Let go and fight, Greb'.

Flowers, he said, finished the tenth round as fast as he began the first. Pulford said Flowers was 'out in front and going away' right up to the final bell, when with a grin, he patted Greb on the back.

There wasn't a single minute when Greb stacked up evenly with the Atlanta streak. He was out-boxed, out-punched and out-speeded from gong to gong. Most of the time he was on the retreat, backing away from the flashy Negro, who took the pace away from him and carried him faster than he has been carried by anyone since he became a national figure in the boxing world.

Pulford said only occasionally did the champion look like the Harry Greb of old. For the most part he was defending, if at times with a degree of mastery. By contrast Flowers, as he advanced, blocked and caught the vast majority of Greb's punches.

> Flowers' judgement of distance was perfect. Time and again Greb missed punches by the fraction of an inch… Apparently he was not hurt by Flowers' blows, although upon at least three occasions he hung on tenaciously and showed a disposition to loaf on the ropes.

Flowers, said Pulford, would make Greb miss, then counter to the body time and again.

Two wire service reports had vastly contrasting interpretations – one gave Flowers seven of the ten the other gave Greb eight. It was rumoured the report in favour of Greb was sent by none other than his manager, Red Mason, who rushed across to the telegraph office to file it, anxious to get his version out first. This fits in with the practice described in a retrospective piece by Al Buck in the April 1949 edition of *Ring*, whereby managers would race each other to the wire services away from the major cities in order to file 'reports' in favour of their man. No doubt Walk Miller did it often enough. On this occasion, perhaps, Mason beat him to it. Lewis Bryer said Mason actually sat on the press row, attempting to influence the opinions of writers, accompanied by two of Greb's 'home town scribes'. One of those would have been Regis Welsh, the sports editor of the *Pittsburgh Post*, who saw it 7-2-1 for Greb, an astonishingly contrary version to that of most of the neutral Ohio writers. Welsh gave Flowers only the second and sixth, with the first even. His newspaper ran the headline, 'Champion Harry Greb Beats Negro Boxer In 10 Slashing Rounds.' Welsh felt Flowers did well for six rounds, then tired and 'grew more timid as the bout wore on, and was at sea against Greb's windmill tactics, speed, and roughhouse…'

The agency copy, probably supplied by Mason that gave Greb eight of the ten rounds was used by the *Washington Post*, the *Oklahoman* and the *New York Times*. The *Sandusky (Ohio) Register* scored the fight a draw, while the *Elyria (Ohio) Chronicle Telegram* went for Greb.

The *Toledo News-Bee*'s Dick Meade, probably not meaning to be disparaging, described Flowers as, 'the ebony hued, rubber bodied son of a Georgia mammy and a Southern Uncle Tom'. Aaron and Lula Flowers, who had raised their son to be a man of principle and faith, did not deserve to be dismissed in those terms, but Meade was perhaps a better boxing writer than social analyst.

Greb was rough from first bell to last, but once the fight was done, he was genial and sporting. According to E. W. Dickerson of the *Grand Rapids Herald*, he said:

Flowers is the greatest boxer I ever faced in the ring. He can beat heavyweight champion Jack Dempsey in a contest of ten rounds. He gave me a fight I will never forget, and showed me a lot of things about boxing that I never knew before.

O. B. Keleer, in the *Atlanta Journal*, wrote:

Let us give the 'Tiger' a square deal. He has earned it. He is unquestionably one of the greatest fighters at his weight in the game today, if not the greatest. He is a marvel as an entertainer, because nobody can loaf or stall with him.

Keleer wrote that he hoped Walk Miller would not find it too difficult to match Flowers in the wake of this performance.' And the next time Flowers gets Mr Greb in the ring with him, if he ever does, put down a bit of change on the Georgia 'shine', if you are that kind of a man.'

One who dissented from the opinion that Flowers won was Hardy Bradburry, the *United Press* correspondent, who wrote:

Harry Greb, master boxer, found in Tiger Flowers perhaps the most difficult proposition in all his ring experiences. The black fellow certainly made good every claim as to prowess coupled with uncanny skill. It would be unfair, unreasonable and unjust to give a decision otherwise than a draw… It was not a spectacular battle, but one wonderfully interesting to the devotee learned in the higher branches of the art of self-defense. It was a battle of defense rather than offense, for every legitimate blow which would have caused considerable damage was blocked skillfully by one or the other. It continued thru ten rounds without a single bit of injury to either and still every round was fought with a determination to win.

The following week in the *Lima News* of 31 August, Bradburry quoted Greb as saying Flowers was 'a tough customer' and declaring that he didn't want to fight the Tiger again 'for any amount of money'. Having had time to think Bradburry suggested that if he had the skill to punch straight instead of concentrating on hooks, Flowers would be even more dangerous. He also felt Flowers was an expert at blocking punches. 'I cannot remember where I have seen a cleverer boxer at this important requirement than Tiger Flowers. Greb could find no weakness…'

Ed Danforth of the *Atlanta Georgian* was not at the fight but said most of the newspapers he had seen had Flowers as the winner.

Walker Miller, manager of the 'Tiger', galloped into this city this morning
with a pocket full of press clippings, and in every one there was the verdict
in black and white: Flowers Wins!

The old heavyweight champion James J. Corbett wrote of it, based on what
he had heard. Unnamed newspapermen had told him that Flowers had
actually carried Greb, which was unlikely, by agreeing to pull his punches.
Corbett was not a good journalist, though he was able enough with words to
write his own autobiography.

Joe Williams, writing in the *New York Evening Independent* the following
November, referred to the fight as even. 'I saw him hold Greb even some
months ago in one of those no decision step-alongs… Flowers should have
won by a wide margin, but he was over-awed. Greb out-awed him.'

James Fair, who wrote the brilliantly entertaining book about Greb called
Give Him To The Angels in 1946, said, from his vantage point two decades on, that
Flowers caught the champion on an off-night and the fight was fairly even.

Jimmy Jones, the biographer of Young Stribling, said some years later: 'The
result was a newspaper decision for Flowers. And the Georgia Deacon was
made. The fight with Greb really launched Flowers nationally.'

Tiger did not allow himself time to dwell on what he had achieved. Eleven
days later Miller wheeled him out for another payday against Tut Jackson
over ten rounds at the League Park in Martins Ferry, a small town on the
banks of the Ohio River. He won in the eighth, putting Jackson down four
times. He was back on the treadmill.

A fortnight after that he was in Columbus, Ohio, for a twelve round
'newspaper' decision over Jamaica Kid. On the same day the *Modesto
Evening News* described him as the 'unofficial middleweight champion of
the universe'. He stayed in town for another twelve round bout with Lee
Anderson at the Fairmont Arena. Babe Adams, for the *Columbus Dispatch*,
reported that Flowers won easily.

Every round went in the Atlanta darkey's direction up to the seventh frame.
Anderson tried to cope with the fleet Tiger but was rewarded for his efforts
with jabs and hooks from varied sources, and in the clinches the New
Yorker appeared bewildered.

Anderson made a big effort in the seventh, throwing low blows, back-
handers and wrestling as well as looking for a knockout punch, but Flowers
was unfazed and went on throwing punches in 'smothering flocks'.

In the final round there was a moment of comedy when Anderson scored
a flash knockdown. As he turned towards a neutral corner, Flowers rolled
over, sprang to his feet and tore in again before the referee, whose name was

Trott, could think about counting. Before the bell it was Anderson who was down from a left swing, and he did need a count.

Incredibly, before the month was out, Flowers had boxed on successive nights at the Canton Auditorium and the Weller Theatre in Zanesville, scoring respectively a second round knockout of Tut Jackson and a four round retirement win over Battling Gahee, who was pulled out with a broken wrist.

In the course of his career Flowers fought sixty-five rounds against Jamaica Kid, sixty-one against Lee Anderson, fifty-four against Battling Gahee and thirty-six against Tut Jackson.

The capacity of these men to go on fighting on this ludicrous, brutal carousel, especially when it meant losing gruelling fights with a man as relentless as Tiger Flowers, was astonishing. What kind of a mindset made them come back, again and again? Yes, they needed the money, or must have done, but there is something about a man who will go on putting himself through pain and sweat in the certainty that no matter how hard he tries, he will lose, and may even be knocked out or pounded until the referee will rescue him.

In October 1924 it was the Jamaica Kid's turn again, this time at the Commonwealth Sporting Club in New York. Flowers wore his man down and stopped him in eight.

Miller lobbied hard to build on the superb performance against Greb, sending out his press releases to anybody and everybody who might hold some influence but it was not his policy to leave Flowers waiting around for big fights to come in.

There had been talk of Tiger fighting Battling Siki in Atlanta in October, but it didn't happen – Siki was always reluctant to box other black fighters because there was usually less money on the table. When Flowers did return to his home city it was to knock out a veteran from Montreal named Cleve Hawkins in three rounds at the auditorium on 21 October. Flowers conceded 11 lbs to an old fighter who had been working the circuit for almost twenty years. The extra weight probably just made Hawkins slower and easier to hit. The next day the Tiger's boots, trunks and robe were packed again and he was on the move, north through Knoxville, Lexington, Cincinnati and finally arriving in Hamilton, Ohio, for a fourth round, low blow disqualification victory over Joe Lohman, whom he had outpointed over twelve rounds in Harlem only four months before. In twelve days, Flowers had fought three times and travelled by road or rail more than 1,350 miles.

The money was still rolling in steadily but at times even this most durable, optimistic, ambitious and religious of human beings must have been so very tired.

Still the journey went on. A week after beating Lohman at the Moose Arena in Hamilton, he was back in the confines of the Commonwealth Sporting Club in Harlem, entertaining the patrons by outpointing George Robinson over twelve rounds. The *Atlanta Constitution* reported:

Tiger Flowers rushed George Robinson off his feet from first to twelfth and last round, and won the decision at the end of the speediest and more scientific match of the season... Flowers was always (the) aggressor, while Robinson, a natural phenomenon in defense, failed to get [sic] his speedier opponent in a single round.

From New York it was on to Philadelphia Arena on 10 November, where he found himself boxing twice on the same night. He was scheduled to box Jackie Clark of Allentown, Pennsylvania, over ten rounds but the medical officer ruled Clark unfit because of a split ear. The promoter, Jules Aronson, who earned his real money dealing in furs and jewellery, could not find a suitable replacement for a ten round fight, so did the next best thing he could think of. No doubt with the approval of Walk Miller, he hired two novice-level men to box Flowers over five rounds each. That way, his customers, who had paid to watch the new middleweight contender from the Deep South, would not be disappointed – or at least would not have grounds for asking for their money back. First, Flowers beat a black fighter named Jerry Hayes on a second round knockout. Local writer James C. Isaminger said the Tiger played with poor Hayes in the opening session at the end of which Hayes was told by his cornerman, who was either crazy or stupid: 'That fellow has nothing, go in and finish him.' Hayes ignored him, tried to box on the move, but Flowers got down to work, shook him up with a left hand to the mouth, chased him and knocked him down with a short right to the jaw. Referee Lew Grimson stopped it and as soon as Hayes had been taken away, they brought in Flowers' second opponent, a white light heavyweight from Gloucester, New Jersey, named Hughie Clements, sometimes written Clemons. Flowers had weighed 167 lbs, and while Clements' weight was not announced, he looked about ten pounds heavier. The extra weight could not help him. Flowers, warmed up by his first contest, pinned Clements in a corner with a burst of punches, then to entertain the crowd stood stock still and let his opponent hit him back for about three seconds. While this strange, rather daft act of kidology worked in one way in that he was not shaken in the slightest, a right hand did cut his lip. Flowers merrily went back to the attack and dropped Clements, who was still on the floor when the bell rang with the count at seven. He pulled himself up and made it to his corner, came up for the second only to be nailed by a right hand that buckled his knees and put him down again. Referee Grimson did not bother to count, just raised the Tiger's arm in victory as the towel was thrown in from the loser's corner in a belated, futile gesture of surrender.

It was after this that Joe Williams, in the *New York Evening Independent* of 22 November, included Flowers in his list of leading pound-for-pound black boxers.

… in action he resembles a cross between an agitated whirlwind and an enthusiastic typhoon. Speed is his metier. Next to Greb, the champion, he is probably the best middleweight in the game today.

Williams, who was at times an astute judge unafraid to put his neck on the line, wrote that Flowers' tendency to slap left him short of the very highest level, of those who will be considered in the pound-for-pound top ten for decades to come.

On 27 November 1924 Flowers was in Canton, Ohio, at the city auditorium, pounding out a one-sided, bloody twelve round newspaper decision over a heavyweight trial horse Clem Johnson, who fought out of New Orleans and then New York, but who was born in a small community on the west bank of the Demerara River in Guyana.

Johnson had raised his profile by stopping the forty-year-old, half-blind Sam Langford in thirteen rounds in Mexico, and had lasted into the twelfth with top heavyweight contender Harry Wills. He was strong, and had the ability to absorb punishment without complaint – and was no match for Flowers, whom local writer Vance Dolan described as, 'the dynamic black man from the land of cotton'. The Tiger won every round, and by the closing stages seemed almost tired of hitting the big man. Dolan said:

> … if any man ever took plenty of good, hard socking, Clem did last night. His face was a gory spectacle when the bout was over. The crimson flowed generously and the New York heavyweight's face was puffed up like a toy balloon… We will say this for Johnson. He is game and can take more punishment and stand up under it better than any man we have seen in a ring, but he will never get any place as a pugilist. He has no ability whatsoever and he is too slow.

The Afro-American said Flowers took things at his own pace, cranking it up over the first five rounds, responded whenever Johnson did land a blow by raising the pace even more, and overcame a low blow in the seventh that 'crumpled him up for a bit', pouring it on even more. By the last three rounds, this writer agreed with the Canton man, that Flowers was tired from his own efforts.

> In the face of a 30 lb handicap in weight, the Southern Tiger swarmed all over the easterner and won by several miles, but he could not bring Johnson down. In fact, Clem did not appear to be hurt, although he left the ring with a face that was battered raw and bled freely from eyes, nose and mouth… Flowers is a real fighter. He exhibited one of the greatest two-fisted attacks we have ever seen and his speed was amazing.

For Clem Johnson fighting for a living was all too often grim and painful. For the next four years he would go on trying and losing until eventually his willpower, his ability to withstand the punches, left him. According to the best records available on the superb BoxRec website he was stopped inside three rounds of five of his last six fights. He went to the well for the final time in December 1928 when he was knocked out by the 28 lbs heavier, infinitely better George Godfrey in Richmond, Virginia.

Four days after handing Johnson a drubbing Flowers was fresh enough to take out poor, washed-up Battling Gahee in a couple of rounds. The *Lima News* reported, 'Tiger Flowers, Atlanta Negro, scored a technical knockout over Battling Gahee, Youngstown middleweight, in the second round of the scheduled twelve round fight. Gahee was on the floor unwilling to fight and referee Trott stopped the fight.'

And then, finally, came the booking he had waited for since the great night against Greb. The word came through to Miller offering a fight with former world middleweight champion Johnny Wilson ... at Madison Square Garden.

CHAPTER 11

'Blessed Be The Lord My Strength'

Johnny Wilson was born Giovanni Panica in New York City on 23 March 1893, was raised in the Italian section of Harlem and began boxing for a living as a teenager. He changed his name to John Panica and then settled on Johnny Wilson. Like Tiger Flowers he was unusual in that he was a southpaw – he fought left-handed, with his right leg and right glove forward. He won the world middleweight title with a twelve round points decision over Mike O'Dowd, the St Paul Cyclone, at Boston Armory in May 1920. He was managed by Marty Killilea until March 1923, when Killilea suddenly retired from the sport, claiming he did not approve of the way the New York State Commission did its business. Both Wilson and Killilea had been suspended the previous year for not honouring a contract to fight Harry Greb, which Killilea insisted was made under duress. As a result of that Wilson was no longer recognised as champion in New York. Strangely, given that Killilea was retiring, a man described in the news report as a 'horseman and sportsman' named Frank Marlow paid $50,000 to buy him out of his contract with Wilson. Once Marlow had the contract, Wilson suddenly became champion again in New York. It was perhaps not inconsequential that Frank Marlow's real name was Frank Gandolfo. The 'horseman and sportsman' label translates into illegal bookmaker and Broadway nightclub owner. Gandolfo, who had become Marlow, paid protection money to a Brooklyn mob boss, Frankie Yale, for whom Al Capone had worked as a waiter in a Coney Island bar, before moving to Chicago. Yale, who controlled Gandolfo AKA Marlow, was born Francesco Ioele. He worked for the Masseria crime family. His business was extortion, prostitution, boot legging and also 'legitimate' fronts, including, ironically, an undertaker's. Yale AKA Ioele was killed in 1928, shot while sitting in his bulletproof car. The dealer had somehow omitted to bulletproof the windows.

Johnny Wilson lost the middleweight championship to Harry Greb at the Polo Grounds in August 1923. He always said the decision was pre-arranged. Wilson said the fight was a good one, but at the last minute the ringside judges were changed. He said as he was warming up, 'connected' fight manager Broadway Bill Duffy came into the dressing room and warned him 'they' were going to take away his title. Wilson remembered telling Duffy, 'I don't think they'd do that to me.' Wilson felt he had won, but the decision went to Greb. It's not unusual in boxing for a man to believe he has won, only for the verdict to go the other way, and it doesn't mean the fight is crooked – or that the verdict was a bad one. However, Wilson said afterwards he was invited to an expensive Italian restaurant on 46th Street where the mood was unexpectedly joyous. 'You'd think I'd won the title or something the way he champagne was flowing,' he said, in an interview with writer Peter Heller, when he was in his seventies. Wilson, incidentally, called the mob men he knew 'nice guys'.

Greb also beat Wilson at Madison Square Garden in January 1924, after which Wilson appeared to lose some heart. He was thirty-one years old, still capable of mixing with the best, but the momentum had gone, and his training became erratic. When the call came for him to fight Tiger Flowers he had not boxed for three months, since it was considered he had come off worse in a no-decision fight with Jock Malone in St Paul, Minnesota.

Millicent Hearst, wife of the newspaper magnate William Randolph Hearst, was raising money for her charity, which aimed to provide free milk for the poor of New York City. Tex Rickard, anxious to ingratiate himself with Mrs Hearst and her social set, and so to deprive them of a small fraction of their bank balance, began running boxing promotions to assist the Milk Fund, just as he had at the beginning of the decade with Anne Morgan. By attending the Garden at the corner of 26th Street and Madison Avenue, Millicent Hearst and her friends and acquaintances gave Rickard's business a renewed veneer of respectability. Suddenly he seemed, not a promoter of legalised violence, but a philanthropist with a sense of social responsibility. Boxing was chic. It was also shining proof that any mud that had been clinging to him following his 1922 acquittal of sexual crimes against young girls had well and truly been washed away.

Rickard booked Flowers for the show on 9 December but initially could find nobody to fight him. Eventually, through a tame newspaperman, Bill Farnsworth of the *Boston-American*, they offered Johnny Wilson $7,500 to do it. Wilson was probably of minimal interest to the Mob now he didn't have the title and wasn't training with any great commitment. He agreed, trained for a week, and fought to reduce his weight to the match limit of 160 lb. He managed it, scaling 159½ lb on the day of the fight, but what it took out of him is anybody's guess. Flowers, as usual, was fit and sharp, and in great form. More than 13,000 turned out to swell the charity fund. Gross receipts were given as $107,599, with expenses of $52,665 – a big night for Mrs Hearst and her companions, and for Rickard. It was a big night for Flowers too. The *Afro-American* report shows he came out throwing punches from the first bell and Wilson was overwhelmed. 'He pressed Wilson hard from the starting bell, repeatedly forcing the former champion to the ropes under a steady fire throughout the first two rounds, while Wilson missed like a novice.'

In the third Flowers staggered Wilson with a looping left and southpaw right hook.

> Flowers continued the battering, working Wilson before him along the ring ropes until the former champion was rendered groggy in Flowers' corner. A right to the jaw crashed home cleanly and Wilson slumped forward. Then a left swept to the jaw and Wilson was practically out on his feet. Instinctively, however, he lurched forward and grabbed Flowers about the neck with the grip of a wrestler and held until the bout was stopped.

Referee Eddie Purdy called it off with five seconds left in the round but while the decision 'did not meet with the unanimous approval of the crowd', the Afro-American writer considered it justified and believed the victory put Flowers high in the list of the world's top middleweights.

Wilson, who later would run nightclubs in New York and Boston, had lost inside the scheduled distance only once before, and that was more than ten years before. His pride was hurt, and the defeat still rankled almost fifty years later. 'Just stale, not in shape,' he told Peter Heller. 'He didn't hurt you or nothing. The only thing he did that made it look good, he throws a million punches. But there's no steam behind it. And it looked one-sided and the referee stopped the fight. He was throwing all the punches and I was just doing the blocking.'

Six days later Tiger was back before an 8,000 crowd in Philadelphia going over old ground once more in the name of a payday, stopping Jack Townsend in five rounds. Townsend, whom Flowers had beaten in eleven rounds in New York at the beginning of August, had once fought the great champion Jack Johnson within the confines of Leavenworth jail in Kansas.

Back in 1913 Johnson had been sentenced to a year and a day in prison and fined $1,000 for a contravention of the Mann Act, which allowed prosecution of men who took women across a state line for immoral purposes. Instead of serving his time Johnson fled the U.S.A. and stayed away for seven years. He defended his title in Paris, moving on to Argentina and then Cuba, where he lost his title to Jess Willard, and on to Spain and then Mexico. In July 1920, following political changes in Mexico, he had run out of road and agreed to return home. He served his time in Leavenworth, where he gave at least six exhibitions, one of which, on 15 April 1921, was against Townsend. In spite of the 'exhibition' status, Johnson had won on a sixth round knockout.

Now, more than three years on, on 15 December 1924, Townsend outweighed Flowers by fifteen pounds, 185 to 170, but was hopelessly outclassed, according to the *Reading Eagle*, and in the fifth round it was all over. 'After being sent to one knee from a smashing right and left to the jaw, his seconds tossed in the towel before referee Lew Grissom could start the count.'

There was no break for Christmas celebrations in Atlanta. On Boxing Day Tiger was at the Broadway Auditorium in Buffalo, New York, way up near the Canadian border, slugging out a six-round draw with Frankie Schoell, a twenty-four-year-old local ticket-seller. Schoell had won the vast majority of more than seventy professional fights, was a valuable commodity to the Buffalo promoters and if the fight with Flowers had been anything like close he would almost certainly have been awarded a victory that would have drawn him attention. We cannot be sure but the fact that Schoell was given a draw probably means that Flowers was, as he should have been, the better man, and that anywhere else but Buffalo he would have been given the decision. He probably didn't worry about it. An agency report reprinted by the *Atlanta Constitution* suggested it was a typical Flowers fight. He bulldozed Schoell to the ropes and into the corners, although Schoell held him off well at times with a fast, stinging jab. Flowers hurt him with body shots in the third, but he rallied again in the fourth and then they slugged it out toe-to-toe over the last two rounds.

W. C. Vreeland, writing in the *Brooklyn Daily Eagle*, said Flowers had developed to the point where a fight with Kid Norfolk would be the best bout that could be made between 'colored artists'. He felt the knockouts Norfolk had scored over the Tiger in 1922 and 1923 were no longer a fair guide to form. 'Flowers has improved so much in the past year that there is scarcely any comparison between what he was and what he is now.'

The win over Wilson had impressed Rickard, who complained to New York writers at the turn of 1925 about fighters who wanted big money yet couldn't draw fans. 'The little fellers have been spoiled and they're not much good anyway. You give 'em the earth with a diamond belt around it to get 'em into a ring and then they can't draw the customers.'

By contrast the great promoter liked the fact that Flowers would fight anybody and tried to sell himself as an attraction. 'I want fellers like this Paul Berlanbach, or Tom Gibbons in my shows, or this Tiger Flowers, the colored man from Atlanta.'

Rickard talked about Berlanbach, Gene Tunney and Mike McTigue, and then added:

> Flowers is the kind of fighter I like. I've got a contract up in my safe with his name on it, agreeing to fight any man in the world bar one. That one's Willie Stribling. The only reason Flowers bars him is that he might whip Stribling and then he wouldn't dare go back to Atlanta.

Meanwhile, Walk Miller announced he had been advised by his lawyers to sue the Atlanta Commission for $100,000 over the seizure of gate receipts from a show he had promoted headlined by world light-heavyweight champion Mike McTigue and Jimmy King on Boxing Day 1924. He had not been in Atlanta because he had been at Flowers' side in Buffalo for the Frankie Schoell fight. In his absence the show had 'bombed' and there had not been enough taken at the gate to pay McTigue his $3,000 guarantee. Miller had sent word to call off the show when the financial implications had become obvious but the Atlanta Commission had insisted it should go on, presumably because of the late notice. In the end it was a row about nothing. Miller found the money from somewhere to pay McTigue when the Irishman returned to New York.

On New Year's afternoon, 1925, Flowers was in Brooklyn at the Rink Sporting Club, hammering out a three round stoppage win in a rematch with Joe Lohman from Toledo. Matchmaker Lew Raymond said Lohman was not only the best opponent he could get for Flowers but the only one 'that dared face the new black sensation'. The fight drew a detailed preview in the *Brooklyn Eagle*, which referred to 'the dusky Mr Theodore Flowers' and, 'this gentleman of color'. The writer also considered the fight with Lohman a foregone conclusion.

> If Flowers is the goods – if he is really the colored cyclone they say he is – Lohman should hit the canvas and stick there within five or six rounds... Lohman is a big, hulky specimen whose main asset is the ability to absorb considerable punishment before saying 'Good night'. He is slow, not much of a boxer and not much of a hitter... Still the mere idea of seeing this so-called dusky demon in action will doubtless cram the Rink arena and it is likely that few will be dissatisfied with the result of the bout with the exception of Lohman.

The unnamed writer also said it was within the past year that Flowers had risen to prominence – in other words, since he'd been boxing in New York City.

> He came north and knocked out a number of opponents at one of New York's smaller fight clubs. He journeyed into the Midwest and mopped up an Ohio ring with Harry Greb, our esteemed middleweight champion... Now Flowers literally sits on top of his world. It is current opinion that only the task of luring Greb into a decision bout stands between the Georgia Negro and a world's championship.

As had been predicted, Lohman was incapable of giving the rapidly improving Flowers any kind of fight. Jack Farrell of the *New York Daily News* said Lohman was showered with punches and knocked down four times before referee Eddie Forbes waved it off. Lohman was on the floor from a left uppercut in round two, down again from a left to the body in the second, down from what Farrell called 'a light tap on the shoulder' in the third and then finished off with a final left to the body. Forbes did not bother to count. An agency report printed in the *Reading Eagle* said Lohman could not deal with 'the unrelenting attacks of the colored man'.

Next it was north to the Mechanics arena in Boston, where Flowers was matched with Billy 'The Kansas Cyclone' Britton over ten rounds on Monday, 5 January 1925. It lasted to midway through the fourth before Britton was rescued. The *Associated Press* reported:

> Flowers swarmed all over Britton from the start, landing at will with stiff right jabs and left hooks to the jaw and body. Britton landed an occasional right but was unable to do damage. The Tiger's blows seemed to lack power, however, failing to put Britton down for the count. Britton was weakening fast after a fusillade of rights and lefts as the referee ended the bout.

That win sat well on the Tiger's record. In his next fight Britton would give Harry Greb a tough night in a no-decision bout that went the full ten rounds, with Greb only really turning up the heat in the last.

Two days before the Britton fight, Flowers talked to Lawrence Sweeney of the *Boston Globe* and revealed that he and Willie Mae were expecting an addition to the family. 'All my fighting these days,' he was quoted by Sweeney as saying, 'is being done for Mrs Willie Mae Flowers, for little Vera (sic) Lee Flowers and for another little Flowers that we expect pretty soon in Atlanta.'

What happened is uncertain. If Willie Mae was pregnant, either she miscarried or the child was stillborn. Or it's possible, if the *Atlanta Constitution* was right and they had indeed adopted Verna Lee, they were planning to adopt again and that the idea came to nothing.

From Boston, Flowers moved on to Marieville, a suburb of Providence, Rhode Island, where only forty-eight hours after the Britton fight, he stopped Dan O'Dowd in eight. Again, the result was impressive. O'Dowd was a so-so Boston heavyweight but he had mixed with the best and had taken Gene Tunney the distance.

By then Flowers had won nineteen consecutive fights since the fight with Greb which had made his name. Tiger had gone forty-two fights in sixteen months without defeat, back to that strangely passive withdrawal against Fireman Jim Flynn in Mexico in September 1923. He was now acknowledged as one of the best middleweights in the world. No black fighter had ever held the world 160 lb championship but it was obvious that if he kept up the form he was in, kept appearing regularly in New York and Boston, and remained the dignified, humble, unprovocative man he was, sooner or later he must get his chance.

He was so busy that when Tex Rickard called Walk Miller to book him to fight Jack Delaney, another middleweight with a great deal of talent, at Madison Square Garden on 16 January, it was Tiger's fourth fight of the month. Even by his standards, it was a mad schedule. Today, a manager who had Flowers on the brink of a championship fight would be persuaded only by a serious amount of folding money to take on a young, dangerous puncher like Delaney with nothing at stake. In those days, life was different. Flowers never avoided anybody in his life, and Miller had shown in the past that he had a reckless disregard for shrewd, or even sensible matching. He drove as hard a financial bargain as he could, but by and large took whatever fight was on offer, wherever it was, and seemingly in the end for whatever money they could get. The Delaney fight, for example, was called off at one point because Miller was asking for too much money, but they came to a deal in the end. It is likely that, under the weight of Rickard's powers of persuasion, Miller had to reduce his price.

Delaney, called by more than one writer Bright Eyes because of his ability to attract female fans, was a capable boxer, shrewd and experienced, with a heavy punch. He was a French-Canadian from Quebec, whose birth name was Ovila Chapdelaine. His ring name came about when he was a preliminary fighter – an announcer asked him what his name was, misheard Chapdelaine and called him Jack Delaney. It stuck. The son of a lumberjack, who moved the family to Bridgeport, Connecticut, Delaney had boxed on the undercard when Harry Greb had won the middleweight title against Johnny Wilson at the Polo Grounds and was making his name among the regulars at the Garden. When Rickard matched Delaney with Flowers he made a fight of considerable significance.

Paul Gallico, in his book *Farewell to Sport*, wrote of Delaney:

> He was married to a pale, pretty wife whom he seemed to adore. He was ostensibly a child of nature who loved to fish and hunt in the wilds, and when his training and his fights were over he would retire to a woodland lodge he owned in New Hampshire on Lake Winnepesaukee...

British writer Gilbert Odd said Walk Miller felt something was wrong before the fight when money suddenly began to flow in on Delaney. He knew they were still the out-of-town boys and that Flowers, as a black man, might easily be considered expendable, but a hunch was all it was. Delaney came out before the crowd of around 15,000 to a reception that reminded some of the golden days of the great lightweight and New York favourite, Benny Leonard.

The Tiger attacked in his usual rushing style in round one and seemed to be enjoying himself. One body shot appeared to slow him momentarily, a testament to the power the Canadian carried, but the round was his beyond argument. Delaney had employed the same kind of tactics against Paul Berlanbach ten months before, defending, waiting then exploding into life. He had beaten the inexperienced Berlanbach in four rounds. He let more heavy right hands go against Flowers in the second, missing wildly sometimes, but looking more dangerous. Then Flowers made a weird error, echoing the 'go on then, hit me' tactic he had used against the novice Hughie Clements in Philadelphia the previous November. He dropped his hands, stuck out his chin, moved it side to side and began as if to laugh. Before he could enjoy the joke, Delaney smashed home a right uppercut and the Tiger crashed down on his back. He tried to get up at seven, but his legs folded again and referee Jack O'Sullivan completed the count only forty-three seconds into the round.

Ed Danforth of the *New York Sunday American* went to the dressing room to ask Flowers what had happened. By attempting to write down the way the Tiger spoke, he enforced the stereotypes of the day, but also revealed a little of Flowers' character.

'What happened to you up there, Deacon?' said Danforth.

'Well, suh, I spec I got knocked out. Yessuh. Though I don't know jus' exactly how, yet.'

Danforth tried to give Flowers a fair shot at explaining himself, but his transcription was pretty stilted stuff. Flowers partly regained his senses in his corner and at first thought the fight must be over because he had won, and only fully came to when he stepped down from the ring. Many fighters who have been knocked out cold with a single punch have said they felt no pain, and when they woke it was as if nothing had happened. They felt as if they could go straight back in the ring and fight on. Flowers said it was the first time it had happened to him, that he had been hurt in the past by Panama Joe Gans and also with a body shot by Kid Norfolk, but nothing like this. It reminded him, he said, of being shaken awake by his brother as a boy. He told Danforth that in round one he felt at ease and suspected he must have grown over-confident. He remembered Miller telling him in the corner after round one, 'Tiger, he's the biggest bum we ever fought.' It does sound as if complacency had led to his crashing fall.

Miller didn't see it that way. Maybe he was saving face, maybe he couldn't face what had happened, or maybe he genuinely felt they had been carved up, but he was already screaming loud and long that Delaney must have had a loaded right glove, an iron bar or spring, known as a gimmick, which he said must have been put there in the interval between rounds one and two. Danforth asked Flowers for his opinion on that.'I dunno, suh, but I do know one thing he had in his glove. He had his fis', yes, suh.'

Flowers did not want to play Miller's game and was generous to Delaney, saying that anybody who hit as hard as he did could be a world champion. He went to the Canadian's dressing room, wished him well and said he hoped he would make a lot of money and win a world title. He also showed his wit, and an endearing ability to accept defeat, when he said later that he went out to buy the newspapers the next morning, something he never usually did. He still had no recollection of how he came to be knocked out and wanted to read about it, and see any photographic evidence for himself.

> So early nex' mawnin', I got a papah and saw a pictah... and there was a man standin' up... and offah the canvas was a leg stickin' up, and I knew that mu' be me.

Why writers wrote like that, I can't understand, but we get the gist.

Miller would not let the situation drop. There is a difference between a legitimate argument that a manager might have a chance of winning and an unprovable claim that will serve only to provoke hostility. At this time it would have been best for Miller to hold his hands up, take some of the blame for the match itself, and for leading Flowers into the complacency that made him stick his chin out, and say the Tiger would, in time, prove it a freak result. Miller was never that subtle. He took Flowers before the New York commission, and told them to look at an ugly, swollen mark on the bridge of his nose. It could not, he argued, be the result of a conventionally gloved fist.

Miller, the boy from Atlanta still considered wet behind the ears by the long-serving cynics of New York City, was making himself a pain in the backside. He was making enemies of the men who ruled the business from their offices in the Flatiron Building where Broadway and Fifth Avenue meet at 23rd Street, and quite possibly the men who liked to think they ran the sport from other offices on Broadway and from backrooms of nightclubs, speak-easies and dance halls. Newspapermen began referring to Walk as 'Squawk' Miller.

The sports editor of the *Afro-American* laid the blame for the defeat squarely on Miller's lack of discretion in an angry, mixed-metaphor blast.

> This human dynamo was, after all, made of flesh and blood and the terrific strain of fighting two and three times a week for the last year took its toll... Because he could fight and the fans fought for the opportunity to swell the gate returns when the Georgia Tornado was going in action, Walk Miller killed the goose that laid the golden egg when he sent his 'pitcher' to the well once too often without a let-up. In meeting a polished boxer like Delaney, Flowers should have had a rest of several weeks and trained for several more... this ought to be a warning to the fighter's manager.

If he heard any criticism, Miller ignored it. The show went on.

Danforth said Flowers had already signed for another New York fight with Paul Berlanbach, while the Afro-American said a Berlanbach fight might happen in Baltimore on 26 February, the winner to box Delaney. Perhaps Miller's lack of tact had made New York cool on him and his fighter, if only temporarily. The Berlanbach idea was dropped, as was another plan to fight Mickey Walker, then the reigning world welterweight champion at the National Sportsmen's Club in Newark, New Jersey. Both sides had agreed, with Walker's side stipulating Flowers must not weigh more than 160 lb, but the plan was shelved.

Tiger went home to Atlanta on the afternoon of the 19 January, to see Willie Mae and Verna Lee for a short visit, in lieu of Christmas and New Year. His mother-in-law, Mamie Spellars, who lived with them at the family home at 282 Parsons Street, Atlanta, had been ill for the past year and on 12 January suffered a stroke. He also had time for a public engagement at a white theatre where his home citizens gave him, according to the brief mention in the *Afro-American*, a tremendous ovation. The information would have come from Miller, who also said he had turned down an offer for five fights in Boston for a total of $15,000 plus a percentage of the gate, on the grounds that he preferred to negotiate each fight as it came. Miller didn't like tying the Tiger to one place or one promoter when other offers might come in from elsewhere.

Miller agreed his next fight for Boston at the Mechanics Building on the 27 January, against Tommy Robson, a local scrapper known as the Malden Mauler. By then, agencies were reporting that Flowers also had fights lined up against Jamaica Kid and, on the 26 February against Johnny Wilson. The *Afro-American* printed a cartoon of two men looking up at a giant billboard with Flowers' schedule of fights written across it. One man says: 'Can he hold up under it?' The second man replies: 'He will have to be an iron man.' Even in those tough times, the rate at which Flowers was fighting was a subject for concern. At the foot of the cartoon was the headline 'Walk Miller, Money Crazy, Has Flowers Fighting Every Week'.

A respected trainer named Dixie Kid – not the old welterweight champion who fought under that name – expressed his concern that not only did Flowers need a rest, he might be struggling to stay at middleweight. In his first fight of the year against Lohman in Brooklyn, Flowers had been 168 lb, but had made it down to 161½ lb, still 1½ lb above the middleweight limit, when he lost to Delaney. The Dixie Kid told the Afro-American that more than once recently Flowers had been forced to reduce weight and was 'drawn too fine' against Delaney.

> What the Tiger needs is a layoff of several weeks or he will be shot to pieces in less than two months. He is a great scrapper and it is a pity that his manager can't see that human endurance can only stand so much.

His knockout defeat by Delaney had been bad enough for modern day doctors to have placed him on a medical suspension of at least four weeks, but defeats came and went without restriction in those days. Only eleven days later he mauled the Malden Mauler, Tommy Robson, in eight rounds. The *Afro-American* reported:

> Hundreds of followers of Robson begged and pleaded with voice and gesture for Tommy to go in and fight but the Boston man stood doggedly... and took a lambasting such as has been handed few men in the prize ring.... As early as the end of the fourth Robson was whipped, but as the bell tolled for round after round he came out grimly, doggedly and gamely, only to take more and more punishment. In fact, as the fray continued, Flowers grew weary himself from pounding his man... Finally in the eighth when the local man's face had become a red ruin and he was practically helpless from the barrage of blows that had been rained upon him by the Atlanta firebrand, the referee stepped in.

From Boston the Tiger was on the move south to Providence, Rhode Island, and forty-eight hours later he knocked out a raw no-hoper from Cleveland called Bill Savage in two rounds. Incredibly, that was his sixth fight in the month of January alone, including the knockout by Delaney.

February began with another excursion into genuine world class against the British middleweight Ted Moore at the Sussex Avenue Armory arena in Newark, New Jersey on the second day of the month. The match had been made before Tiger fought Delaney and was initially cancelled when he lost, but the promoters changed their minds.

Moore was a good fighter from Plymouth, Devon, who had been trying his luck in the United States for more than a year. He had challenged Harry Greb for the middleweight championship at Yankee Stadium in June 1924, but had not come close to winning, even though Greb had shed around 15 lbs in the ten days leading up to the fight. Greb had won thirteen of the fifteen rounds.

Technically, Flowers-Moore was a No Decision contest, but the *Afro-American* called it a spectacular fight that Flowers won easily in spite of the bravery and stubborn resistance of the Englishman. 'Flowers took an early lead and was never headed. Moore, who was handicapped from the start with his battered nose, tried hard to the final bell.'

At the end Flowers was fresh enough to give the crowd a back handspring while Moore earned their applause for being 'game under fire'.

From Newark, Flowers travelled on to Dayton, Ohio, for an extended workout three days later against old rival Jamaica Kid, whom he stopped in the tenth round of a scheduled twelve. Flowers won every round.

Jamaica Kid, whose real name was James Buckley, would become one of the victims of the sport. The tough fights, the hard sparring with Jack Dempsey, and no doubt others who were too good and perhaps too big for him, the relentless treadmill of training and fighting eventually broke him. He lost his sight and his health. Nat Fleischer wrote:

> For several years he became a familiar and pathetic figure in front of New York boxing clubs, ekeing out a bare living on the charity of sports fans. He would stand before the club, a sign across his chest reading: I AM TOTALLY BLIND. PLEASE HELP JAMAICA KID, FORMER SPARRING PARTNER OF JACK DEMPSEY. His plea did not go unanswered, for sports followers are sentimental folk, and many of them remembered the Kid in his prime, an honest fighter who win, lose or draw, always gave his best. On several occasions I saw Jim Corbett hand Jamaica a five-dollar note and an encouraging 'Keep your chin up, Kid'.

Jamaica Kid collapsed in the street on 3 June 1938, was taken to hospital in Harlem, but died twelve days later.

There was talk of Flowers fighting Battling Siki in Atlanta on 9 February, Lee Anderson on the 18, Berlanbach on the 26, and Mickey Walker and Johnny Wilson in March. None of them happened, but Flowers was being written about, his reputation rising. People wanted to know who and where he would fight next.

By this time Miller had an office in Manhattan from where he could lobby and hustle for Tiger's work. Boxing had become a boom industry. The market was attractive for any fighter or promoter who could put on a good show, and Flowers was an entertainer who pulled in crowds and made them want to come back and see more. His dressing gown with the large motif of a tiger on the back identified him as much as his gold-toothed smile. Miller made as much as he could out of Flowers' Christian faith and his habit of reading his Bible every day. Aside from the toll that fighting so often, without time for the bruises to heal, without taking into account if he were even slightly sick, would inevitably take on the boxer's health, they were good for each other. Miller was white, Flowers was black, but they were both from Atlanta. They understood their ways of life better than any 'outsider' would. And they were, more than ever, men in a hurry.

On 14 February 1925 Flowers boxed Jackie Clark, whom he should have taken on in Philadelphia the previous November, when he ended up boxing two men on the same night. This time the match was made for twelve rounds at the Commonwealth Sporting Club – and Flowers won without difficulty in five.

Forty-eight hours later the gravy train had pulled into Boston for a return to the Mechanics Building and a fight with one-time title claimant, Lou Bogash, an Italian immigrant whose family had made Bridgeport, Connecticut, its home for almost twenty years. Lou, whose original name was Luigi Bocassi, sometimes spelled Buccasio, was tiny for a middleweight at 5 foot 5 inches, and a fair-haired bundle of aggression. His elder brother Patrizio had boxed as Patsy Bogash. Luigi, or Lou, had claimed New York recognition as middleweight champion when Johnny Wilson was suspended in January 1923. Bogash had stopped Charley Nasbert in eleven rounds to stake a claim but few took any notice. As a nineteen-year-old back in 1920, he had also fought a draw for the welterweight championship against Jack Britton. In the autumn of 1923 he had fought a No Decision bout with Harry Greb. Lou knew his trade.

In 1925 Flowers and Bogash slugged out an exciting four-fight series, beginning that night in Boston on 16 February when the Tiger was disqualified by referee Jerry Moore for hitting Bogash low with a left hand in round three.'Bogash went down suddenly as the pair were involved in a fast mix-up near the ropes... Bogash was completely out.' This according to the report in the *New York Herald-Journal*.

Bogash was content to wait for each of the four matches with Flowers to come around, but Tiger crammed in the paydays as usual. He had been matched with Paul Berlanbach and Johnny Wilson on 26 February, but both fell through and instead Walk Miller's screaming loud and long about foul play in the Delaney fight earned them a rematch at the Garden. The New York commission gave him an assurance, for what it was worth, that they would be especially vigilant over the behaviour of Delaney and those around him in his dressing room and in the corner.

Miller's sensational claims made good copy. The *Afro-American* wrote: 'Whether Miller was right in saying Delaney had a horse shoe in his glove on the night of their last meeting will be proved Thursday night.'

If Flowers and Miller had learned anything from the first fight it didn't show. The Tiger gave it his usual charge and Delaney tucked up into a tight defensive shell and waited. For three rounds the Canadian did nothing more than try the occasional, exploratory pot shot while Flowers hustled and bustled his way into an early lead. Then in the fourth Flowers was caught leaping in with his chin exposed and Delaney's right hand landed flush. Tiger crumpled back halfway through the ropes. He pulled himself back inside the ring and, plainly still dazed, dropped to one knee. Referee Patsy Haley ordered Delaney to a neutral corner, and picked up the count again. Flowers struggled to his feet at around four, then dropped down as Delaney steamed forward and let fly. The *New York Age* said a left hand landed before Flowers went down, but other reports said that as Flowers dipped down, a right hand was already on its way. Those who saw it said Flowers was on his right knee when the right hand completed its arc and connected with his head. He keeled over, badly hurt, and Miller once again screamed for retribution. Referee Haley seemed undecided about what to do and, once Flowers was on his feet, ordered both men to their corners. As it became clear that Haley was considering disqualifying Delaney, and that he might already have done so, discontent erupted and the fans 'set up a howl that has seldom been equalled at the Garden', said the *New York Age* writer. The crowd threw whatever came to hand into the ring. Programmes, fruit, newspapers all rained down. Some irate customers even tried to storm the ringside area. They booed, they jeered, they shouted abuse and even in the expensive seats gentlemen in evening dress joined in the protest. Pete Reilly, Delaney's manager, argued with referee Haley that the punch had already been on its way when Flowers chose to kneel down again, and he reminded him that dropping down without taking a punch was a disqualification offence even in the old bare-knuckle days. Haley waved Reilly away but went and stood to think in a neutral corner as the arguments continued to rage. After a few moments, in which he also consulted with deputy commissioner Walter Hook and, for some reason, ring announcer Joe Humphreys, Haley came to an astonishing conclusion. He said that as it had been a double foul, or at least one foul by Flowers, i.e. going down without being hit, closely followed by another by Delaney, i.e. landing a punch when his opponent was down, he would declare round four null and void. They would he said, therefore have to start the contest again from the beginning of a new round four.

Obviously Walk Miller should have screamed loud enough for the roof to have flown off the Garden. No manager in their right mind, let alone one who purported to care about his fighter as a friend, would put him back out after he had been so badly dazed, especially against a big puncher like Delaney. Miller was not prone to such sensitivities. He returned to the corner, took a look at Tiger who, as fighters will, wanted to box on. Miller, weakly, stupidly, let it happen. The New York commission, whose remit even in those rough and tumble days was to ensure as far as possible the safety of boxers working under its jurisdiction, should have intervened, but did not.

The sign that Flowers was still badly shaken came when the fight resumed. It was not in his nature to box on the run, but he tried to circle the ring, hardly throwing a punch. After almost a minute of non-action, Delaney feinted to throw a left to the body then smashed a right hand over the top to Flowers' chin and the Tiger dropped in a heap, out to the world. There was no point in counting, but Haley did anyway, completing the bizarre proceedings after sixty-five seconds of the round. The *New York Age* man said the knockout blow, 'rolled him in the resin dust with the blood pouring from his nose and mouth'.

Ed Van Every, an early biographer of Joe Louis, recalled, or recreated on hearsay, the tension in Delaney's dressing room when the door opened and Flowers walked in. Rather than complain or accuse, the Tiger said, 'Mister Delaney, I'm here to tell you I had nothing to do any of them things my manager said about you unfairly. Any time us two meet, you are the better man and that's all there is to it.'

Flowers bowed and turned to leave, but Delaney got up, asked him to wait and threw an arm around his shoulder, then shook his hand. 'Deacon,' he said. 'I'm going after the light-heavies from now on and I hope some day you win the middleweight title – and I mean it.'

There were other similar versions of the incident, with other similar quotes, but the gist was the same. Flowers had gone in and congratulated Delaney, which brought an end, or should have done, to the controversy.

Miller tried to cover up his terrible piece of misjudgment by blustering. The next morning he was outside the Flatiron building before the commission office opened ready to file a complaint that, once again, Delaney's gloves were loaded with an iron bar. He also filed complaints about referee Haley, and against Pete Reilly, whom he said had intimidated the official. Haley, he said, had broken the rules, and boxing tradition, by changing his mind after the initial disqualification decision. The commission listened, took its time, called Haley before them to explain himself, and as commissions usually do, they came out in support of their licensed official.

Knockout defeats in those far-off days meant less to a man's career than they do now because boxers worked more often and could more easily consign them to the further recesses of memory. Nevertheless, this was the second time that Flowers, who at the turn of the year was to some people's mind the uncrowned middleweight champion of the world, had been knocked out heavily in the first two months of 1925. His reputation had taken a serious dip. Miller, by accusing his opposing camp of chicanery, not once but twice, without any evidence whatsoever, had ostracized himself. The men who mattered on the New York fight scene might have tolerated if not exactly welcomed Miller, but by this time he had the reputation of a troublemaker. He was on the outside, not to be done any favours.

Flowers needed time off for the sake of his own health but also because back in Atlanta his mother-in-law Mamie Spellars was dying. She had not recovered from the stroke she had suffered on 12 January and so he returned home to support Willie Mae. When Mamie died on 10 March, he stayed on to help his wife through the funeral service, which took place back in Brunswick on the following day.

He was out of the ring only eighteen days in all. In Toledo, Ohio, on 16 March, he won a twelve round decision over an opponent from the old days, Sailor Darden, then set off for his second, brutal, dramatic fight with Lou Bogash at the Mechanics Building in Boston on 20 March. The possibility that Delaney had put a permanent short circuit on Flowers' ability to hold a punch arose when Bogash, who was not a particularly formidable hitter, dropped him twice in round two. Flowers fought back to win round three, when Bogash tried to claim a low blow foul, but then Tiger's vulnerability surfaced again in the fourth, when he was down twice more, once for eight. Both times he tore back in, and took over in the fifth and sixth with all-out attacks. The scoring system of the day did not give extra points for knockdowns. Whereas today Bogash would almost certainly have won both the second and fourth rounds by 10-7 margins, in 1925 this kind of mathematical intricacy did not exist. In round seven Flowers was knocked down for the fifth time, but was on his feet at three, once again jumping up smiling as if nothing had happened. His resistance was unshakeable and over the last three rounds it was Bogash who tired, with Flowers dominating. The agency report printed in the *Lewiston Sun* mentioned only three knockdowns, but as mandatory eight counts were not applied, it was easy to misinterpret knockdowns as slips, or vice-versa. The Lewiston report did agree that Flowers fought back strongly each time and swept the last three rounds and pointed out that when the Tiger rallied in round seven, Bogash tried to claim a foul but was ignored.

For the *Boston Daily Advertiser*, S. J. Mahoney wrote:

> Five times the greatest crowd that ever witnessed a fight in Boston madly jumped to their feet with the expected K.O. impending. And five times Mr Tiger Flowers, the tornado of the South, came up smiling. Lou Bogash, his opponent, couldn't produce the necessary wallop to keep the Tiger on the mat. From the opening gong until the finish, in one of the most desperate as well as thrilling fights, Bogash was dangerous, but Flowers always weathered the threatened curtains, and by a thrilling finish won the decision.

Bogash probably wondered how on earth the officials managed to find a way to vote against him. Nobody could have argued if he had been given the verdict, and later Flowers remembered the fight well: 'I had a boil on my nose, my tonsils were sore and my side ached before the fight. Each time I went down I felt terrible. Finally, I gritted my teeth, sailed in and won the decision...'

He admitted, though, that at one point around the fifth round he wanted to die. Illness, minor injury, nothing stopped the Tiger from honouring his commitments, but after this one he returned to Georgia. Perhaps, following the death of her mother, Willie Mae needed him badly. Perhaps, too, as he had already had thirteen fights in the first three months of the year and had been knocked out twice, his recovery from five knockdowns to win that fight with Bogash, had left him drained, psychologically as well as physically. He did not box again for almost six weeks, and when he did, it was no more than a workout not too far from home, a five round win over Sailor Darden in Savannah, just up the coast from Brunswick. He must have felt good after that one because he went across to Macon to knock out Battling Mims in five the next week.

He was soon back in the swing of things and on 18 May 1925 he was in Boston, at the Mechanics Building again, for a ten round points win over a fellow southpaw named Percy 'Pal' Reed, who was the type to give anybody rounds. He had gone the distance twice with Greb and once with Delaney.

Eight days on and Flowers was in the State Street Arena, Bridgeport, Connecticut, for a third fight with Bogash. This time it was in Lou's home town and the unwritten script was obvious. If it was anywhere near close, Bogash would almost certainly get the decision, especially after the events of their second battle. However, this time the Tiger was free of illness and refreshed after his spell at home. At the end of twelve rounds, he was a clear winner.

The *Norwalk Hour* went so far as to predict it was the end of the line for Bogash.

> Time and Tiger Flowers wrote the final chapter in the boxing career of Lou Bogash. Last night at the State Street Arena with fully 6,500 fans pulling for him, Bogash went down to one of the worst defeats of his career, losing every round in his 12-round battle to the slashing, leaping, slugging panther from Atlanta.
>
> It was a sad finish… There stood Bogash, his arms seemingly powerless, overweight and sluggish, blood pouring from cuts over both eyes and streaming from his nose and mouth as Flowers never let up a brutal, relentless attack…

Bogash had a solitary moment of success in round one when a right to the head knocked Flowers on to his heels but by the third blood was running from Lou's nose and mouth. From round four he had a cut over his left eye. In round five it was the right eye that opened up. This cut was wider, longer, than the other over the left. In the eighth referee Dan Buckley wanted to stop the bloodbath but Bogash refused to quit and hung on for another four to the final bell. Somewhere along the way Bogash also damaged his right hand, which robbed him of the one big asset that might have given him some hope.

> Flowers, long, gaunt and drawn, was a perfect specimen of perpetual motion. He waved in and out of Bogash's arms, punching at will, ripping the face of the Bridgeporter into literal shreds, punching his stomach until it was as red as the October sun… Bogash took a terrible lacing. But he bore up under the defeat like a man.
>
> Back in his dressing room after the bout, Bogash with his head bowed and tears streaming down his cheeks admitted his defeat. 'I gave them what they paid for, a good fight,' Louis said. 'I could have crawled into a shell and clinched but I let them see everything the Tiger had. I took my licking like a man. I have no alibis.'
>
> Yes, he took a licking and it was a bad one at that.

While in Bridgeport, Flowers was invited to give the sermon at a local 'colored' church, possibly the Bethel African Methodist Episcopal Church in

Grove Street. He was more aligned to the CME denomination rather than the less integrational AME, but he explained how he could reconcile boxing for a living with his Christian faith. He quoted the passage that had inspired him for so long from Psalm 144: 'Blessed be the Lord my strength, which teacheth my hands to war, and my fingers to fight. My goodness and my fortress, my high tower, and my deliverer; my shield, and he in whom I trust.'

Miller liked to hype up Flowers' devotion to God, saying he always read the old, small well-thumbed Bible that his mother had given him and said a prayer in his dressing room before a fight. Flowers, however, straightened this story out when he could. When the time came for his obituaries, an unnamed *Associated Press* writer recalled a conversation he had with the Tiger that made his position clear. He was quoted as saying:

> I wouldn't pray to the Lord for victory before a fight because I might meet a better man, a stronger man, and lose. Then I might think the Lord hadn't answered my prayers and I might be tempted to doubt Him. So I always wait, and when the fight is over, I thank God for the strength that brought me safely through, and then I read my Bible.

A man's faith is not something to trade in for column inches in newspapers and this was not a man for whom religion was a commodity to be marketed. He would have seen his wife and daughter as a gift from God to be honoured, and his fighting strength and boxing skill as a tool whereby he might bring stability and security for his family and provide financial and spiritual help for his church.

Ed Van Every felt he came to know Flowers as he based himself more and more in New York. At first he, like many wise old journalists who have listened too long to publicists, took the Tiger's devout ways with a raising of an eyebrow, but after getting to know him he said he no longer questioned his piety, 'nor the information that never had he missed a day from early childhood in the reading of three verses of the New Testament'. He wrote: 'Even the more cynical-minded of the press members, as well as pugilists with whom Flowers came in contact, had come to accept the faith of the Georgia Deacon as the genuine thing.'

Walk Miller had no trouble finding him fights now he was back in the flow. Ten days after beating Bogash, Flowers drew a crowd of 12,000 to the East Chicago Arena, just over the state line into Indiana, for a ten round no-decision fight with Jock Malone, a rock solid, stylish opponent from St Paul, Minnesota. This was a landmark promotion because for the first time in that area it featured a 'mixed' bout, between black and white. No doubt, Flowers was pleased to play his part in this kind of progress. The idea had been championed by the *Chicago Defender* newspaper and local promoter James Mullen, knowing that Tiger Flowers was a popular, highly respected man, went with it. Flowers won another 'newspaper' decision at the end of ten rounds in a fight that pleased fans and persuaded Mullen to continue the mixed shows experiment. Malone, whose real name was John Murphy, was a good fighter who had once laid a claim to the middleweight title, during Johnny Wilson's time as champion. He was extrovert and colourful. Before one fight he was so confident of victory he said he would leap off the Charleston Bridge in Boston if he lost. He did lose – and at noon the next day duly jumped off, fully clothed, feet first, and nearly drowned.

At the Polo Grounds, New York, on 2nd July 1925, Greb defended his world championship against Mickey Walker, the welterweight titleholder, in a classic fifteen-round war that people talked about for years.

Flowers was relying on Walk Miller to make enough noise to keep him in the picture. He was doing his part by turning up for battle whenever and wherever required and entertaining crowd after crowd. They knew that Greb did not draw the colour line but if he lost the title his successor might not see the situation in the same way. They needed to get to Greb, who was beginning to look a little ragged around the edges.

Three days after getting the better of Jock Malone, Flowers was in Philadelphia at Shibe Park baseball stadium, handing old rival and one-time conqueror Lee Anderson a ten round points defeat before an incredible crowd of more than 30,000 fans according to the *Afro-American*.

> Flowers kept his left hand continually in Anderson's face, but always protecting himself as far as possible from the New England man. Anderson bled freely from the nose and mouth, but kept on fighting, doing the best he could to score a knockdown blow, but the chance never came and when the bell rang he was a badly beaten man.

A fortnight later Flowers and the no doubt still bruised Anderson put on their show again before the patrons of the Commonwealth Sporting Club in Harlem. This time Anderson, perhaps not recovered from the hammering he had taken in Philadelphia, 'fouled out' in round three.

Then across the Hudson in Elizabeth, New Jersey, the hometown of Mickey Walker, Flowers was matched with Jack Stone, a stubborn, crazy New York middleweight who lost almost every time he stepped into a ring. Stone didn't care who he fought, was fed to a number of top class operators, sometimes managing to hang tough for the whole distance, sometimes not. Flowers knocked him out in round four.

Flowers had three weeks until he fought Pat McCarthy in Boston on 20th July 1925, and arrived early, working out with another of Walk Miller's black boxers, 'Sunny' Jim Williams. They trained every day in George Byers' Gymnasium and it was said Williams was a talented enough counter-puncher to get the better of Flowers in a short spar. Lee Anderson was also there to work out with them both.

The *Lewiston Sun* writer considered McCarthy, a local light-heavyweight who was in a good run of form, a real threat.

> Even the most enthusiastic admirers of Flowers admit the Roxbury Irishman packs enough steam in his right hand to drop the Tiger if he connects squarely on a vulnerable spot. McCarthy is far the classiest opponent Flowers has met in Boston. Pat combines cleverness and punching power...

McCarthy was good but not good enough. Flowers outpointed him in a hard fight over ten rounds in the open air at Braves Field, home of the Boston Braves baseball team.

Four days on and, for the fourth time in five months, Flowers and Lou Bogash faced each other, on this occasion in Aurora, Illinois, west of Chicago. As in their third fight Flowers handed out an increasingly painful battering. The writer for the *Chicago Defender* said:

> Bogash was the worst looking sight imaginable when he left the ring at the end of the ten rounds, after the newspaper men and the ringside experts had yelled for the referee to stop the fight.

An agency report printed in the *Oakland Tribune* said, 'Flowers had an easy time in every round.'

Tiger had earned a rest, went home to Georgia, and didn't box again for a month. The toll their four fights had taken on Bogash was even heavier. Lou was out of the ring for nine months until April 1926 and was finished as a contender.

When Flowers came back it was in Grand Rapids, Michigan, on 21 August 1925, and a ten round battle with Allentown Joe Gans, a competent but unsung black middleweight, brought the Tiger another newspaper verdict. Gans' real name was Joe Hicks. Sometimes he boxed as Gans, sometimes as Hicks. He is pretty much forgotten now, but was talented enough to hold Jack Delaney to a split decision and to draw with the British pair Frank Moody and Ted Moore, as well as Jock Malone. For Tiger, the offers of work continued to come in, and it seems as if neither he nor Walk Miller, like the ambitious freelances they were, burdened themselves with the inclination to pick and choose. As hard as it must have been, there is no evidence to indicate that Flowers wanted to turn down a payday or slow the pace at all.

A week after beating Gans, he was back in front of the fans at Braves Field, Boston, going over old territory once more by outpointing Jock Malone on a show run by the Suffolk Athletic Club. A photographer recorded the two fighters standing in the centre of the ring before the first bell, with referee Joe O'Connor. Miller, as well as managing Flowers, often still worked his corner. S. J. Mahoney of the *Boston Advertiser* scored seven rounds to three for Flowers, giving Malone the first, eighth and last. Malone's left eye was cut in round seven, but neither man was close to going down as they slugged away to the end of the tenth round.

From Boston the Tiger travelled to Cleveland, Ohio, to fight the Englishman, Ted Moore, over ten rounds at Taylor Bowl on the Labor Day holiday of 7 September 1925. Flowers had won the newspaper verdict over Moore seven months earlier, but improved on that in the return. The Tiger's persistent attacks left Moore helpless to the point that referee Matt Brock stepped in to stop the fight in round six. Then there was confusion as the verdict was widely reported as a No Contest.

As summer turned into autumn a fight with Greb for the title looked no nearer. Flowers made do with a third meeting with Jock Malone, this time in St Paul, Minnesota, Malone's home city. Tiger almost lost it, too. Twice Malone during the ten rounds was offered the chance to be awarded the fight by disqualification after Flowers had fouled him, but each time declined. The newspaper verdict was that Flowers had won clearly. Even the St Paul local paper, the *Pioneer Press*, acknowledged that Flowers had dominated. Afterwards Tiger went to Malone's dressing room and said, 'I want to thank you, Mr Malone. Everybody else seems to be against me, but you get me good purses and fight me hard and treat me like a man.'

Malone replied, 'That's all right, Tiger, but don't forget that some day I'm going to get lucky and put these old knuckles on your chin.'

'I suppose you will, Mr Malone, and when you do it's all right with me. You sure deserve to beat me some time.'

Back in East Chicago, at least there was some variety in that Flowers fought somebody he had never met before, Chuck Wiggins, a light-heavyweight known as The Hoosier Playboy, from Fortville near Indianapolis. Wiggins was a rough handful, in and out of the ring. He had had fought the previous month against heavyweight Johnny Risko, and had hit him so low that Risko had to be carried from the ring in agony. Risko was given twenty-five minutes to recover and box on. When he said he could not, Wiggins was awarded the win by knockout.

Flowers could handle himself when the rough stuff began to fly. He was a gentleman outside the ring and preferred to be one in it, but he was hard enough mentally and physically to look after himself in the clinches and when the fouls began to get a little too extreme. Wiggins and Flowers hammered away at each other for the full ten rounds without let-up, without complaint. It was a No Decision contest, and is usually perceived as a draw.

Flowers was mostly fighting over ten and twelve rounds, but after a month's break he came back a little more gently, with a six round workout at the Broadway Auditorium, Buffalo, against a win-one, lose-one type named Benny Ross. Flowers won on points.

By then the Tiger was thirty-two years old, and had toiled through some desperately hard battles in nearly 150 professional fights. He had been knocked down, knocked out, he knew the taste of his own blood, he knew all about pain and its variable thresholds. Before he fought the Welshman Frank Moody, on 10 December 1925 he talked to the *Boston Evening Transcript*'s LeRoy Atkinson about his career. He said when it was over, hopefully after he had won the world championship, he wanted to settle down back in Atlanta and run a chain of delicatessens and bakeries. He already owned one bakery in Atlanta, which his elder brother Carl ran.

As to keeping in shape between fights, he said he enjoyed swimming and running, but took care when he did his roadwork in a city. It was a rare moment when he talked openly about the problem of being a black fighter in a white world.

> When I runs and nears a corner where a gang loiters, I slows right down and ambles by. I don't want nobody to remark at me.
>
> I never yet had a real fight outside the ring, and I'm not aiming to have one if I can avoid it.

He talked about Verna Lee as well, though LeRoy Atkinson wrote that she was nine, when she was four or five… it may be that the writer misheard, or misread his notes from the interview when he came to transcribe it. Tiger enjoyed telling a story about how his tiny daughter was punched in the mouth by a little boy called Willie Moore and he had sent her back outside to deal with it. She must have inherited her father's genes because she went out and tore into poor Willie Moore.

'I gave 'em both some candy to square matters,' said the proud dad.

He said he had a fight planned for the following week in Syracuse – there is no record of one happening – after which he was looking forward to going home, where Willie Mae and Verna Lee were to meet him, as Atkinson put it, 'in the family's new motor brougham'.

Atkinson met Flowers in Jim Toland's gymnasium in the town, on the fourth floor of an old building on Hanover Street. Atkinson described Flowers as 'almost a millionaire', though that was unlikely at that point, and said he found him to be 'a big, 170-pound, good-natured, bashful darkey'.

> His face shines, he interrupts his Southern drawl with vast gestures and at one point stretches full length on the floor to illustrate how Willie Hooper once knocked him out. [In sparring, we assume.]
>
> When he sits down, he ties his gangling legs into inconceivable knots, remains quiet a second and abruptly untangles himself.

Flowers told Atkinson that he went to church on a Sunday whichever town he was in. Atkinson already knew that he had given the Butler Street CME Church in Atlanta $1,275 for repairs, new chairs and other alterations.

Now and then, said the Tiger, he did some 'speaking', by which he meant preaching.

Atkinson reported that Flowers neither smoked nor drank alcohol, nor did he swear or keep late hours.

Flowers beat Moody on points over ten rounds, did as he pleased, according to British writer Norman Hurst. In a 1977 interview Moody's brother Glen, also a fighter, said Flowers cut him over the right eye in the first round but after that deliberately avoided hitting the cut again. There was also an apocryphal tale repeated on a genealogy website from somebody that knew the Welshman. The story ran that Moody felt he was doing very well, until Tiger whispered into his ear in a clinch that the party was over and proceeded to give him the worst beating of his life. The excellent Welsh boxing writer Gareth Jones said Moody, who let's not forget also fought Greb, believed Flowers to be the best man he boxed in his 200-plus fight career. He knew the Tiger had carried him in the later rounds.

Since his second defeat by Jack Delaney, Flowers had not been invited back to Madison Square Garden or any other major New York venue. Miller's angry, unsubstantiated claims about the Canadian fighting with loaded gloves had lost them what friends they had. At the beginning of November, the situation worsened –Miller suddenly found himself suspended indefinitely in New York because of the slurs he had cast upon the business. A week later on 11 November 1925 a chastened Miller made a public apology and retraction.

Hype Igoe reported in a syndicated column that Miller appeared 'before the fistic fathers' – which we assume to mean the commission – and the New York press to say he now understood that Delaney had nothing in his gloves but his fists. No blackjacks, horseshoes, no flat irons, no dumb-bells. Miller was humble to the point of deference, going as far as to say, 'He was simply too good for my man and always will be.'

Miller also said he had been offered fights for Flowers against Frank Moody, Dave Shade and Jimmy Slattery but would even forego his end of the deal if he could lure Harry Greb into a title defence. The ban was lifted – and Flowers was duly offered the opportunity to box in the Garden again, not against any of those Miller had mentioned, but against Mike McTigue, the former light-heavyweight champion of the world, two days before Christmas.

McTigue wasn't Harry Greb and this wasn't for the middleweight championship, but it was a chance to show the sceptics at the Garden, who had twice seen him flattened by Jack Delaney, that he was for real. And it was a chance for Miller to show he could behave, to fall into line with what was expected of him as an outsider in New York.

A ten round No Decision fight with McTigue had actually been proposed earlier in the year, to take place in Canton, Ohio, on or before 4 July, with the Irishman earning $50,000. McTigue, it was said, wanted $65,000, and it didn't happen. He found Tex Rickard's terms, whatever they were, more to his liking.

CHAPTER 12

Of a Boy Bandit, Booze Barons and a Bad Decision

The fight Tiger Flowers needed, that he had no doubt been waiting for, his return to Madison Square Garden, was a charity show planned by the *New York American* newspaper, aimed at providing Christmas meals for the city's poor. Mike McTigue's influential, British-born manager, Jimmy Johnston, had suggested McTigue fight Flowers, but the Irishman's spoiling, defensive style was not popular, and there was still the worry that the crowd would not turn out to see a black fighter, particularly one who had been knocked out in two of his three appearances in the Garden. *New York American* sports editor Sam Hall had been delegated by the newspaper to liaise with promoter Tex Rickard to guarantee the success of the show, but while neither of them was over-enthusiastic about the match, they decided it was the best they could do at that time of year.

The charity was a good promotional exercise for Rickard but to his shock any chance of making a decent profit for himself was ruined when the New York Commission suddenly ruled that fifty per cent of the gate receipts at all charity shows must be lodged with them, and they would oversee the payment to the designated charity. Paul Gallico reported that this caused 'a fearful squawl,' but made the shrewd, if acidic conclusion that 'this will be the first charity show in years in which the charity will get more than the boxers'. Or, he might have said, the promoters.

Mike McTigue had been a fortunate light-heavyweight champion. He had been given what was generally regarded as an unfair twenty-round decision over the African, Battling Siki, in Dublin in 1923. The Irishman was a notoriously defensive, cautious fighter. He had also been suffering from a troublesome broken bone in his right thumb that would not heal. When he was matched with Flowers, McTigue had boxed only seven times in two years. In one of those fights he had lost his world title to the popular New Yorker, known as the Astoria Assassin, Paul Berlanbach. That was in May 1925. His most recent fight was a twelve round decision over Tony Marullo in Brooklyn in August. Very few fight fans had missed him in his absence.

McTigue's side of the deal was taken care of by Jimmy Johnston, the New York hustler born in the Edge Hill district of Liverpool.

Johnston, a small, noisy man who dyed his hair black, had been running shows in New York for ten years when he teamed up with McTigue. He liked to put about a story that he had personally beaten up two serious-level New York hoodlums, known around town as Gyp The Blood and Lefty Louie. Their real names were Harry Horowitz and Louis Rosenberg.

According to Johnston, the two bad boys decided to occupy ringside seats, for which they had not paid, at his first show in the 'old' Garden. After a physical confrontation he had personally ejected the pair of them, he said. It was a good story, but that was all it was. Gyp The Blood and Lefty Louie were arrested on 14 September 1912 for the murder of a gambler, Herman Rosenthal, outside the Metropole Hotel the previous July. They were both executed in the electric chair at Sing Sing prison on 13 April 1914. And that was a year before Johnston began promoting at the Garden. The story, of course, served Jimmy's purpose, as did the tale he told about winning a biting-gouging-butting brawl with Owen Moran, the world-class bantamweight from Britain, in the lobby of the Nadau Hotel in Spring Street, Los Angeles. He did have the good grace to say Moran had been drunk for at least two days, in which case there might have been some truth to it.

Johnston did appear to have friends in high places. He avoided doing time for his poor memory in the little matter of paying the US Government its due in tax on ticket sales for a show in New York in 1921. It was, no doubt, a specimen charge, but somehow the accusation that he had deliberately defrauded the Government disappeared, even after he had been ordered by a Federal judge to hand himself in to a jail in New Jersey. Instead of being locked up, Johnston was reminded to pay what he owed and move on. Johnston, who enjoyed being labelled 'The Boy Bandit of Broadway' was also a close friend of the head of the New York State Commission, James A. Farley. Some cynics said it was Johnston, not Farley, and not Tex Rickard either, who ran the commission, which consisted of Farley, the old wrestler and strongman William Muldoon, and a businessman named George Brower.

Norman Hurst was at Walk Miller's meeting with Rickard to discuss Flowers' end of the deal.

> Tipping his hat back on his head, and banging his clenched fist on the desk, he said, 'That new Madison Square Garden holds near on twenty thousand people, and eighteen thousand of them would be voters for Good Old Mike McTigue, with just a few coloured boys, and unbiased sports rooting for the Tiger.
>
> I would need a referee like old Bat Masterson to be able to stand against the argument that eighteen thousand voices would give. Tiger will have to nail him down to win.'

Still, Tex persisted, and Miller gave way when the purse was satisfactory. He did try to make sure that, whatever verdict was given, it would be an honest one. He insisted on, and Jimmy Johnston agreed, that two sporting gentlemen should act as judges, with a professional referee to be inside the ring to handle the fight.

It seems Miller turned down a string of suggestions as to who should judge the fight before agreeing, in an astonishing demonstration of naïvety, to a commission suggestion of Bernard Gimbel, a wealthy New York businessman, and Peter J. Brady, a banker who was involved in New York politics. While both were regulars at fights, neither had judged one before. And Johnston's influence on the commission was widely understood. A much later British promoter, Mickey Duff, once said in *Ring* magazine, 'Honest judges sometimes will do out of stupidity what you could never get dishonest judges to do.' The major problem that should have been screaming out at Miller, was that there was no proof that either Gimbel or Brady, as honest as they might have been, knew what to look for when scoring a fight.

But for good or bad the deal was done and on a bitterly cold night Flowers and McTigue walked into the Garden arena to do battle for the poor of the city. Heaters had been installed, and the presence of thousands of people jostling together made it warm enough.

McTigue, a dull fighter but an Irish one, received a terrific reception, while Flowers, an exciting fighter but a black one, was no more than politely received. Hurst wrote:

> What a contrast as they stood in their corners. Mike, his typically Irish face set in serious lines, broke into an occasional wide grin as he nodded to a friend close up to the ringside. He chatted with his handlers. Over the other end of the ring, the long, lithe, well-muscled black figure of Flowers was as a statue, fashioned from weather-battered bronze. Film stars, producers, and motor magnates mixed with top ranking booze barons in the ringside seats... Green flags were waved, and a stentorian voice, which was to be heard throughout the contest, yelled, 'Up the County Clare!'

McTigue fought with his left hand hanging low, while Flowers was a little more square on than expected. Hurst wrote:

> Stiff-legged as a young horse trying to unseat his rider, Flowers was in and away like a flash. His long black arm flashed round and up and his glove connected hard to Mike's body. Before the surprised son of County Clare could realise what had happened, Flowers' left hand had wanged its way to the side of the head. Mike went after Flowers, mad as a wasp, but Flowers glided like a black shadow out of range.

Hurst was not as far as I know an unfair, prejudicial or racist man, but he repeatedly referred to McTigue as Mike, and only rarely, almost for the purpose of variety, altered from calling Flowers by his family name to using Tiger. Small things, maybe, but just a part of the whole.

> There was no grin on Mike's face as the contest progressed. There was none of the raillery with which he usually kidded his opponents. This was a serious McTigue, with a stiff job in hand, and well he knew it.
>
> 'Come on and fight', he once spat at Flowers. The words were hardly out of Mike's mouth before the Tiger responded to the invitation. His muscles tensed, his black eyes flashed dangerously, and with arms flailing he was upon the surprised Mike like a human tornado…

Hurst said at one point Flowers was staggered by a right hand but tore straight back in, hooking and jabbing with speed not commonly seen. Another time a body shot made him dip at the knees but when McTigue moved to follow up, a right to the nose stopped his advance.

> … Flowers fought with a cold and deadly purpose. Sometimes it would be speed that would defeat Mike, at other times it was brainy, well thought-out ring strategy that made the fighting Irishman fall into traps.

This was the first time the writers who frequented the Garden, but who did not, as a rule, bother about the smaller shows in Harlem or Brooklyn, had seen Flowers in a long fight, and so at his best. Previously they had seen him overwhelm Johnny Wilson in three rounds and lose to Jack Delaney in two and four, but this time they were witnesses to the full treatment. McTigue could make good men look ordinary, but Flowers was just too fast for him, too busy, too inventive. One newspaperman said to Norman Hurst, 'This guy ought to fight with one hand tied up.'

So convincing was Flowers' superiority that in the last round some people who had backed McTigue reportedly settled their bets without waiting for the formality of the verdict. One writer told his copy-taker over the 'phone before the final bell to send his story over to the sports desk because Flowers was such a big winner that it could not possibly go the other way. Hurst heard him and tapped him on the shoulder.

'What if Mike should land a K.O. in this round?' he said.

'What if I should be President?'

And the final bell sounded, and the writers, the crowd, the fighters, heard, after a minute or so, the announcement, 'The winner… McTigue.'

It was a split decision. The referee, the experienced Eddie Purdy, scored for Flowers. Purdy knew what he was watching. He had been a fighter himself, and had refereed the Greb-Walker middleweight title fight the same year and had himself mysteriously been knocked down twice in the clinches.

At the announcement Flowers, maybe with his 'Be Nice, Don't Let Them See You Cry' mask very firmly in place, crossed the ring, smiled and congratulated McTigue. Backstage, after they had returned to the dressing room, followed by the press, Miller began to make a strong complaint, but Flowers asked him to talk to him in private a moment. Miller did, then returned to offer the writers their quote. 'The Deacon says it was God's will – and to let it go at that.'

The decision, however, raised the ire of the fans – and even many years later Nat Fleischer, the editor and founder of *Ring* magazine, was still cross, when he remembered that night.

> It was really a ludicrous ruling… by no stretch of the imagination could the Irishman have been given more than two rounds. There were many critics around the ringside who didn't even give McTigue a round.

Madison Square Garden's official records said 13,777 people paid $49,976 to watch, and most of them knew they had just witnessed an appalling robbery.

Were Gimbel and Brady ignorant of how a fight should be scored, biased, or had somebody got to them? We'll never know.

Gimbel was a respected, forty-year-old businessman who took a great interest in boxing. His family ran a chain of department stores, including two in Manhattan, as well as radio stations in New York and Philadelphia. He was, or came across as, an old-fashioned enthusiast, who was confident enough in his opinion to discuss tactics with Gene Tunney before Tunney out-boxed Jack Dempsey for the world heavyweight crown in September 1926. Tunney did not need Gimbel's opinion, of course, but was a gentleman and would never have made the businessman feel small. Tunney said he was in the shower after his great win when Gimbel burst in, fully clothed, to offer his congratulations. On another occasion Tunney, who towards the end of his career had one eye on boxing and the other on climbing the social ladder, indulged him in a sparring session.

> Whether he was negotiating a multi-million dollar deal, devouring a gargantuan platter of corned beef and cabbage, jogging five miles before breakfast, or betting on a horse race, he did it with a verve and gusto that was pure joy to watch.

Gimbel did not suffer rejection in the boxing world for his strange reading of the Flowers–McTigue fight… in fact, it could be said that he was rewarded handsomely. In 1930, the year after Tex Rickard died, he joined the board at

Madison Square Garden and remained in a position of power and influence for a quarter of a century. He resigned with five other directors when the involvement of James D. Norris, head of the International Boxing Club which controlled the Garden's fights, with career criminal Frankie Carbo and his cronies became public. Gimbel, by then chairman of the Garden, was in the thick of it. 'I do not know the man (Carbo), nor do I know who he knows or what he does,' he told *Time* magazine.

However, another of the resigning directors said, 'We figured we'd get out while the going was good.'

Peter J. Brady had no such interest in boxing tactics or in being involved in its promotion. He was a labour leader and aviation enthusiast who set up the Federation Bank & Trust in 1923. He was twice an alternate delegate for a Manhattan ward to the Democratic National Convention, in 1924 and in 1928. What he knew about boxing was, and is, open to debate.

When the hostile newspaper reaction to their judgment hit the streets, both attempted to justify themselves in the *New York Daily News*.

Brady claimed, contrary to what most others had seen, that McTigue had landed the cleaner and harder punches. He relied on a tired argument that is still, from time to time, handed down by administrators when their officials are criticised – that is, that the irate crowd were not demonstrating against the decision but against a poor fight. Brady argued that McTigue had not just won, but won clearly. 'My point score at the end of the contest showed that McTigue had hit Flowers more often than the Tiger had hit the Irishman.'

Gimbel's argument was along the same unconvincing lines. And he added: 'Mr William Muldoon had asked us to officiate and we were glad to oblige him.'

Jimmy Johnston, whose influence over the New York Commission was an open secret, was at the Flatiron building office the following day, when McTigue walked in and presented him, in addition to his manager's cut of his purse, a gold watch inset with diamonds as a 'thank you'. McTigue was not a fool.

The decision became, said the *Chicago Defender*, the laughing stock of the pugilistic world but that didn't matter to McTigue. The record books would show that life had been put back into his fading career. He would go on to box once again for the world light-heavyweight title, Johnston securing the chance for him ahead of other contenders, and with the New York Commission's backing. Tommy Loughran outpointed him in that 1927 title shot in the Garden.

The press fall-out from the McTigue-Flowers decision was damning. Paul Gallico, the *New York Daily News* man, declared it 'one of the rankest decisions ever rendered against a colored man'. He also said it was

the most outrageous decision ever rendered in a town where poor decisions are nothing extraordinary. The crowd let out a roar that could have been heard to the East River. If ever an inefficient, blind, idiotic verdict was turned in at the end of a bout, this was it.

Ed Sullivan of the *New York Evening Graphic* also called the verdict outrageous, John Kiernan, Joe Villa and the legendary Bert 'Hype' Igoe, whom Damon Runyan described as the best informed writer on boxing who ever lived, all slaughtered it.

Gallico said that but for Flowers' exemplary sportsmanship in congratulating McTigue when the decision was announced, the ten-minute demonstration as the crowd booed and hollered might well have become a full-scale riot. The building was cleared by special police officers but people still gathered outside to complain.

Jack Kofoed, in the *New York Evening Post*, was slightly less demonstrative than the others, suggesting the best McTigue might have hoped for was a draw. According to Kofoed, McTigue did outbox 'the Methodist deacon from Georgia', but added:

It was Flowers who came tearing in continually, unloosing a multitude of blows. True, Tiger suffered the only real casualty of the fight, a cut eye, but it did not slow up the attack. He ripped in just as strongly afterwards as he did before he received it. The basis of the judges' decision rested, evidently, on McTigue's ability to tie his enemy up at close quarters and the body belting he handed out in several rounds.

Kofoed called McTigue lucky and described Gimbel and Brady as men of unimpeachable character. In his opinion the decision was, therefore, one of those things that happens from time to time in boxing and not a result of outside interference or corruption.

Tiger went home to Georgia for the holiday, then settled back into training. What he felt in his solitary moments, those unspoken, quiet times when everyone must reflect on what life is serving up, we cannot know. Perhaps he was frustrated, disgusted, anguished at the injustice, perhaps he felt in his heart this was about race, about blatant or underlying, deep-seated prejudice, or maybe he understood Johnston's relationship with the New York Commission better than his manager had. Or perhaps he was able to smile and shrug it off, as one more piece of the journey, one more example that the Lord his God did indeed work in mysterious ways his wonders to perform.

Meyer 'Mickey' Cohen, another fighter who appreciated the details of the way the business worked, suggested that at one point in the 1920s the racketeers had six of the eight world champions. Later Cohen worked with Bugsy Siegel and after Siegel's murder in 1947 he took over mob interests in Hollywood and Las Vegas, so he knew what he was talking about.

Flowers was a loyal man, a Methodist, living by a code that excluded the use of alcohol, and would have understood well enough the nature of the business of the smiling gentlemen in the sharp suits, whom the Englishman Norman Hurst boldly called 'booze barons'. Did he know the extent to which they spread their influence? It's always a difficult issue. Is a bad decision just that, a mistake, a momentary aberration by an otherwise good judge, or referee? Or is that official in on the plot, if only in a subtle, unspoken favouritism, a view of a situation affected by an understanding of what those who are perceived to be in positions of power want to happen?

In too many parts of the world it is still the case that the administrative commission or federation survives mainly because of the taxes and fees paid by the major promoters, and it is by no means unknown for pressure to be put on the authority by a promoter who is unhappy with a decision that has frustrated his man's progress to the extent that he says a certain referee or judge should not work his show. Therefore, the official might well understand the best way for him to get more work, to earn more and raise his own profile in the business, is to favour the 'house' boxer over the man who is brought in as an opponent. Ask a judge and none will accept that they are a part of this system. And it is true that some are not, some do retain their independence. Others seem more vulnerable. Whether or not Gimbel and Brady had any ambitions at all in boxing – and it seems Gimbel did – both would have understood that Jimmy Johnston carried more clout in New York than Walk Miller ever would. It's easier for a fighter to lay that consideration to one side, at least until his career has finished and he has a broader perception of what has, or might have, happened to him. It's not only easier for him to concentrate on his own job and trust others to do theirs, but essential that, in a business as tough as fighting for the entertainment of others, he becomes single-minded in his quest to be as good as it is possible for him to be.

Nobody had showed much interest in giving Flowers a shot at the championship when he was winning, but after the hostile reaction to the McTigue decision a sense of righteous injustice broke out among those who controlled the business in New York. Tex Rickard also had cold commonsense in abundance. He knew that if publicity like this was turned on its head, interest in Flowers fighting Harry Greb would be huge, and the unthinkable could be worked for his promotional benefit: in the minds of those less prejudiced, the black man from the South could even become a sentimental favourite. The path to the return with Greb, this time with the middleweight title on the line, suddenly opened up. This is the way of things in boxing sometimes.

Paul Gallico followed this line of argument, and wrote that the McTigue decision was so bad that justice demanded Flowers be given the compensation by way of a shot at Greb for the championship.

The Commission, appearing to bow to the pressure, duly obliged, on 2 January 1926 ordering Greb to accept a challenge from Flowers within thirty days or be suspended in New York State. Flowers, or rather Miller on his behalf, posted a certified cheque for $2,500 to secure the match, and Gallico went through the formalities of praising the Commission. Tex Rickard first contacted Greb in Los Angeles to offer to stage the fight, then brought the two sides together, Red Mason for Greb, Miller for Flowers, and sealed the deal for the fight to go on at Madison Square Garden on 26 February.

The *Chicago Defender*, which served African-American readers, later reflected on why Tiger had not been given his chance earlier, and concluded it was a straightforward act of racism.

> … the commissions of various states put a taboo on it by evading the issue, simply because they figured the championship would slip out of the hands of a white man.

On 12 February 1926 Flowers returned to New York, refreshed from his visit to Willie Mae and Verna Lee in Atlanta, and settled to his final preparations, working out in the Garden, where the public could go in and watch.

Both he and Walk Miller had made enough money, and were spending so much of their time in New York, that it made sense to have premises there. Miller moved into a new suite of offices (nos. 904-7) in the heart of Manhattan at 140 West 42nd Street, on the corner of Broadway in the Knickerbocker Annex. The one-time pool-hall operator from Atlanta had made it big at last. He had a prestige address in the heart of the city that mattered more than any other in boxing. He brought an old friend from El Paso, Dr. Carl J. Studer, across to Atlanta to look after business in Georgia. Studer, a chiropractor by trade, had worked as a referee on fights in Juarez in the old days.

Flowers, too, had an address in New York. He lived in a house, 58 West 140th Street, in Harlem. And his moment of destiny, his chance to carve out a lasting place in boxing history, was almost upon him.

CHAPTER 13

'Maybe Mother Will be Just a Little Proud of Me Now'

Harry Greb was blind in one eye and had imperfect sight in the other. In spite of his genius, his instinct for how to fight, he was as ready for the taking as any man could be.

Gene Tunney was one who was sure that Greb had slipped some way from his peak. Tunney said after they fought for the fifth and last time, in St. Paul, Minnesota, on 27 March 1925, Greb told him, 'Let the other guys have a dose of you from now on.' He was right in that Tunney had weighed 181½ lb to Greb's 167½ lb and with the talent that Gene possessed it was too much for him to give away. However, Tunney also knew that in the old days Greb wouldn't have given the little matter of conceding 14 lb a second thought. This was the man who ripped into Jack Dempsey in sparring and gave him hell, the man who demanded to fight Dempsey for the heavyweight championship itself. Tunney wrote in his autobiography:

> The frankness of this statement touched me. It was an acknowledgement of started decline, the dread of all boxers. My heart went out to Harry. He was slipping, and what is more pathetic, he knew it. The Greb of 1920, 1921, 1922, 1923, would never have admitted the superiority of anyone. He was getting old. There is something heart-rending about noticeable disintegration in a gallant warrior.

By the time Greb arrived in New York, and set to work at the gym of his old friend, Philadelphia Jack O'Brien, he had boxed six times over a total of fifty-seven competitive rounds in as many weeks from the start of the year, taking in Toronto, Omaha, Los Angeles, where he fought twice in four days, Oakland and finally Phoenix before heading east a fortnight before he was to step into the ring with Flowers. It was a crazy schedule for a man whose thirty-one-year-old body had almost 300 fights on its clock. It was almost as if he wanted to cash in on being champion while he still could. Not that a man like Greb would have contemplated losing to anybody in the middleweight division over the fifteen-round championship distance. In around 100 fights going back to the beginning of 1921, the only men to beat him in decision fights were Tunney, the talented, skilful light-heavyweight Tommy Loughran, on a ten round decision in 1923, and his old adversary, Kid Norfolk, on a foul in 1924.

Greb was 165½ lb by the week of the fight. Rumours spread that he was struggling to make 160 lb. He sparred eight rounds a day against southpaws to familiarise himself with the problems associated with the 'wrong way around' style. Boxers who fought out of the left-handed stance were far more of a rarity in those days than now, and Flowers, because of his fitness and the fast pace he set, was more awkward than most. Greb larked about, playing handball, but did his early morning runs. With two days to go the champion was down to 162¼ lb, and by the time he had dried out, he came in at 159½ lb. Flowers was 158½ lb.

Flowers revealed his diet for the week, in addition to running eighteen miles twice – at the same time scotching stories that he was, in addition to a Methodist tee-totaller, a vegetarian.

Breakfast: Stewed prunes, not more than five. Baked apple, without milk or cream. Two soft-boiled eggs, two slices of dry toast. One cup of weak tea. No water.

Lunch: Cornflakes, bran or equivalent. Vegetable soup with rice. Rye bread, crackers, one glass of water.

Dinner: Choice of two pork chops, piece of broiled steak or lamb chop. Rye bread or toast. One slice of apple or peach pie. One cup of tea or water.

Nightly: Half-an-hour before bed, one teaspoonful of beef essence in a small cup of hot water. No eating at night!

The Afro-American said Harlem to a man backed Flowers to beat Greb and there were plenty who were ready to lay their money down. They pointed out that Flowers' friendly personality was a primary reason why he had been given his shot at the middleweight title, while the more remote Harry Wills had been more easily avoided by heavyweight champion Jack Dempsey.

Flowers never refuses to give reporters interviews and on one occasion the Tiger got out of his bed after midnight to talk to an Afro-American newspaperman.

Another piece in the *Afro-American* suggested Flowers' lifestyle and faith had touched something even in those black people who normally took no interest in prizefighting.

The whole Methodist church, North and South, will listen in and wait with abated breath the outcome of Steward Flowers' battle with Harry Greb in the new Madison Square Garden for the middleweight championship of the world.

James R. Fair, in *Give Him to The Angels,* remembered that the Pittsburgh fight crowd turned up to swell the gate, backing Harry with 'vocal cords, money, fists and blackjacks'. Any idea that Flowers might be a sentimental favourite in the arena itself was soon dispelled. He walked to the ring almost unnoticed while the majority of the paying customers in the Garden on that night of 26 February 1926 stood in a noisy salute the moment Greb began his walk to the ring. Tex Rickard had done good business on the back of the McTigue decision and on Greb's reputation. Records of the size of the house, and the amount of gate receipts varied. According to one set there were 16,337 paying customers, according to another 17,756. Money at the gate added up to somewhere between $95,577 and $105,134. A report the week after the fight said Flowers received $11,219 and Greb earned $33,659. Another estimate quoted in an IBRO newsletter put it at $37,500 for Greb and $12,500 for Flowers. According to one of the many inflation-based conversion tables available on the internet today that would mean Flowers earned around $112,000 and Greb around $338,000. Confirmation that the fight was filmed came with the statement that 'picture rights' could net Flowers as much as $25,000 more, so trebling his gross fee.

Ring writer Jersey Jones said Greb was not his usual confident, cocky self in the corner. He fidgeted and fussed during the introductions, while Flowers seemed to be taking it all with a degree of nonchalance. He smiled broadly when he was introduced – to what Jones described as 'a lively reception'.

The first bell sounded at nine minutes to ten. The referee was the old heavyweight Edward 'Gunboat' Smith, who had fought in world class, but whom Greb had knocked out in a round back in 1920.

Fair said Greb tried to crowd in on Flowers, bulling his way to close range (where he could see him) but he was slow and his timing off.

> Flowers was as nervous as a butterfly with an itchy tail and he flitted about like one, wrapping his arms around his head as he jerked his jitter-bug frame all over the ring... It was not a cleverly waged bout, but it was exciting and it was pathetic – pathetic because a washed-up Greb was exerting every ounce of his waning energy to hold off an inferior opponent. It was as though Caruso, his voice a thin whisper of what it once had been, were competing with a bierstube tenor for a singing waiter's job.

This was unkind, exaggerated, probably inaccurate, but then Greb was a hero figure to Fair and he, not Flowers, was the subject of his attention. For Fair, the logic ran that Greb lost because he couldn't fight any more, not because the Tiger was actually a top class fighter himself. That, and the fact that he was working from memory twenty years later, clouded his judgment, but that memory does still have some value.

> Flowers was using a right hand that was a feeble attempt at a hook but was nothing more than an off-balance sideswipe. But he scored with it. As the bout moved into its final stages his fright disappeared and he got rough. Greb was too contemptuous to rough him back. But when the roughing continued and it was apparent Flowers was challenging his mettle, Greb went close and gave him the works – backhand, elbows, thumbs, head, knees – fast like that. Flowers jumped back and protested to Gunboat Smith, who just looked at him.

The contemporary report in the *Chicago Defender*, as an African-American newspaper, concentrated its attention on Flowers and his attempt to become the first black middleweight champion of the world. The *Defender*'s writer accused Greb of using 'every foul means known to the ring game' and pointed out that Gunboat Smith did not even warn him, even when it was so obvious that even the crowd could see it and began booing.

> Greb held the back of Flowers' neck with his left and yanked the Georgian towards him as he would uppercut him with his right hand. In the tenth and fourteenth rounds Greb deliberately pushed Flowers through the ropes and in other rounds he used his elbow with telling effect. But Flowers would come back in each round, strong, scoring enough points with his lefts and rights to win easily.

The film of the fight has long been lost, which makes a detailed description of the action hard to pin down. Writers at the time had their own agendas, their own views of what happened. While the Afro-American had a slant towards Flowers, Regis Welsh, the reporter from the *Pittsburgh Post*, was Greb's friend and saw the whole thing from the opposite perspective. At the end most writers felt it was a close fight, whichever way they felt the decision should have gone, but it perhaps says all we need to know about Welsh's impartiality that he gave Flowers only three of the fifteen rounds.

Welsh did point out, probably fairly as Flowers tended to do this, that he was slapping while Greb punched more correctly, with the knuckle part of the glove.

However, piecing the fight together as best we can, it seemed to go as follows. Greb made a slow, almost shocking start. Twice in the opening minute he was staggered as Flowers settled straight into his rhythm and threw a shower of punches. Greb pulled himself together and drove the Tiger on to the defensive with a right hand flush on the chin, following it with a furious barrage but the Tiger responded and it was Greb who winced from a left hand to the body near the bell. Flowers finished the first round cut over the left eye.

A crack of heads near the end of a second round that seemed to sway one way then the other left Greb with blood flowing from a cut on the left eye. It was the first time he had been cut since he fought Bob Roper on New Year's Day 1923.

The blood still ran freely from both in the third, with Flowers driving himself on, working the body and Greb defending much of the time. Flowers' relentless attack continued in the fourth round and both men fought on after the bell which was completely drowned out by the noise from the fans. According to Welsh, Flowers seemed dazed at this point but if that was the case he recovered well in the interval, for he went out and won the fifth beyond reasonable doubt. The blood from Greb's cut was running into his eyes, which impaired his vision, his judgment of distance was poor and he swung wildly, missing as Flowers scored well at long range.

Greb made a real battle of it in the sixth but it appeared a quieter round. Greb landed one solid right hand in round seven, but Flowers avoided taking another shot flush and responded in the eighth, opening it with body attacks and then a series of short right uppercuts which sent the champion's head flying back. Greb, perhaps trying to find more power by sacrificing movement, sat down on his punches more and had successes from time to time through the middle rounds but mostly Flowers outpunched him, particularly to the body.

In round nine Greb grimaced after shipping a left to the face. By the tenth the pace had slowed, and Greb's visual problems would perhaps have been evident had anyone suspected how severe they were. His punches lacked timing and fell short. Every so often he would find a solid punch, as with a right hand in round ten. Greb attempted to rush Flowers in the eleventh but Flowers timed a hard right to the jaw as he came in and Greb backed off.

Greb showed his champion's heart with a big surge to win the twelfth, driving Flowers back with a terrific attack of the type he excelled in during the years of his prime. A right hand spun Flowers round and the champion landed eye-catching uppercuts inside. Flowers looked in trouble. That, however, was Harry's last big effort. The crowd got on Greb's back when he rushed and wrestled Flowers through the ropes, and he looked tired in the thirteenth, when he was backed on to the ropes, spoiling Flowers' work as best he could. Again, he dug into his resolve and charged but his punches were more like pushes.

The fourteenth seems to have been slower, as if both men were gathering themselves for a big push in the last. The writer from the *Washington Post* considered that Flowers deliberately boxed defensively in this round, then raised the pace again in the last. Greb tried to take control but was off balance, missed badly with wild, almost desperate swings and appeared to lose the round.

The round-by-round report in the *Afro-American* offered something of the drama.

Fifteenth round. The men shook hands. Flowers slapped his right to the face and to the body and head as Greb rushed in. Flowers slapped a left and right to the head and almost upset Greb with a right to the jaw. Greb rushed in but was wild. Flowers hooked a left to the body as Greb missed a right to the head.

They exchanged lefts to the body and clinched. After falling short with a right for the face, Greb drove a right to the body. Flowers jabbed his left to the face and in a clinch they exchanged rights to the body. Flowers hooked a left to the body and they clinched. They exchanged rights at the final bell.

At some point in the fight Greb thumbed Flowers and swore at him, which led to a story going down in boxing folklore. Greb told writers afterwards, with a mixture of amusement and amazement, that in a clinch, Flowers had admonished him. The beaten champion said:

> What do you think Flowers says to me when we fell into a clinch? He says to me, 'Thumb me in the eye if you has to, Mister Greb, but please don't take the Lord's name in vain.'
>
> I thought he was kidding but damned if he didn't mean it. I did stop cursing him. Say, and I also quit trying to give him the thumb, but that was because he wouldn't have paid any attention if I did. So, what the hell.

At the final bell, with the crowd making a terrific noise, announcer Joe Humphreys walked to his position at the centre of the ring and spread his hands. At first Regis Welsh took this as a sign that it was a draw, which would have meant Greb had retained his title, and claimed that Flowers looked relieved. Humphreys, however, was merely signalling for quiet and after glancing at Greb and giving a little shake of his head, shouted, 'The winner... and new middleweight champion of the world... Tiger Flowers!'

Hype Igoe, who had Greb two points up at the end, 7-5-3 in rounds, wrote that Humphreys' announcement was met by a deathly silence in the great arena. Maybe fans were suddenly aware they were witnessing an extraordinary moment in boxing history, not only the dethroning of a champion, and one of the great maverick entertainers of the business, but the arrival of a new era, one where black men would not out of social necessity be deprived of victories and championships they deserved. Igoe wrote, 'To some it was a just verdict. To others it was unfair to Greb.'

It was a split decision. Referee Smith had Greb ahead, but the judges, Charles Mathison and Tom Flynn, had called it for Flowers.

Greb, said Welsh, was close to tears in his corner.

The *Washington Post*, while not disagreeing with the verdict, had sympathy with the fallen champion. Greb had not been knocked down, had never stopped trying, but was 'so far off his accustomed form that it seemed as though his name was not Greb'.

Frank Getty of the *United Press* stated that 'many experts figured that the worst the former champion should have had was a draw, for Greb was the stronger puncher and at times had Flowers in real trouble'.

The *Chicago Defender* celebrated Flowers' triumph and pointed out rather sanctimoniously that those gamblers who had wagered heavily on Greb had been cleaned to the bone.

The *Afro-American* sports editor saluted the new champion.

Flowers is a fighter and a gentleman. His victory over Greb was a popular one. The 20,000 fans received the new champion with shouts and plaudits. There is no cause to fear that the Georgia churchman will cause his crown to become tarnished or use it for questionable purposes. Wine, women and song hold no part in the life of the modest Southern steward. Long live the king.

The same newspaper's main report accused Greb of serial fouling.

It appeared from the press box that Greb was using his head as a battering ram in the clinches and on more than one occasion he was guilty of heeling Flowers with both hands and was guilty several times of poking the Tiger in the eyes with his thumb.

The Associated Press report, which was without a by-line, seemed neutral enough.

Greb was not what he had been in previous defenses of his title for after four rounds he forsook his windmill attack and poised his right hand for a damaging blow. The blow never landed and Flowers, lashing out continually, gained the verdict for aggressiveness and a willingness to fight throughout.

The AP man said some argued the fight was so close Greb should not have had his title taken away, that a draw would have been the fairest option. He then set out the case for the official verdict.

… the New York State Athletic Commission has ruled that fights shall be decided by the number of rounds won and under this ruling the decision last night was made.

He had canvassed ringside opinion and felt the most popular interpretation was that Flowers had won by a round, six to five with four even. He noted that the Greb camp were not creating too much of a fuss.

Red Mason, manager of the former champion, said after the contest that if Flowers had won then he was the victor by the narrowest of margins. Flowers' manager, Walk Miller, said that his boxer would have shown to better advantage had not Greb locked arms and his opponent from the ninth round to the end.

James Fair, obviously writing years on, said in the dressing room Greb put on a brave face. 'What the hell, Tex is gonna give me another fight with Flowers. I'll take a good rest, then I'll come back and beat that jig so bad even the judges will have to admit it.'

Ed Sullivan, remembering the fight in the *New York Graphic* the following year, said he was among the writers who trooped in see the new champion. They found him in unusually expansive mood.

'Don't be too hard on Harry,' said the Tiger. 'He was a good champion, and he said a lot of things in the ring tonight that he didn't mean. He fought everyone while he was champion, and that is important.'

Sullivan also gave us a glimpse of how Flowers had not only survived but actually thrived in mixed society. Sullivan quoted Flowers as saying,

I always fight to win, but I never strike an opponent in anger, even when he fights foul. And I pay no mind to anything insulting that's said to me, except when they take God's name in vain. Then I ask them please not to, but if my opponent don't stop I close my ears to the things he says and fight harder.

When all the crookedness, the external interference, is stripped away, the core of boxing – that is, those men who put themselves on the line again and again, round after round, fight after fight, year after year – is good and its heart is big. Flowers, once again, came over as one of the nice guys in boxing history and Greb, no matter how close to the edge of the rules he had drifted at certain times in the fight, had lost with honour and dignity.

James Butler, the British writer, also said Flowers referred once again to his mother's disapproval of boxing as an activity in which a Christian man should not participate. 'Maybe mother will be just a little proud of me now, and forgive me.'

Flowers spent his first Sunday as champion in the First Methodist Church (now the Mount Calvary Methodist Church) at 140th Street and Edgecombe Avenue, and at his house three blocks away at no. 58 with Willie Mae and Verna Lee. He read his Bible and played his violin as Willie Mae played the piano.

There was never any suggestion that outside interference had affected the decision. It is possible that after the volatile reaction to the McTigue verdict, and given that the racketeers did not appear to hold a piece of either Greb or Flowers, it was felt best to let this one take its course. Both Mathison and Flynn were considered good enough officials, and Gunboat Smith knew how to work and score a fight.

The next day Greb reiterated what he had said in the dressing room, that he would like a rematch on the plain and simple grounds that he believed he could win it. However, he also said he had not felt the same since he had been hurt in a car crash the previous year. He refuted stories that suggested he would retire. He said he would go home to Pittsburgh, then holiday and recuperate at Hot Springs, Arkansas, and come back to fight Flowers again. Hot Springs was a good-time town, then developing into a fun and relaxation resort where, for a decade and more, pretty much anything went. Owney Madden was to own the Hotel Arkansas there. Al Capone enjoyed staying at the Arlington Hotel. Madden eventually retired from the front line of crime to potter about in Hot Springs in his declining years.

If Greb had a realisation that he was not the fighter he once was, he had no intention of revealing that to a press man, doctor or commissioner. Unlike his biographer, James Fair, he was also aware of how good Flowers was. He told Regis Welsh

> I feel that I am a better fighter than I was last night and a better fighter than Flowers was. I'm not squawking… the verdict was a shock to me, but then you must figure that Flowers is a great fighter.
>
> I knew that and said it when we met at Fremont two years ago, as his awkward style with his abundance of speed makes him one of the toughest fellows in the business. But there are no good middleweights except us, and we will meet again, sure as you're alive. Then will come my chance… and I will retire as the middleweight champion who came back and proved that he had the stuff in him.

The stilted phrasing of these words makes them sound like prose not conversation, but no doubt Greb said the gist of it. And he also appeared to accept that, while he disagreed with the decision, he did not feel it was an outrageous robbery.

> I couldn't get going early last night and when I did it was only in flashes. But even at that I thought I did enough to protect my title. I was surprised by the decision but hope that when the time comes those who are now feeling sorry for me will learn that I can fight back.

Jack Dempsey did not hide his own racism when speaking to Welsh five days after the fight. He said he would drop in to see Greb when he could, and added, 'He was, and I believe, still is a great fighter, but for the life of me I can't understand why he gave a Negro a chance to take that title away from him.'

Even though he was the new middleweight champion of the world, Flowers did not for a moment lose his head. The social barriers that existed, particularly in the South, the lines he knew he must not cross, were etched in some kind of invisible scar beneath his skin. He knew what would offend white people at home - and would know that how he behaved, or was seen to behave, could have a direct impact on the lives of his family in Atlanta and Brunswick. He would not have needed reminding of the reaction of influential white people to Booker Washington's meal with President Roosevelt in the White House. Yes, that was a generation earlier, but ordinary African-American people were still being burned alive, or hanged from trees, or drowned, cast into chain gangs for the most minor of offences, if offence there was. And so, when the white-dominated sports press of New York arranged a dinner for championship belts to be presented to several champions, including Flowers, he declined the invitation to attend. He said, 'White people'll be mostly there, and some of them might not like breaking bread with a Negro.'

He was assured that if any man should raise such an objection their invitation would be withdrawn and that he, above all others, deserved to be there. Still, he wouldn't do it. 'I sure appreciate your nice invitation,' he said, 'but if I came the feelings of some might be hurt and I don't want to hurt their feelings. Let my manager, a white man, accept my belt in my place.'

Back in Georgia, Flowers was a hero. The *Savannah Journal* ran an editorial to celebrate his success and used him as an example of a man whose earthly reward had come as a result of the purity of his lifestyle,

> A Negro, for the first time in the history of pugilism, has been acclaimed champion of the world's middleweights – Theodore 'Tiger' Flowers. This distinction, gained at Madison Square Garden, New York City, when Harry Greb, titleholder, was dethroned, was not the result of mere brute force, ring cunning or foul tactics, but the outcome of clean living.
>
> Theodore Flowers stands out pre-eminently in the American life today as an example of living a clean, sane life. The stamina that carried him through fifteen rounds of fierce fighting against an opponent who was booed for his unsportsmanlike conduct, was made possible through a life that knows not the cabarets, the white lights, pool-rooms, poker table or shine joints.

The editorial writer wanted black readers to be encouraged by the example Flowers had set, and to understand that progress for any of them was possible if life was lived with discipline and devotion.

Temperate in all things, devoted to his church and family, modest in the midst of his ring triumphs, safe in his investments from ring returns, 'Tiger' Flowers easily becomes a safe pattern for others of our group.

Whatever may have justly been said about other Negroes who rose to fistic championships, only to be dethroned by riotous living, Theodore Flowers has given character to the fight game. And should he ever be dethroned from the high pinnacle on which he now stands it will not be said that the dethronement came as a result of nightlife with its attendant evils.

This theme was developed by Henry Grady Edney in the biography he wrote with the permission and help of Willie Mae Flowers in 1928. Edney was clear that the Tiger's victory was a result of his clean life, perseverance and faith.

Tiger had, in the very sinew of his physical make-up, the determination to win. He had faith in himself. 'The Lord will sustain me' – again and again these words ring in our ears... He had faith in his Maker.

A week after the fight, Miller and Flowers went to the Garden to talk business with Rickard, and by chance or design Greb and his manager, Red Mason, were there. They sat down and discussed a rematch. It was Jess McMahon, one of the brothers who ran the Commonwealth Sporting Club in Harlem, and by then the matchmaker for Rickard at the Garden, who drew up the agreement for them to box again on 21 May 1926. When the fight contracts were signed before the gathered newspaper writers Flowers told Greb:

You gave me a chance to be a champion. Now I'm going to return the favour and let you have a chance. All I want is enough time in between to let the doctor work on me for a few minor operations and engage in a few little bouts. Then you and I will be at it again.

This is the first reference to the toll that boxing was beginning to take on Flowers' health.

Jack Conway of the *New York Mirror* applauded the new champion for agreeing a rematch. 'It's been quite some time since champions conducted business in such quick fashion and without quibbling.'

In a letter to an acquaintance soon afterwards Miller said Tiger's nose had been fixed – an obstruction cleared – and they planned to travel to Brunswick for a week or ten days to do some fishing. After that he planned to 'start him on a few matches that will tune him up for his fight in New York in May in defence of his title'.

Jess McMahon, by the way, thoroughly enjoyed his time making matches for Rickard. In contrast to the secretive, under-stated promoter, McMahon, along with Jack Delaney's manager Pete Reilly, brought a raucous sense of humour to the Garden. They once installed an electric chair in the waiting room outside McMahon's office. A prospective manager waiting to lobby for a match on behalf of his fighter might be ushered to it. McMahon would then press a button in his office and listen gleefully to the bellows of shock from the other side of his door.

Even as Flowers fulfilled his ambition and stood on top of the middleweight world, the lumps and bumps were becoming evident. He made little of them in that conversation with Greb, and certainly did not see the injuries as career threatening, but at the same time there were problems that needed attention. Given the battles he had fought on the long road to the championship, it was an understandable and perhaps inevitable hazard of the trade. It was also an indication that the Tiger's time at the top could not last. He was champion of the world but he was also just past his thirty-third birthday and had competed in around 120 professional fights in the past half-dozen years. He had zigzagged around the country for an incredible 60,000 miles travelling by road or train (and that figure would rise to 77,000 by the end of his career). He was using his money by investing in fruit farms – the Edney biography includes a photograph of him with a caption 'Gathering peaches on one of his numerous farms' – and he would soon move Willie Mae and Verna Lee into the newly built mansion on Simpson Road. His mother would have her own house nearby.

The tributes to Tiger's achievement continued. *United Press* sports editor Henry L. Farrell wrote on 11 March 1926:

> Among his predecessors there may have been greater middleweight champions than Tiger Flowers but certainly there were none with more patience and perseverance…
> After seven years of painful labor through the minor leagues where recognition was scant, competition hard and pay poor, the new champion finally got into the big money…

On 17 March, three weeks after the marvellous victory over Greb, Flowers returned with Miller to Brunswick, Georgia, where he and Willie Mae had grown up, had met and begun their married life. The returning hero was greeted at the station by a brass band and throngs of people. There was a parade in his honour and a banquet reception at the Selden Institute, which included the Mayor (Andrews), former Mayor (Emanuel) and the editor of the local newspaper, C. H. Leavy.

Crowds swarmed around him in Atlanta, too, when he returned there and he posed with his championship belt in front of his home, looking slick in a suit and bow tie.

It was his time.

CHAPTER 14

'The Tiger Is All Right. I Got Nothing Against Him'

Tiger Flowers said when he spoke to Harry Greb in the offices of Madison Square Garden that he wanted time to get some injuries sorted out and to cash in a little bit on his world title. Six weeks after his career defining win over Greb, he was back on the circuit, with his new status and no doubt correspondingly higher fees, boxing Allentown Joe Gans at the Armory in Wilkes-Barre, Pennsylvania, over ten rounds. Allentown Joe could fight, and perhaps the achievement of reaching the top, as well as the physical problems to which Flowers had already admitted, had taken a temporary psychological and physical toll. He won, but only on a split decision, and worse, he finished with a cut on his left eye that troubled him enough to keep him out of the ring for another eight weeks.

A story emerged in the Los Angeles Referee in July that he had been offered $40,000 for a fifteen-week engagement on the vaudeville circuit, but he had turned it down, stating that he was a boxer by trade not an actor or variety performer, and preferred to be known as a fighting champion. What Walk Miller thought of that isn't known. Perhaps they both felt that he could earn more than that in the ring.

When Flowers' cut eye had healed, he came back on 16 June 1926, for another ten round workout, this time a No Decision contest, against a heavyweight, Young Bob Fitzsimmons, son of the old three-weight champion, before 15,000 fans at Boyle's Thirty Acres in Jersey City. This was the huge arena built by Tex Rickard for the Jack Dempsey–Georges Carpentier million-dollar epic in 1921. Flowers gave away a chunk of weight to Fitzsimmons, 166½ lb to 184 lb, but won as he pleased. The old heavyweight champion James J. Jeffries, who once said he would never defend his title against a black man, and who never did, was ringside to see, in the words of the Associated Press writer, Flowers toy with the son of the great old fighter whom he beat to win the title in 1899. 'Flowers… handed the heavyweight a scientific demonstration of all the finer points of the art.'

Ten days later he was performing at Braves Field, Boston, in a ten round points win over another heavier man, a twenty-two-year-old from Jersey City,

Ray Newman, also spelled Neuman. Young Ray was, not for the first time in his career, in too deep. He came into the fight off the back of five consecutive defeats, the last to the Georgia Peach, Young Stribling. He had also been a sparring partner for Jack Dempsey on an exhibition tour the previous year but was one of a multitude of good solid fighters who were matched too hard too young.

After giving his Boston fans a look at him as world champion, Flowers returned to Juarez, over the Mexican border from El Paso, Texas. It was, after all, the city where he had first made some kind of a name for himself. On paper it seemed an acceptable workout against old rival Lee Anderson, who had actually beaten him when they had first met in Juarez in 1922. However, Anderson had long accepted that Flowers had his measure, and it turned into a farcical exhibition which ended in round two when Anderson fell down from what seemed an innocuous punch and was counted out.

From there it was across to Los Angeles, with Willie Mae proudly accompanying him along with Walk Miller. Edney, the mouthpiece for Willie Mae, said that when he took his wife on one of his journeys, he was 'as happy as a child'. A crowd of around 3,000 thronged around the platform as their train drew into the station. His opponent was a light heavyweight, 'Sailor' Eddie Huffman. Originally from Mississippi and then based in California, Huffman was a legitimate contender – he had just fought a draw with Georges Carpentier in Madison Square Garden, and earlier in the year had taken heavyweight hope Jack Sharkey ten rounds to a decision. Tiger trained at the Main Street gym where he struck up a bond with a veteran trainer called Joe Willmore, who was known as Old Folks. When Willmore died mysteriously of a fractured skull in Portland, Oregon, in 1930, the *Ring* writer Theron Fiske wrote of him:

> Old Folks came from the South. When or what part, nobody seems to know. Around a gymnasium it doesn't matter much where you come from or what your name is as long as you can deliver. Old Folks was a trainer and a mighty good one and he could cook too – and how. Old Folks has rubbed and broiled steaks for some of the best in the business. His favourites were Jack Dempsey, the late Tiger Flowers... Old Folks also liked his fighters to drink his special beef tea. He had a way all his own of making it and thought it better than anyone else's.

Writers called the downtown gym the Main Street workhouse. By the time it closed in 1951, it had been a temporary home for all the great fighters who visited the city. Joe Louis, Ray Robinson, Harry Greb, Tony Canzoneri, Barney Ross, Fidel LaBarba, Ike Williams, Henry Armstrong – and Tiger Flowers – all trained there. When its doors were shut for the last time, Ring's Californian correspondent wrote, 'It was not unusual to see more than one hundred boxers there in a single day, with as many as thirty or forty training there at a single time.'

The fight, on 24 July 1926, was at Ascot Park, an open air arena built on an old city dump south of downtown in Gardena. It was about as far removed from the glamour of the Hollywood film studios as it was possible to be. Usually it staged dirt track race meetings. There were 7,500 seats in the rudimentary stands, and for boxing, more could be set out on the inside of the track. One estimate put the crowd at 12,000. Tiger struggled. He won but had to get up from a knockdown in round two to do it after shipping a heavy right, and as usual Huffman was still on his feet at the final bell. Still, the payday came to $10,000. The writer for the *Los Angeles Referee*, praising the Fighting Deacon as wearing the championship with 'a great deal more grace and dignity than several other champions', called his win over Greb 'the most sensational upset of recent ring history'.

> Flowers is a devoted son, husband and father, and looks forward to the day when he can hang up his gloves and retire to one of the farms he has acquired in his native state of Georgia. Members of his race staged one of the greatest demonstrations in the history of the city when he arrived in Los Angeles last week, indicating the tremendous popularity the champion enjoys. He is the greatest drawing card in the boxing game aside from Jack Dempsey, and holds practically all the recent records for attendance in Eastern cities.

The Associated Press, however, recorded that the Tiger had 'skidded close to defeat' when after punishing Huffman severely he had been dropped heavily by the right hand. This report said it was in round three, not round two, that Flowers got up groggily at seven, but that Huffman missed his chance to finish the fight by being over-eager.

Flowers said he was returning to New York for the rematch with Greb, which had been postponed until August because of Greb's protracted fallout with his manager Red Mason. Tiger also said he would like to box Jack Delaney again. Delaney, who had knocked him out twice, was now the world light heavyweight champion following a points win over Paul Berlanbach in Brooklyn. The writer for the *Los Angeles Referee* also said,

> Both Mr Miller and Mr Flowers and their families like Los Angeles and don't be surprised to hear that they have purchased a slice of Los Angeles real estate before many months roll along.

Instead of going straight to New York, Theodore and Willie Mae returned to Atlanta, where he acted as corner man for his younger brother, Cecil, in a fight with a Memphis middleweight, Happy Hunter, at the Paramount Theater.

Cecil, who sometimes fought as Baby Flowers and Young Tiger Flowers, lost in the fifth round. It is not easy to see where Cecil fitted into the family. He had not been mentioned on any of the previous census returns, but was later mentioned in Theodore's will, so there is no doubt that he was his brother. By the 1930 census Cecil had moved to Florida. Perhaps it was Cecil that their mother Lula was visiting when Theodore had the altercation with the policeman in 1925 when he said he was travelling to Florida to collect his mother.

At the beginning of August there was also talk that Flowers would be one of nine men selected to spar with Jack Dempsey when the heavyweight champion returned to training before his defence against Gene Tunney in Philadelphia on 23 September. Associated Press reported this on 6 August. Some of the nine would help Dempsey in the initial stages but it was proposed that Flowers and light-heavyweight champion Tommy Loughran would join Dempsey in the later stages at his Saratoga Springs training camp. It is interesting that after being out of the ring for three years Dempsey left himself only a six-week training camp – and perhaps that had some bearing on the fact that Tunney outpointed him with a degree of ease on that rain-sodden night at the Sesquicentennial Stadium.

Flowers had been world middleweight champion for almost six months, his place in boxing history was secure, his achievement honoured at home in Atlanta and Brunswick, and across America itself. He was celebrated as a role model to African-Americans, honoured as a dignified, courteous man who lived clean and set a fine example to any black person who wanted to better themselves in a tough world. He gave to his church, to universities and colleges, and might also have been something of a soft touch.

One dubious character who claimed Flowers as a backer was the eccentric would-be airman Hubert Julian who planned a solo flight from New York to Liberia on the west coast of Africa, from where the ancestors of so many black Americans had been taken into slavery. Julian took off once in a seaplane from the Harlem River but a few minutes later settled somewhat gracelessly on Flushing Bay. A re-run never, as was said with wry amusement at the time, got off the ground.

James H. Jones, reflecting half a century later on the Flowers he knew at this time, wrote in *Ring* magazine that it seemed the champion was struggling to cope with his wealth. Perhaps he felt the guilt that some do when they are luckier than most, or that their lives work out when times are hard for so many of their friends and acquaintances. Jones wrote,

> Visitors, as a rule, found him sitting on his glass-enclosed porch or in his parlor, reading his tattered testament and fearful that Jehovah in his wrath might send a bolt to blast him from his palatial surroundings.

There was also the not insignificant problem of being a successful black man in Georgia. While nobody was about to lynch him or members of his family, there would have been pockets of resentment among those for whom life was not working out. And the Ku Klux Klan, while not as powerful as it had been just a year or two earlier, remained an attractive proposition for poor, embittered white farmers, businessmen or the kind of crazy folk who attach themselves to any cause that brings with it a uniform and some physical and psychological power. Atlanta's black community was relatively safe, but it would not have taken much for a criminal element to have, for example, kidnapped his wife or daughter, burned his farms, damaged his new house, or the one he had bought for his mother. Harassment, suspicion, bias, were still routine – and it would stay that way for generations to come.

Walk Miller was busy. Tiger Flowers, the middleweight champion of the world, was his dream meal ticket. Like so many whose job it is to promote a product, Miller exploited the best-selling lines when and where he could. Most writers lapped up the 'Fighting Deacon' line *ad nauseam*. Paul Gallico found it intensely irritating. 'They press agented the Tiger's church connections and Bible quotations until the theme was threadbare. I never cared much for that.'

Miller also wrote and produced a film, which he called *The Fighting Deacon, The Life of Tiger Flow*ers. It was a 35 mm movie in five reels, featuring the two of them talking. The American Film Institute catalogue of motion pictures lists it as follows. 'Episodes from the boyhood and early manhood of Theodore Flowers are presented, including his experiences in the United States Army during World War One.'

Presumably Miller, anxious to avoid any possibility of the kind of 'slacker' label that had haunted Jack Dempsey in the early part of the decade, wanted to head it off with this piece of fiction. What part in that Flowers played is unclear, but on the Government census of 1920, he did not tick the box that covered war service and in no interviews that I have found did he ever refer to having served. There is no record of it, though he did fill out the US Draft eligibility papers. At the time of the war he was working in the shipyards in Philadelphia. He was contributing to the war effort but was not in the forces. The AFI description continued. 'Following the Armistice, Flowers turns to boxing and, under the training of Walk Miller, becomes the middleweight champion, beating Harry Greb for the title.' The film was screened at African-American theatres, including the Elmore in Atlanta, where it was accompanied by vaudeville artists, including Vader and Hunter 'the fast steppers', and Jennings and Reed, a 'creole musical novelty act'. Archie Moore, who became the world light heavyweight champion a quarter of a century after Flowers had passed on, said he remembered seeing the film when he was a boy in St Louis, Missouri. He would have been about nine years old. Unfortunately, the movie is now presumed lost.

Miller's own reputation had risen now that Flowers was champion. He guided the Australian heavyweight George Cook, whose wife told the English writer James Butler that she and her husband thought very highly of the Tiger. 'The colour of his skin doesn't matter,' she said. 'He's the whitest man I've met. Outside and inside the ropes he is a gentleman.'

This theme of Flowers, in spite of his black skin, being 'white inside', was repeated often. Gene Tunney and Nat Fleischer were two who reiterated it, as if it was the greatest compliment they could give an African-American. A phrase for the times of course, but one that said so much.

Flowers kept on working, just as he had always done. Maybe at thirty-three he felt like slowing down, maybe not. Maybe Miller, maybe both of them, sensed his time in the high-earning bracket would not be especially long, and that they had to make what they could while the going was good. Or maybe Miller just booked him out as the opportunities arose and Flowers felt obligated to him to honour each and every one. Certainly, boxing had given him its greatest reward in the shape of a world championship, and had allowed him to rise up the social ladder as far as it was possible for a black athlete to rise, but he had long proven that he was not stupid. He would have been well aware that it was a cruel business and the big paydays could disappear overnight.

Although the Greb rematch was only twenty-six days after his ten round battle with Eddie Huffman in Los Angeles, he managed to fit in one more payday. On 10 August 1926, back at the Atlanta Auditorium, he made a goodwill gesture to his local fans by appearing in a workout against a heavyweight from North Carolina by way of Boston named Battling Jim McCreary. Flowers won in the third round when referee Jake Abel disqualified McCreary for a low punch. McCreary was known in Boston as the Battling Preacher but that was the result of a colourful piece of writing by the Boston Globe's Lawrence Sweeney who noted 'the large number of black church-goers' who would turn out to watch his fights. Whether that was true, or indicated a link to any particular church, or if McCreary did any preaching at all, is unclear.

Two days later the Cohocton Tribune reported that the low blow that Flowers had absorbed against McCreary would not delay the Greb fight. He had recovered well.

And so it was back to New York City, to the house in Harlem, and to preparations for the return with Harry Greb with the middleweight championship on the line at Madison Square Garden on 19 August 1926.

Walk Miller walked straight into a row when he said he had been told the fight was 'in the bag' for Greb to win, in other words, a pre-arranged fix. Greb's contractual dispute with manager Red Mason had led to Jimmy Johnston being involved in making the training arrangements for Harry and to work his corner on the big night. Mason was removed, then reinstated, but in name only, with a financial cut due him. Miller knew all about Johnston's reputation, and remembered only too well the events of the McTigue fight and probably felt that by making a noise he could discourage anyone wanting to influence the outcome.

Greb must have known he did not have much left. Since losing the title he had boxed twice, both times in June, points wins over Art Weigand and Allentown Joe Gans, in Buffalo and Wilkes-Barre respectively. Before the rematch he said, according to James Fair, 'I've got one good fight left in me. And I'm gonna whip the Tiger sure as hell.'

The crowd in the Garden this time was lower, although there was a big walk-up, according to the Universal Service agency report.

> There was a furious last minute rush of customers that astounded the ticket snatchers at the portals of Madison Square Garden... The boys and girls came clattering forward in such numbers that the traffic cops were submerged.

Maybe there were less people from Pittsburgh prepared to travel in, having seen Greb beaten in January. The crowd was 14,125 – or 15,367, depending on your source – and gate receipts, it was agreed, were $75,176. Maxie Rosenbloom fought on the undercard, and beat a Texan named Chuck Burns, whose deal for the fight had been done by Walk Miller. Also fighting was KO Phil Kaplan, who knocked out one of Max Hoff's fighters, Dick Evans, in the second round.

At the weigh-in the challenger looked fitter, and more lively than he had first time around. He had been training outdoors and his body was tanned and fit. Flowers seemed his usual self.

In the dressing room before the fight a man stepped up to Greb and handed him a letter. 'Something for you,' he said. It was a summons in an action for $250,000 brought against him by A. H. Bronis, charging alienation of the affections of his wife, Sally Bronis, with whom Greb had been romantically involved some time before. Sally Bronis, in a separate case, also sued for $100,000 for an alleged breach of promise.

Jimmy Johnston had far more emotional difficulties to contend with. His wife, Ida, had died only three days earlier from heart disease. Maybe her illness had left him too preoccupied or drained to do any 'leaning' on the Commission. The referee was Jim Crowley, the judges Charles Mathison, who had officiated in the previous fight in February, and Harold Barnes. The officials were straight.

Crowley would be hauled before the New York Commission twelve months later for disqualifying the Spanish heavyweight Paolino Uzcudun against Jack Delaney but went on to referee the world heavyweight title fight between Jack Sharkey and Max Schmeling in 1930, when he disqualified

Sharkey for a low blow. Coincidentally, Mathison and Barnes were both appointed to that fight too. Barnes, an optometrist from Flushing, New York, was actually a referee and judge from the early twenties until 1958, when he resigned, declaring boxing to have fallen into a state of 'moral turpitude and physical derogation'. He went so far as to call for the sport to be abolished. Five years on, he was still campaigning. He said,

> If anyone doubts the dangers of boxing to its participants, I'd like to have him come out to my house and look over my horror file – of boxing suicides, murderers, lunatics, blinded, paralyzed and killed.

Barnes displayed no such scruples in 1926, though he might have been less comfortable had he understood that the Human Windmill from Pittsburgh could not see anything out of one eye. Of course, as usual, Greb had passed the Commission's medical examination. After Greb's death, when rumours began to circulate that he hadn't been just partially blind but actually had a glass eye, a doctor solemnly declared, without any apparent sense of irony, this couldn't have been the case as he would have noticed that during the pre-fight medical. In fact, the glass replacement was not put in until a month before Greb's death.

Traditionally, a champion is afforded the respect of coming into the ring second and being announced second. It is just one of those small things that do not mean a great deal in themselves, but which have become a part of the ritual, that places, until the fight starts at least, the champion in a higher position to his challenger. Flowers was not afforded that respect. It probably did not bother him, but he was first into the ring, this time well received. Once again, Greb received an ovation. Regis Welsh wrote in the *Pittsburgh Post* that Greb ducked between the ropes into the ring and immediately walked across to greet Flowers like an old friend.

This time the livelier, fresher Greb made a fast start, anxious to make an impression and prevent Flowers finding an early rhythm. It worked. Flowers was seen to stagger under an attack inside the first minute. However, this was only the preliminary moments of forty-five minutes of fighting. Flowers stayed cool and began to work Greb's body. Already, though, Greb looked sharper than he had in February. 'Harry swarmed all over Flowers with rights and lefts flailing away from all angles and the Tiger seemed bewildered,' wrote Jersey Jones. Opinions differed as to who won the round. The Universal Service, whose account was detailed, reported that Tiger had the better of the exchanges, his blows more effective.

Greb certainly won round two. Harry brought the house to its feet with a series of blows to Flowers' head.

And then in the third disaster struck for Greb. His left eye, his good one, or at least not his blind one, was bleeding. It was obvious that he couldn't see too much, but his fighting heart was as strong as ever, and referee Crowley didn't notice his impairment, or didn't feel it was having any major bearing on his ability to handle himself. Flowers worked the body well on the inside. 'Harry kept clinging to the Tiger and even the referee found it difficult to pry him away.'

Should Flowers have switched angles, kept the fight at long range, bamboozled and bewildered him with punches he couldn't see coming? Maybe, yes, but Greb really was an incredible fighting machine. He knew what to do, and he had been battling away with this handicap for years. It just didn't faze him. Jersey Jones wrote in a retrospective piece for *Ring*,

> The scrap developed into as rough a fracas as the Garden probably ever has housed. It was a back-alley brawl in which everything went. Greb, master of rough-and-tumble tactics, found Flowers more than willing to meet him at his own forte.
>   The rivals slugged, butted, heeled, hit on breaks, gouged and shoved each other all over the premises.

In round four Flowers twice complained to referee Crowley that Greb was trying to gouge his eyes out, Crowley ignored him, so the Tiger set to work with his own fouls. Greb landed a stinging right to the head, but Flowers threw three back. Greb landed one more then went on the run. 'He kept this up until the referee stepped in. Both boxers were waiting for something to happen but nothing happened.'

Round five was easily Flowers' round, according to the agency. His body punching was more hurtful as he crowded and outworked Greb.

In the sixth Flowers was cut. Greb had Flowers stumbling into the ropes with three right hands to the body, and when the champion came off the ropes it was into the path of two left hands. However, the crowd booed Greb for some blatant holding and hitting.

Both were warned for hitting low in the seventh, but again Flowers, according to the US writer, out-generalled and even outclassed Greb, who took to complaining to the referee. To his old admirers that was unthinkable. The man who had made a reputation out of accepting that boxing was a rough business by nature and fighters were best left to get on with it wanted the support of the referee.

In round eight, according to Greb's *Pittsburgh Post* friend, Regis Welsh, the champion was knocked down by a right to the chin. He rolled over and jumped straight back up, and on they went. In retrospective James Fair thought it was not a knockdown but a slip and Jersey Jones did not recall it as a knockdown either, saying Flowers got his feet tangled up and sat down with a bump. The contemporary agency said simply: 'Flowers slipped to the floor at the start of the round.'

Flowers dominated the middle part of the fight, chasing Greb and swinging away, sometimes missing by a distance, but piling on the pressure. In the ninth he forced Greb to the ropes and hammered away at him with both hands. 'Greb finally fought his way into the centre of the ring and they sparred. Greb caught Flowers with a couple of haymakers but Flowers came back with a volley of rights and lefts and won the round by a long margin.'

The tenth was quieter for the first half – 'they did a lot of dancing and all the punches that arrived were without sting' – but Flowers closed the round better, pressing Greb into a corner and 'pasting away at the one time rubber ball'.

Flowers was rocked in round eleven as Greb rallied with big, bold attacks and landed at will, but to the agency writer at ringside Harry was still well behind.

Then they stood toe-to-toe and fought – and fouled – it out. 'With a perfect half-nelson Flowers threw Greb at the start of the twelfth', a move that earned him a telling off from the referee. The crowd were showing their disapproval of the mauling action by the thirteenth, by which time Greb was also cut on the right eye. Greb pushed Flowers over, but there wasn't much in the way of clean punching.

This time, however, it was Greb who found the bigger finish.

Apparently realizing he was losing, Greb threw everything he had left into the two remaining rounds. He plunged in recklessly – swinging, butting and wrestling in a last desperate effort to swing the verdict in his favour. It was a spectacular finish, typical of Greb at his peak.

Fair suggested Flowers was struggling by the closing rounds. 'Flowers actually turned and ran. Two or three times, when Greb caught up with him, he doubled him over the ropes and pounded him dizzy.'

The US agency man said, 'Greb now had blood streaming from cuts over both eyes… Greb seemed to have got his second wind.' His punches carried more weight, and there were more of them, but Flowers didn't hear the bell to end round fourteen and kept slugging back. And Greb also outfought Tiger in the last, twice almost shoving him out of the ring in his anxiety to keep the attacks going.

Greb had, indeed, produced one last great fight and his big finish made some forget how Flowers had dominated round after round earlier on.

The Pittsburgh faithful believed they had seen their city's favourite son regain the title, and when ringmaster Joe Humphreys said, once again, that Flowers was the winner, the fans stormed to ringside and threw bottles, hats, paper and any bits of trash they could find in the general direction of the ring.

'Little did the crowd, which littered the arena with straw hats and torn newspapers in noisy disapproval of the decision, sense it was seeing Harry Greb for the last time,' said Jones, but the *Ring* stalwart had Flowers in front 7-6-2 in rounds and saw nothing wrong with the split decision in favour of the Tiger.

Greb told Fair that at the end referee Crowley, who had voted for him only to be overruled by Mathison and Barnes, said to him, 'Tough, Harry. A tough one to lose. It was your fight.'

The Universal Services agency report, reprinted in the *Milwaukee Sentinel*, had Flowers ahead by an overwhelming margin of 11-4, having given the Tiger the edge in most of the close rounds.

In the dressing room Greb had a sob in his throat, and seemed more bitter than he had after the January fight. He said, 'Well, that was one fight I won, if I won any. The Tiger is all right. I got nothing against him. But he's not a champion. He'll lose my title the first time he defends it against anyone who can fight.'

He also announced that he was through with boxing and that he wouldn't fight again.

Ed Sullivan of the *New York Evening Graphic* considered Greb and Flowers to be similarly styled fighters, even allowing for the fact that the Tiger was a southpaw. They fought at a high pace, could look awkward but both had a great deal of ability. He also felt Greb, as a white man, could get away with fouls that Flowers would be pulled up about, and so fought dirtier. Flowers, however, could withstand being fouled, as could Greb, and possessed amazing levels of courage and mental and physical strength.

The *Chicago Defender*, as resolutely pro-Flowers as ever, claimed Tiger won clearly, 'beating the white boy unmercifully in fifteen rounds of furious fighting'. However, their writer did attempt to put the fight into a wider perspective.

> Greb was not the Greb of old. His legs are gone. He again used foul tactics, which drew boos from the big crowd. Even with all this, referee Crowley voted for Greb, but this time the two judges thought that Flowers had won, and so did the rest of the public, including the press representatives.

Well, not so.

Regis Welsh, not surprisingly, had it 9-4-2 in rounds for Greb, only slightly closer than he'd scored the first fight. The United Press International writer Frank Getty also felt Greb won. Gene Tunney, who had watched at ringside, felt the decision an unfair one but presumably did not keep a running tally and William Muldoon, one of the New York commissioners, agreed, but said he would not change it.

Two months later Harry Greb was dead at the age of thirty-two. He had the eye which had been sightless for five years removed and replaced with a glass one in September. And then in Atlantic City on 21 October he had surgery on his nose, which had been damaged, he said, when he crashed his car in Pittsburgh in early October. If this was the case, what on earth was he doing behind a wheel? Red Mason, his estranged manager said Greb faked the accident, that it was a story to cover the fact that he was going under the knife in Atlantic City for cosmetic purposes, to have his nose straightened and his scar tissue tidied up now that his career was over. The old champion joked to friends, 'I'll be back in a few days looking better than ever.'

Greb was given nitrous oxide and oxygen gas, and had a fragment of bone removed from the back of his nose. According to a Dr Weinberg, it was the removal of the piece of bone that led to his death because it released a blood clot that had formed behind it, and that blood rushed to his brain, causing a haemorrhage. This explanation was given in the *Washington Post* on 26 October. Greb's operation was completed, but the next morning his condition worsened and he died, at 2.30 p.m. on the 22nd, eighteen hours after surgery.

At the weekly show at the Pittsburgh Motor Square Garden they hung coloured portraits of Greb draped in black over the ring and after the traditional count of ten bells, the crowd stood in silence, head bowed as a bugler sounded 'The Last Post'.

A month after retaining the championship against Greb, Flowers was in Memphis, Tennessee, for what amounted to an exhibition against a fighter who competed under the name Happy Hunter. Maybe Theodore felt it was necessary to satisfy family honour, as Hunter had beaten his brother Cecil in five rounds at the Paramount Theater at the end of July but whatever the reason it was a bad match. Tiger won in three.

Then it was back to serious business. At the Mechanics Building, Boston, on 15 October 1926, the week before Harry Greb died, Flowers lost on a ninth round foul to 'Slapsie' Maxie Rosenbloom in an over-the-weight non-title fight. Rosenbloom would win the world light-heavyweight title four years later.

Rosenbloom was too big to get a return for the middleweight championship, and so Flowers' next defence of the title was agreed for Chicago Coliseum on 3 December 1926, against Mickey Walker, who had been world champion at welterweight (147 lb) before moving up and playing his full part in a fifteen round classic with Greb for the middleweight title the previous year. Greb had won on points.

Illinois had not yet staged a mixed bout. The other Chicago experiments had been in the city's sprawling outer reaches, but over the state line in Indiana. After due consideration, with appreciation of Flowers' reputation as a gentlemanly athlete, the Commission accepted the idea. What, or who, persuaded them to take the unprecedented step is not known.

Flowers' appearance in Chicago excited the black community, and a banquet was held in his honour at the Ambassador Club. Jack Johnson attended. Eubie Blake, pianist and co-writer of the Broadway musical *Shuffle Along*, and songs like 'I'm Just Wild About Harry' and 'Memories of You', played a few numbers.

Flowers was given a warm-up for the Walker fight at the Chicago Coliseum on 22 November against the white fighter, Sailor Eddie Huffman, who had given him a scare when they had fought in Los Angeles the previous July. On that occasion Huffman had floored him for a count of nine but this time when the 10 lb heavier Sailor finally landed his big right hand Flowers' chin held firm and he stayed on his feet. At the end of ten fairly one-sided rounds referee Jimmy Gardner held up the Tiger's glove. There were no problems. Chicago fans, white and black, had accepted the match readily enough – and enthusiastically acknowledged his superiority. The *Indianapolis Recorder* said it was a boxing lesson that Huffman would long remember.

> Huffman... openly boasted that he would wipe the Deacon and his Jumping Jack tactics. Flowers moulded Huffman around the ring for ten rounds, winning every round. After the fight Flowers was given the greatest ovation ever given a fighter in a Chicago ring.

Local writer Harry Hochstadter said promoter Jim Mullen under-estimated the popularity of Flowers among the black community and did not have enough turnstiles open at the stadium. The consequence was that frustrated ticket-holders were milling around outside in long queues.

> There is no denying that the Tiger is one of our ring's greatest showmen. He may not hit so hard, but he bounces them around the enemy's anatomy so often that he makes the average fan wonder where he gets his technique. Just to show the 6,000 cash customers who fought and battled to enter the Coliseum, the Tiger did a couple of nips on the canvas in the first two rounds, when he slipped. Just to show everyone that he was still fresh as a daisy after ten rounds with the sailor, the tiger turned a half-somersault to close the show.

On the same night in Boston, Mickey Walker also took part in a warm-up, outpointing Jock Malone to clear the way for the championship fight.

Walker, known as The Toy Bulldog, was born Edward Patrick Walker in Elizabeth, New Jersey, in 1901. He was shorter than Flowers at 5 foot 7 inches, and a rough, aggressive bundle of energy. He had held the welterweight title from 1922, when he outhustled long-serving, thirty-seven-year-old Jack Britton over fifteen rounds in the old Garden, and had stayed champion until Pete Latzo had outscored him in a ten round title fight in Scranton, Pennsylvania, in May 1926. Walker was managed by the shrewd, cunning Jack

Kearns who had guided Jack Dempsey all the way to the heavyweight title. By this time the relationship with Dempsey was all but broken. Dempsey was living in Hollywood, doing a little movie work, playing out his celebrity lifestyle as the living proof of the American Dream, while his wife, Estelle Taylor, tried to build an acting career of her own. Kearns was more in tune with Walker, who saw life as a roller-coaster party wherever, and however late, he laid his head. They particularly enjoyed the carousing temptations of New York. Kearns said, in his autobiography *The Million Dollar Gate*,

> Mickey and I were kindred spirits who were always ready to juice it up together... we painted the whole town, from LaHiff's to Legs Diamond's Hotsy Totsy Club, Dutch Schulz's Embassy, Texas Guinan's 300 Club, and Owney Madden's Cotton Club. And we did it with a likely string of fillies – the beautiful, blonde Margaret Quimby, who later became a motion picture star; diamond-draped Peggy Hopkins Joyce; showgirl Peggy Lane; the shapely May Devereaux; creamy-skinned Pearl Germaine; and, at one period, Madame Dora Dena, one of the best of the shimmy dancers.

Kearns and Walker might as well have lived on another planet to the disciplined, calm, devout Flowers. They knew the bad boys, they ate, drank and made merry at their clubs. While Flowers dutifully honoured his tithe to his church, the only charity Kearns cared about was the one that ensured the quality of the lining in his pockets.

Walker had actually retired after losing his welterweight title and then getting flattened by a future champ called Joe Dundee. Kearns persuaded him back, got him some wins and then paid Walk Miller a call at a house Flowers was using on Chicago's South Side. He took Walker with him, instructing him to look sad and say nothing. He persuaded Miller that Walker needed the fight because he was washed up and broke. Kearns told them Walker would quit for good after the fight, but they could be sure of a big crowd because of his name. He recalled saying to Miller, 'You guys will make a bundle.'

It was a trick that was as old as prizefighting, but Miller listened, and then agreed as Kearns said he would run the show himself, fronted by Jim Mullen, and would say that Flowers was being paid $50,000 to attract the newsmen. In fact, Kearns suggested they split the proceeds down the middle.

Miller should have been wiser, should have known better than to trust a hard-nosed sharp-talker like Kearns.

The fight was also scheduled for only ten rounds, which did not suit Flowers, and was to be handled by a referee, scoring alone without the help of ringside judges, which left another hole for Kearns to exploit. Ten round world title fights were not uncommon at around this time: both of the Jack Dempsey-Gene Tunney heavyweight championship bouts, in 1926 and 1927, were over ten rounds, and Harry Greb had fought Bryan Downey in a middleweight championship defence over that distance in 1923. Walker had defended his welterweight crown over ten rounds against Lew Tendler at the Baker Bowl in Philadelphia. But if it was not unusual, it was not to Flowers' advantage, as the naturally bigger man, to have a shorter fight. The likelihood was that it would take time for him to establish his superiority. Old-timers, meanwhile, must have wondered what their old sport was coming to. Why, only as recently as 1915, the world championship fight between Jack Johnson and Jess Willard was scheduled for forty-five rounds and ended in the twenty-sixth. Jake Kilrain, who fought John L. Sullivan in the last of the bare-knuckle heavyweight championship fights in Mississippi in 1889, was still alive, and only in his late sixties. He and Sullivan had fought for seventy-five rounds spread over two hours sixteen minutes and twenty-three seconds.

Rumours began to circulate that Flowers would not be treated fairly. Charlie Rose, an old fight figure who knew the seamy side of boxing well enough, said Flowers, or Miller, would not sign a contract until Kearns agreed to an immediate rematch clause: that is, that if Walker won he would give Flowers a return before defending against anyone else. Rose remembered in his book *Life's A Knockout* in 1953:

> Rumour became busy. One piled on the other to the complete mystification of everybody outside Kearns' circle. Referee after referee turned down the job to handle the fight. It was alleged that in despair Kearns approached a certain Captain of Artillery, who replied: 'I'll act if you'll allow me to station my company round the ring… fully armed.

The commission eventually selected Benny Yanger, a former featherweight. Yanger knew boxing through and through, but of course that is no guarantee of his or anyone else being a competent official. In his own career, he once beat Abe Attell in a fight advertised for, but not generally recognised as being for, the world featherweight title, and boxed the great George Dixon twice. His real name was Frank Angone. Born into an Italian-American family in New York City, he had lived in Chicago since his early teens.

The fight drew $77,127, the largest gate in Chicago boxing history up to that point. 'It was a smash,' said Kearns, who was also said to be privately whispering to friends to 'put the old bank roll on Walker'.

Flowers was a narrow favourite. He worked off the last of his weight before the weigh-in at three o'clock on the afternoon of the fight – it was increasingly tough for him to get to 160 lb but he could manage it. The Pittsburgh Press assessed the fight. 'Flowers is figured to outspeed Walker, while the former welterweight champion hopes to outslug the middleweight champion.'

The local *Telegraph-Herald* declared, 'Chicago is the capital of pugilism today and a wild, fight-mad capital it is… It will be the most important fight staged here since the rebirth of legalized boxing in Illinois.'

The fight itself was described by James P. Dawson of the *New York Times* as sizzling and savage. If Miller and Flowers believed that Walker was there for one last payday, it took less than a round to show them how wrong they were. The fight was only in its preliminary exchanges when Walker put Flowers down. It was only a flash knockdown, and Tiger jumped straight up without taking a count, but the point had been made, and the fight was on.

Flowers came on in the second and Walker suffered a cut over the left eye. The third was close, Walker's extra welterweight speed might have edged him the fourth, but then the Tiger got into his stride and dominated from the fifth to the eighth. Walker's face was a mess, his lips swollen, and blood ran from his nose and mouth.

But the Toy Bulldog knew this was for everything – the middleweight title, his fighting pride and his whole career. He lay all he had on the line, and somehow found space for a left hook in the ninth that caught the champion off balance and put him over. Again, Flowers jumped straight up and waded in. And so it went on to the final bell, at which point the fighters fell into a clinch that turned into a congratulatory hug. Referee Yanger prised them apart – and raised Walker's arm. The Chicago, pro-Walker crowd celebrated noisily, jubilantly. Police officers swarmed into the ring, but there was no trouble.

The majority verdict from the writers at ringside was that if the decision wasn't quite as bad as that in the Flowers–McTigue fight, it was still wrong-headed. Yanger later said he had penalised Flowers for slapping and that Walker's punches, while there were less of them, were cleaner. Not too many bought his explanation.

For years a rumour ran that Al Capone was behind the decision, that he was making a financial killing on a Walker win. Maybe, maybe not. Doc Kearns knew Capone well enough. He claimed in his autobiography, written with Oscar Fraley near the end of his life, that he had visited Capone when he was in Cook County jail in Chicago in January 1932, awaiting the outcome of the income tax case that finally brought him down. Capone ordered fifty tickets for his friends for a world welterweight title fight between Lou Brouillard and Jackie Fields in Chicago at the end of the month. Kearns took them to him and was ushered into his cell, where there was a radio playing, a soft quilt on the prison bed and whiskey and cigars. According to Kearns they spent a couple of hours drinking and telling stories.

The pro-Flowers *Chicago Defender* was outraged by what it perceived as the robbery inflicted on Flowers and blamed Yanger, later also reporting that the Illinois Commission put out a statement to say the referee 'erred', but adding that they would not, or could not, alter the decision. The commissioners were apparently embarrassed enough to say that in future they would not let a referee score a major contest without the aid of ringside judges.

While James P. Dawson of the New York Times saw the fight close for Flowers – by just one round – Paul Gallico bluntly stated that the title was stolen from the champion, while pointing out that the Tiger never once complained or behaved in anything other than a sportsmanlike manner. Ed Sullivan said when the verdict was given, Flowers smiled. James Butler remembered him saying, 'The referee says Mickey won and what he says goes.'

Ed Van Every said Flowers reflected simply, 'It is God's will.'

This version is borne out by Edney, or Willie Mae. 'He did not rebel. He did not register a 'kick'. It was satisfactory with him. He was content to abide by the decision.'

The Defender, however, said that according to Tiger's friends in Chicago the verdict had 'sorely worried him' – it would have dawned on him that rematch clause or no rematch clause he was nothing but a contender again, and a black one at that. The *Afro-American* newspaper also said most of the city's writers viewed the decision as a blot on the game in Illinois.

Trevor Wignall, in his book *Prides of the Fancy*, said that for every person who thought Walker had won, there were six who felt Flowers should have kept the title.

Initially, Walk Miller seemed to accept the verdict, as if he was stunned by it.

I must bow to the decision. The boxing commissioners had a good man as referee and he said Walker won, and Walker must have won. At the same time, however, there is no denying that Flowers was fouled several times during the battle.

I have an iron clad agreement which binds Walker to defend his title in a return bout within three months in a city other than Chicago. Walker cannot fight any other challenger until he fights a return with Tiger. Of course, the match will be held in New York City.

There was something almost too compliant in the tone of this as if he was initially reluctant not to upset anyone else after the shambolic episodes that surrounded the Delaney fights of 1925. Perhaps to be fair to Walk he was stunned by what had happened and embarrassed that he had been so easily duped by Kearns. After time to think, he declared himself 'amazed and incensed' and campaigned to have the decision reversed.

At first the Chicago Commission seemed so disorganised that they couldn't even call a meeting to discuss the complaint. One commissioner, Paul Prehn, was out of the city. Another, O. W. Huncke, appeared to have resigned and not been replaced. Miller announced, 'It is my honest belief that a serious mistake has been made and since the commission is looked upon to uphold the sport, that body should take some action.' He said he believed referee Yanger to be honest but incompetent. 'I am convinced that he was not a fit official to judge a contest.'

His comments were published, thanks to an agency report, around the country, including the *St Petersburg Times*, but they were futile. Nothing was done. The boxing world moved on.

According to Edney, Flowers believed that the friends he had made, both among the nation's boxing fans and leading administrators, would mean there would be enough public pressure for him to be granted the rematch. Kearns said in his memoir:

> Flowers was so steamed up at the remarkable manner in which Mickey had come back from the old man's home that he held us to the terms of the contract, and we had to pay him $50,000. After expenses, we didn't have much of a profit. But we had won the middleweight title and were back on top of the heap.

As Miller did the talking for the Tiger, it was probably his outrage that Kearns remembered but it is possible that behind closed doors the deposed champion had let his feelings be known. For his part Walk knew he'd been made a fool of.

Walker, in his autobiography, *The Toy Bulldog*, ghosted by Joe Reichler in 1961, said, 'It was very close. There were a lot of people who thought I didn't win the fight. In fact, Walk Miller, the Tiger's manager, screamed that his fighter had been done out of the title...'

The new champion stuck to his view that the verdict was fair and not crooked.

> The fact remained that it was I who had Flowers on the floor, even though I couldn't kayo him. The Tiger was a good fighter, but he didn't win that fight...
> Flowers himself never complained. He was a tiger in the ring, but outside of it he was a kindly, good-hearted man... I liked him personally and promised his manager a return match.

Walker said the uproar in the newspapers didn't bother him. After all, he had what he wanted. He was a world champion again.

Miller, probably believing there was nothing to lose, kept up the complaints, even to the point where he tried to suggest there was something wrong with Kearns having allegedly gambled $50,000 on Walker, which of course mattered little to anybody but Kearns and the bookmaker who had to shell out. A Capone-inspired sting, of which Kearns would have had prior knowledge given his connections, remains no more than an intriguing possibility.

Miller, having made mistakes in accepting the fight, put out copies of the fight contract to sports editors, claiming Kearns and Walker were about to renege on the rematch clause.

On 1 February 1927, Walker returned to the ring, not against Flowers, but in Fresno, California, for a non-title workout against a mediocre middle-class dreamer named Mickey Wallace. He won that in three rounds and then, for a guarantee of $120,000 took off for England where in June 1927 he knocked out the Scot, Tommy Milligan, in the tenth round of his first championship defence at London Olympia. Miller's rematch clause didn't trouble Kearns and Walker in the slightest. They had the title and were doing what they wanted with it.

CHAPTER 15

Lumps, Bumps, Headaches, Dizzy Spells

What else could the Tiger do but go back out on the road?

Flowers took the rest of December off and was at home for Christmas and New Year, which was probably a welcome relief from the rigours of earning a living – and offered him some time to come to terms with the loss of the title he had held for only ten months. The lumps and bumps might have been hurting more because his body was almost thirty-four years old and needed longer to recover than when he was young. In their hearts Miller and Flowers probably knew they could not enforce the contract they had from the Walker fight, or at least not in the short term. They knew that even after all this time in the business they had been tricked into taking the fight, and then deprived of the title by a decision they felt was at best incompetent and at worst corrupt. Miller knew he had no alternative course but to complain as loudly as he could, to live up to his nickname of Squawk Miller, just to get one more chance.

And so it was back to the circuit, picking up paydays on the strength of the Tiger's reputation. The miles on the railways, on the road beckoned. He had some money set by, had his properties, but wasn't ready to retire and pick up another project, like the delicatessen or bakery idea. The Walker defeat would have been too fresh in the mind, too harsh a memory. And no doubt, given who he was, Flowers wondered what else God might, in his mercy and wisdom, have in store for him.

They began 1927 against old Tut Jackson in Grand Rapids, Michigan: an easy two round knockout in spite of conceding 24 lb.

Then it was on, more than 2,000 miles to Wrigley Field, Los Angeles and a much tougher job, a ten round fight with a fresh, capable twenty-three-year-old middleweight from Aberdeen on the edge of the Washington State forests named Leo Lomski on 22 January. The Deacon wasn't at his best, and Lomski not only gave him all the trouble he could handle, he got the verdict as well... which outraged the writer from the *Afro-American*, Jimmie Smith, who considered it a robbery to match that of the Walker fight. He said Flowers had won eight of the ten rounds. Lomski was also knocked down by a left hand after missing with a wild right in round three.

Smith wasn't alone in his assessment. He pointed out that Harry Grayson, the white sports editor of the *Los Angeles Record*, wrote,

> The decision to Leo Lomski over Tiger Flowers at Wrigley Field was the biggest hold-up since Three-Fingered Jack stuck up his last stage during the winter of '87. Those who accept a referee's decision as being final and were not among the 10,000 persons present, will never know how the fight came out. Flowers won that from dear old Atlanta and back again.
>
> How'd the crowd take it? How does a guy act when belabored over the head with a blackjack? The majority were stunned, speechless.

Jimmie Smith also praised another white writer who had the guts to say what he saw, a black man winning in a mixed bout. This was Paul Lowry of the *Los Angeles Times*.

> It was pretty hard to figure how big Harry Lee [the referee] figured that the ebony slapper was behind on points although there is little doubt that the victor was the superior puncher and did more damage when damage was done. But as for rounds Flowers won five, Lomski four and one even. In those which Flowers won he outhit his rival almost three to one.

Lowry, unlike Grayson, saw it as a close fight not a robbery.

The United Press report, published in the *Milwaukee Journal*, said even a whirlwind finish from Lomski over the final two rounds had not appeared anywhere near enough to earn him the verdict. The unnamed writer scored 6-2-2 in rounds to Flowers.

Unlike Smith, this writer suggested the crowd had accepted the verdict well enough but it had come as a surprise to most at ringside.'Until the seventh Flowers had Lomski completely puzzled by his awkward style and the northern Pole seldom landed a blow.'

Was it pure coincidence that immediately after this fight Lomski signed a deal with 'Broadway' Bill Duffy, who had been friends with Owney Madden since they were in Sing-Sing together? Less than a year earlier Duffy had been arrested and then released for lack of evidence on suspicion of the murder of a singer, Elsie Regan. He fronted clubs for Madden and Dutch Schulz. Lomski and his manager, Eddie Eicher, were persuaded to sign with Duffy and an associate, Pete 'The Goat' Stone, who had been around the business since the time of Stanley Ketchel.

Flowers left Los Angeles the following morning, probably feeling the boxing world was beginning to turn against him.

No matter how just or otherwise the decision in the Lomski fight, they were really up against it. Flowers had lost three of his last five fights: on that ninth round foul to Maxie Rosenbloom, and then the decisions to Walker and Lomski.

Worse, according to the Georgia writer Jimmy Jones, who knew him, it was after the Walker fight that he experienced the dizzy spells that were to develop into head pains as the year wore on.

Incredibly, Miller booked him another fight only three days after he had lost to Lomski in Los Angeles – 1,000 miles away, at altitude in Denver, Colorado, against Lee Anderson whom Jimmie Smith referred to as the Tiger's 'regular set-up'. It was only a four round workout, virtually an exhibition, but what was really to be gained beyond a few more dollars? In January alone, beginning in Atlanta, Miller had Flowers travelling almost 4,000 miles to pick up three paydays.

The Tiger managed to take a few days rest at home, a little matter of 1,700 miles away but on 18 February he was back in Boston taking on Lou Bogash. Another defeat, on the east coast, might have had far greater repercussions than did his loss to Lomski in L.A., but he pulled it together and beat the admittedly faded Italian from Connecticut over the full ten rounds.

There seems something sad about all this now, and the signs were that he was beginning to suffer. He had six weeks off after the Bogash fight, during which he was in Brunswick to see elder brother Carl's second marriage, to eighteen-year-old Viola Forrester. Carl was thirty-six. Two days later, family man Theodore turned back into the Tiger again, working at the Atlanta Auditorium and taking only seventy-one seconds to knock out a no-hoper from Louisville, Kentucky, by way of New York City, named George 'Soldier' Jones.

Almost as soon as Flowers was an ex-champion Miller had signed a managerial deal with fellow Georgian, W. L. 'Young' Stribling, who after losing a light-heavyweight title shot to Paul Berlanbach the previous June, was now hoping for a fight with new heavyweight champion Gene Tunney. Miller signed him up on 3 January 1927, exactly one month after Flowers had lost to Walker. It seems Miller persuaded the Stribling family that he possessed the clout, via Tex Rickard, to get W. L. the opportunity against Tunney. He did not. Miller believed he had persuaded the great promoter to include Stribling in an elimination contest, but Rickard had not taken him seriously. Rickard did book Stribling for the Garden, but only to box Eddie Huffman. It drew a small crowd, and was a boring, slow fight. Many of those who did attend spent their time booing and shouting for action. Miller's contract with Stribling meant he picked up an astonishing seventy-five per cent of any purse money above $5,000 that the boxer earned, but the soporific fight with Huffman was followed by some low-key, small-money bouts and then the strapping Georgian was easily out-boxed by Tommy Loughran in Brooklyn on 3 May. Miller's dreams of earning a fortune with him were already evaporating. He was picking up all expenses out of his seventy-five per cent. In a desperate attempt to turn the Stribling story in his favour, he had set up a training camp on the roof of a Newark hotel. He was working with him on a daily basis along with his old friend, brought in from Atlanta, Carl Studer. Flowers, the man who had made his name, was no longer Walk's main focus.

In April 1927, Miller received a letter from an officer in the US Army, A. P. Watts, who was stationed in Chicago. Watts defended the honour of the Illinois Commission over the way they had conducted themselves in reacting to the decision in the Flowers-Walker fight. Watts predicted that should the two men box in Chicago again, the Tiger would win, then complimented Miller on his management of his boxer.

> I am a Texan – and during the World War commanded a Negro regiment of 3,400 men, and on my return I even convinced my father, an old Confederate soldier, that the Negro, when properly handled – and I believe I did handle them properly – is all right. The same can be said of the Negro fighter, and the most striking example is the Tiger under your most able management. Both the Tiger and yourself stand forth today bigger than ever before, and on account of the unswerving fairness displayed in the raw decision here I feel sure you have made friends and a following that will pull for a fairer and just decision next time.

Watts' paternalistic view of how a man, particularly a Southern man, should handle 'a Negro' is another graphic illustration of the way things were – and offers us an insight into the probable balance in the supposed friendship between Miller and Flowers.

In spite of his concentration on Stribling, Miller continued to lobby for the rematch with Mickey Walker, announcing that he was confident the New York Commission would 'use every means' to force Walker to honour the agreement he had signed. Tex Rickard, according to Miller, was also on side and wanted the fight to happen.

April and May brought Tiger a pair of hard, ten round fights with Indiana heavyweight Chuck Wiggins, the Hoosier Playboy, who was as rough as they come. Flowers won the first on points in Buffalo, and got the better of the second in a No Decision fight in Grand Rapids.

In Boston he beat Eddie Huffman for the third time, on points over ten. Flowers had the luxury of almost a fortnight to prepare for that job, travelling straight across from Grand Rapids to work at Jim Toland's Gymnasium.

In Detroit on 17 June he beat a local ticket seller named Bob Sage, from the tough Irish section of the city, Corktown, on points over ten rounds. Sage was an unusual character, not particularly talented but durable enough to have lasted the full ten rounds in a No Decision fight with Harry Greb, when Greb was still champion, in January 1925. He had a law degree from the University of Detroit, was billed as 'The Boxing Barrister'.

By the end of June 1927, Miller was disillusioned with Stribling. The New York experiment was over and far from earning Walk a fortune, Stribling was working small towns in Kansas, Nebraska, Indiana and Oregon. In Omaha, Stribling was actually arrested and thrown in jail for participating in a fake fight against Leo Diebel. Walk's big money gamble had cost him dearly. He switched his attention back to Flowers and, probably with a degree of bitterness, left his contract with Stribling to expire.

Miller booked the Tiger for a rematch with the light-heavyweight Maxie Rosenbloom, who had beaten him on a foul nine months earlier. At Comiskey Park, Chicago, on 4 July 1927, the Independence Day crowd saw a tight, hard fight at the end of which both men's gloves were raised in the signal of a draw. It wasn't the result Walk wanted but at least it was a major fight and he earned a cut of some decent money.

Before the month was out, Flowers had breezed through ten one-sided rounds against Bing Conley at an amusement park in Norwalk, Connecticut. Conley, from Lewiston, Maine, had hoped to mount a challenge to light-heavyweight champion Jack Delaney. The local paper called him one of the gamest boxers ever to come out of his home town who had 'outfought every man in Maine'. Not enough, unfortunately. In a 1961 reminiscence piece Conley said he said something he should not have to Flowers before the first bell, and paid for it.

> It made him sore, even if he was a deacon in the church... so after five rounds [referee] Dave [Sloman] was going to stop it but I talked him out of it, and then I said to Flowers in a clinch 'I never thought a deacon would want to kill a man...'

Conley claimed he took advantage of Tiger suddenly relaxing to land a left hook to the belly and right that dropped him, but then again paid for it. 'I already had a black eye [from a recent fight with Paul Berlanbach], he closed the other eye and chopped up my mouth.'

Then August began with another ten round draw with the wild, rumbustious Chuck Wiggins. They really were getting to know each other too well – and fighting Wiggins was always a bruising night's work.

Miller booked Flowers two fights out in the northwest. In Portland, Oregon, at the local Ice Coliseum, Flowers drew a crowd of 6,500 for a ten round win over Harry Dillon, a twenty-three-year-old Canadian from Winnipeg, whose real name was Joseph Darbell. It was a record gate for a boxing match in Portland; more than $13,000. Five days later, the Tiger was earning again in Seattle, at Dugdale Park, for a six-round near-exhibition against Jock Malone, a low-key event that contrasted with their wars of just a short time ago. Malone had been in good form, but couldn't handle the Tiger. He was cut in round four and did not win a round.

If he was to stay in the picture as a world championship contender, it was important to remind New York fans, and the commission, that he still existed, and that was possibly in Miller's mind when he booked him to box Joe Anderson at the Garden on 1 September 1927. It was not a major fight, but still drew 8,856 paying customers with gate receipts of $16,248. Flowers beat Anderson clearly. The *Milwaukee Sentinel* agency report recorded, 'Although fighting back gamely all the way, Anderson could not cope with the busily bouncing, weaving Tiger. Experience scored over youth.'

The report said Flowers dropped to his knees in round four when one of Anderson's swings caught him off balance – this was not considered a proper knockdown – and in the tenth Anderson went down for an instant when he lunged, missed and fell over.

> In the final round the dusky Deacon waded in for a knockout and had the youngster in obvious distress. Hitting blindly and always staggering forward, the Kentucky boy warded off the kayo… Anderson took plenty of punishment and showed it. Banging away with the left, Flowers opened cuts above and below his opponent's eye, which half-blinded him in the last frame.

Shortly afterwards Anderson was critically injured when after a car crash the driver of the other vehicle stabbed him in the chest. Fortunately, Anderson recovered and was back boxing by the end of the year. No doubt he had medical bills to pay.

According to Edney, Flowers was suffering persistent headaches, more prolonged spells of dizziness and discomfort from the growths on his forehead just above his eyebrows that seemed to be lumps of gristly scar tissue. Neither manager nor fighter was too keen on the idea of surgery after the death of Harry Greb the previous year. During roadwork before his next fight, against former world welterweight champion Pete Latzo in Wilkes-Barre, Pennsylvania, in the foothills of the Pocono Mountains, on 30 September, Flowers' headaches became severe. He tried to ignore them, but they did not stop.

One New York surgeon Miller consulted was Wilford Fralick, who was known as a boxing doctor in Manhattan. Fralick had earned a reputation as an expert with fighters' hands in particular – but there was nothing wrong with the Tiger's hands, or at least no more than might be expected when his occupation was punching other men for a living. Fralick diagnosed a sinus problem and said he would keep an eye on it. Doctors in Atlanta were also consulted. It seems the possibility that his long career might be catching up with him, might be affecting his brain, did not occur to anyone but that isn't too surprising. In those days people barely acknowledged the risk of getting punched in the head, hard and pretty often. Brain damage, while admitted in some severe cases, was not considered a serious possibility for most fighters.

The general advice was that surgery to remove the growths on his face would be helpful but that it would be minor and anaesthetic would not be needed, or at least not in any great strength. Miller booked him in with Dr Fralick, and they agreed on six weeks' time, probably once the Tiger's bookings were cleared. Flowers trusted Miller and so, on Miller's recommendation, Fralick. Jimmy Jones quoted him as saying, 'It is the Lord's will and if you agree with Him, it shall be done.'

A fight with Pete Latzo had first been proposed in the summer of 1927. Latzo had won the welterweight title in an almighty upset against Mickey Walker in Scranton in May 1926 but had lost it on a majority fifteen-round decision to Joe Dundee at the New York Polo Grounds in June 1927 and had immediately moved up to middleweight. About a week later it was said a fight with Flowers was virtually sealed, but it had not worked out – Latzo instead settled into the middleweight division with three fights in August and September, before the deal with Flowers was finally made.

Latzo, who was later used by cartoonist Ham Fisher for his character, Joe Palooka, lost clearly to the Tiger on points over ten rounds in Wilkes-Barre on 30 September. The United Press report, published in the Pittsburgh Press, said Flowers won eight of the ten rounds.

> From the first bell to the last Flowers was the aggressor and with short choppy punches never permitted Latzo to get set for a damaging punch. In the majority of the ten rounds Latzo was given considerable punishment, although in the second and fifth frames he managed to reach Flowers with several hard rights. He had his opponent slightly groggy in the fifth but Flowers came back and cut down Latzo's lead (in the round).

Flowers stayed on to work the corner of his old friend from Miller's gym in Atlanta, Bob Lawson, in his fight at the Motor Square Garden, Pittsburgh, against Yale Okun, on 3 October. He returned to Atlanta and then after a couple of days headed back on the road to his New York base. He was driving north on Highway 81 when he was involved in a tragic accident in the town of Harrisonburg, Virginia, in the Shenandoah Valley. Associated Press reported on 6 October:

> Tiger Flowers, Atlanta Negro and former middleweight boxing champion, was arrested here late today on a charge of running over Jack Logan, four-year-old son of John Logan of Harrisonburg. The boy's legs were crushed and when taken to a hospital he was spitting up blood, indicating internal injuries of a possible serious nature.

Flowers, accompanied by two Negro women, was *en route* from Atlanta to New York when the accident occurred. He was following another car and claims that the boy ran out from behind a parked automobile and that he did not see him until the car was upon him. Flowers' bail was fixed at $5,000 and late this afternoon he was trying to get in touch with his manager, Miller. Flowers retained former Mayor, John W. Morrison, as his attorney.

Bail was lodged and he completed his journey, no doubt mortified and awaiting the outcome of both the boy's injuries and the criminal proceedings. We have no way of knowing who the two women were, whether they were family members or not. Little Jack Logan survived the accident. According to a report shortly after Flowers' death, published in the *Pittsburgh Courier*, the car was eventually put in a garage in Atlanta to be repaired and Miller said it was to be used as a $3,000 bond in a civil suit brought, presumably by the Logan family, over the accident.

In Canton, Ohio, on 17 October Flowers dominated old victim Joe Lohman over ten in a No Decision workout.

The following day Miller travelled to the annual convention of the National Boxing Association to press his case for the rematch with Walker. The NBA had been formed to oversee boxing and had under its wing the interests of twenty-four US states. It did not have influence in Pennsylvania, New York, Massachusetts or California, the four most powerful boxing administrations in the country, but at least it was trying to bring some cohesion to the sport.

Miller produced his evidence that Jack Kearns had agreed, in the event of a Walker victory, to a return within ninety days.

The *Ottawa Citizen* reported that the NBA had given Walker a further sixty days, taking them to 17 December, to defend against Flowers.

If at the end of the sixty-day period Walker has not met Flowers the board's governors will decide whether or not Mickey shall be stripped of his title and barred in the twenty-four states and allied bodies of the association.

In the circumstances it was not advisable to have fought Maxie Rosenbloom again but they clearly felt the impending surgery was just a minor formality and that the headaches were easily explained by the sinus difficulties. Or perhaps, after the loss of the middleweight title and his disastrous financial adventure with Stribling, Miller just didn't care. Flowers battled out another ten round draw with Slapsie Maxie, who at twenty-three was still improving, at the Olympia Arena in Detroit on 9 November. The *Chicago Defender* claimed, with its usual loyalty to Flowers, that he was 'handed another bad deal'. Perhaps he was, as the Defender writer reported, 'The house hissed and booed until the third man was out of sight after the fight.'

Miller, while pushing for the Walker return, was also lobbying for a crack at the new light-heavyweight champion, Tommy Loughran, who had in October beaten Mike McTigue for the vacant title. Loughran turned down the idea on the basis that when he began to box he had promised his father he would never box a black opponent. He told his manager, Joe Smith, to send a message to Flowers that if they boxed it would be in a gym with newspapermen present and a fight to a finish, outside the jurisdiction of the commission and therefore not for the title. It was bluster and drew an immediate response from Miller, who issued a press statement that read,

Neither Flowers nor myself have ever endeavored to force any white boxer to meet a colored one if the white boxer objected. However, since Loughran saw fit to raise the issue, I will state that the Deacon, by his clean sportsmanship, his record of pugilistic achievements and his gentlemanly conduct in everyday life certainly made himself worthy of as much consideration as any of the leading challengers.

The following day, 12 November 1927, Flowers was at the Olympic Club in Harlem, on West 135th Street near Madison Avenue, for a fourth round victory over a 6 foot 2 inch, 200 lb heavyweight, Leo Gates, from North Adams, Massachusetts. Gates was reportedly a Mohawk who fought under different aliases, and whose birth name was Arthur Barrier. That was the Tiger's nineteenth contest of the year and, as he so often did, he made light of conceding weight – and of taking what punches he had to take from a heavier man. This time he conceded 28½ lb.

Flowers' operation was scheduled for the 16th, and Miller's complacency about his boxer's health was indicated by the fact that he booked him to box again on 22 November on a charity show at the Olympic Club in Harlem. Flowers must have been suffering quite significantly, or was wary of the effects of undergoing surgery, because he decided he could not honour the date, and so lodged a cheque – for $100 or $160, depending on the source – with the New York deputy commissioner, Daniel H. Skilling, as a gift to the charity involved, the Colored Children's Fresh Air Fund.

He did not tell Willie Mae that he was going under the knife. Maybe he just did not want to worry her over what was supposed to be minor surgery. Or maybe he wanted to surprise her with his tidied-up face when he returned to Atlanta in time for Christmas. There is no indication that the fact that she had not been informed was evidence of their slipping apart, or that he had a separate life, which is what Walk Miller would be shortly attempting to insinuate was the case.

CHAPTER 16

'If I Should Die Before I Wake'

In the 1920s Wilford G. Fralick specialised in treating broken, chipped or dislocated bones and so was of particular interest to boxers. He had premises in a ten-storey house at 778 Madison Avenue, between East 66th and 67th Streets, one block back from Central Park on the Upper East Side, a very respectable address. When he operated on Tiger Flowers it was at a 'sanitorium' or 'clinic' at his home at 42 West 70th Street. The previous year he had been well heeled enough to take a holiday in Cuba. Referred to by Nat Fleischer and his *Ring* magazine writers as a 'master mender' and 'bone-setter extraordinaire', Fralick worked on the hands of at least five men who held the heavyweight championship; Jack Dempsey, Gene Tunney, Jack Sharkey, Max Schmeling and James J. Braddock.

Yet as impressive as that all sounds, closer examination reveals he was not all that he seemed. There were hints in his dealings with boxers. There was an unlikely claim that he removed a five-inch slither of bone from the right thumb of light-heavyweight champion Mike McTigue; he was said to have constructed an entirely new knuckle for another 175 lbs champ, Jack Delaney, although Delaney's brother said when the doctor, whose name he remembered as Froehlich, treated Jack for a broken right arm in a 'dingy little office', they exchanged swigs of bourbon throughout the four-hour process. 'Jack's arm never completely recovered after that and he had to use it more for protection than anything else,' said the brother. Fralick also put a plaster cast on the shoulder of Benny Bass after the little Ukrainian immigrant had broken his collar bone in a fifteen round fight with Tony Canzoneri for the world featherweight title in 1928. The usual treatment for a broken collarbone is to rest and support the shoulder in a sling. James J. Braddock, later immortalised in the movie *Cinderella Man*, went to see Fralick long before he won the world heavyweight title with that incredible upset of Max Baer in 1935. In the twenties Braddock was a light-heavyweight contender with a right hand so fragile that it broke in more or less every fight. Fralick wanted to charge him $1,400 for breaking and resetting or rebuilding the hand. That is around $18,000 today. Braddock's connected manager, Joe Gould declined to pay. Instead he explained they would come back for a better deal after Braddock's next fight when the hand would almost certainly have broken again. That way, they could save on the breaking part of Fralick's surgery. To Gould's apparent astonishment Fralick, perhaps recognising an opportunist when he saw one, or perhaps aware of the men Gould routinely mixed with, and perhaps worked for, agreed.

So, who was this man, this 'master mender' who had an address on the Upper East Side, but who had a penchant for swilling bourbon while he, at one point at least, worked in a tiny room almost certainly not fit for purpose?

According to his obituary in a medical journal after he had died of cancer in 1931, he qualified at the Royal College of Physicians and Surgeons in Kingston, Ontario, in 1887.

Possibly, but possibly not. According to one US census he arrived in New York in 1890 but in another it was 1883. And according to the family tree published on www.ancestry.co.uk, he was born in Prince Edward County, Ontario, Canada, in 1859, not 1863, as he claimed when he was in the United States. His real name was not Wilford or Wilfred but Charles. And in the 1881 Canadian census, the twenty-two-year-old Charles was living in his parents' home in Kingston – and working as a clerk. His father was a hotel keeper.

With or without any medical qualifications, Charles moved to New York, and was followed by his younger brother, Ralph Simcoe Fralick, who was only sixteen when he arrived in 1892. Ralph told the authorities he was nineteen, presumably to avoid being sent home as under age.

Even Charles Fralick's wife seems to have possessed more than her share of mystery. In the 1900 census she is listed only by her initials, E. M. It was said that she and Charles, by then known as Wilford, had married in 1894. She had been born in New York of English parents. Yet by 1910, the census stated that Wilford's wife of fifteen years was named Florence and had been born in Kentucky. The marriage date suggests they were the same person. If so, why had Mrs Fralick's biographical details changed? And if not, why the deception concerning the marriage date? One answer would be that they were different women and he married one but not the other, or neither, but the information serves to cloud rather than clarify his personal circumstances.

Charles, who became Wilford, and Ralph shared rooms in New York City and set up as doctors. It is possible that neither brother had any qualification beyond what they read and the experience they picked up along the way.

In 1901 Wilford, which is inevitably sometimes written as Wilfred, hit the headlines when he gave a public demonstration of treating two patients with a fluid, similar to blood, that he believed would cure consumption. He had, he said, been working on the project for eight years. He claimed his liquid medicine had also cured two cancer patients and contained compounds that destroyed all known germs. The incident has the hallmarks of one of the

Miracle Cure scams of the snake-oil salesmen who operated out of the backs of wagons in pioneer times. Whatever the merits or otherwise of Fralick's fluid, it did not catch on.

He also made the *New York Times* a little later when it was reported that he had removed the stomach of a cancer patient in a pioneering operation, at which his brother had acted as one of the co-surgeons. From inventing a liquid cure for consumption to surgically removing the stomach of a dying cancer patient is a rather large career jump. It seemed Dr Fralick, perhaps the self-styled 'Dr' Fralick, did nothing by halves.

It is easy for doctors to be believed because, primarily, patients want to be cured and so invest their trust in the doctor's ability to do that. It is possible that Fralick did accumulate experience and mend some broken bones along the way. Obviously, he had a measure of success. It is also possible that sometimes his treatment did very little to aid the healing process. The important thing is that his clients believed he was helping them – and he appears to have been a man of boundless confidence and front.

But given the above evidence, would we consider Fralick a qualified man to be using such a new-fangled procedure as a general anaesthetic? I suggest not but it seems to be entirely within his characteristics to do so.

No doubt Fralick was recommended to Miller as the best man to treat the bunches of hardened cartilage around the Tiger's eyes. However, for three months, according to one newspaper report, he 'watched the condition carefully'. That translates as 'he did nothing'. After that time he decided on an operation. Yet on the one hand we have Fralick suggesting that any surgery would be minor to the point of needing virtually no anaesthetic, and on the other we have him saying Flowers would go under a general anaesthetic and was expected to remain in the doctor's (not cheap) care in hospital for a month after the surgery.

And so, on the afternoon of 16 November 1927, Theodore Flowers, the former middleweight champion of the world, prepared himself for surgery at Fralick's clinic. We have details of what happened on the day from Miller, whose inclination may not have been to tell the truth, the whole truth and nothing but the truth. The Associated Press account has sensationalist, sentimental elements to it that might have a remote possibility of being true, but which might also have been fictionalised by Miller. He did say, however, that Flowers was calm as he waited for surgery in the gown he wore into the ring, the one with the large tiger motif on the back. Miller said it was as if he were going into the ring for an easy fight and they expected no trouble. Fralick, he said, expressed the view that Flowers was in splendid physical condition. That's true. Apart from the lumps around his eyes, the dizziness, and the headaches...

Miller was clear about one thing, that Flowers was so taciturn and apparently lost in thought that day that he spoke only three times before entering the operating room. When Miller spoke to him, he responded with 'yes, sir', and again with, 'sure is'. Then immediately before he walked in for surgery at around 3 p.m. Miller asked him if he had anything he wanted to talk over. The fighter replied, 'No, sir.'

It was written, and perhaps it happened, that as the anaesthetic was administered, with his dog-eared Bible in his hand, Theodore recited the old children's prayer, 'If I should die before I wake, I pray thee, Lord, my soul to take.'

Fralick operated to remove the lump on the right side of Flowers' forehead, visible in photographs taken of him in the previous year or so, and also tidied up other scar tissue, as well as the beginning of a 'cauliflower ear'.

As the process began Miller returned to his office on 42nd Street to wait for news. It seems Fralick did not bother to, or manage to, contact Miller again before the man he had managed through seven years from obscurity on small shows in Georgia through to the middleweight championship of the world died at 8.30 p.m.

Fralick said Flowers began to wake after the operation but did not do so fully. In spite of this he seemed strong and appeared to be recovering well, but then his heart suddenly gave out and he died. Death, apparently, came so suddenly that Fralick, who was in an adjoining room, was unable to reach the bedside after he had been called for by an unnamed second physician, nurse or attendant. Who was this other member of the medical team? Why was he, or she, there? Could it have been Fralick's brother, Ralph? Was it simply a nurse employed to keep a check on the patient? Or a third with another agenda, other employers? Is it right, or wrong, to harbour any sinister thoughts whatsoever about the possibilities? As always the boundaries between corruption, incompetence and unavoidable coincidence are blurred. What are we suggesting, that Flowers was the victim of a hit? Isn't that the stuff of old gangster movies? Well, yes it is and it is likely that by suspecting Fralick of being under the influence of outside forces is adding two and two and making seven.

Except that on the day of the operation unknown to Flowers the New York Commission had ordered that Mickey Walker would have to honour his contract and defend against Flowers in New York. While there is no suggestion that Jack Kearns was a criminal, he certainly mixed with the mobsters and racketeers. He drank in their clubs, was on first name terms, and he, and by now, quite possibly they, had the middleweight championship of the world. Years later Kearns was implicated when he managed Joey Maxim, the light-heavyweight champion, in the famous fight when Ray Robinson retired in his corner suffering from heat exhaustion when a mile ahead on points. On the face of it, a fix seems an absurd suggestion – Robinson was disorientated, almost delirious, and utterly spent. However, *New York Journal* American writer Bill Corum wrote a few years later, 'Ray Robinson, the greatest fighter that I've seen in thirty-five years of watching fights, took a dive against Joey Maxim. Maybe his friends will tell him to sue me, but he won't.'

And if the boys who ran New York were involved with Mickey Walker, who was Tiger Flowers to them anyway? Just a black man from the Deep South whose day had come and gone, and who was out of the picture or should have been. Removing him, if that was ever of interest to them, would have the added benefit of getting rid of the irritant who didn't know how to play the game, Squawk Miller. Or had Miller been making a nuisance of himself in other ways – and was Flowers the victim of the old gangster trick of warning Miller to behave by taking out a person close to him? There is a pattern of thought there if we should choose to follow it through. Do we? For eighty-five years Flowers' death has been accepted as a tragic accident as a result of the general medical naïvety surrounding the use of anaesthetic. Fralick's questionable credentials certainly offer the probability of extreme negligence. Is this the likeliest conclusion? Or were Flowers and Miller really worth the time of the bad boys for some other, undiscovered reason? We cannot know.

We should not be naïve about the influence of the underworld bosses, whose tentacles spread further and further from the 1920s through to Lucky Luciano's alleged influence on the progress of the Second World War, beginning with the sinking of the ship, SS *Normandie*, in the New York docks in 1942. Officially that was an accident caused by sparks from a welding torch during the conversion of the *Normandie* into a warship, to be named USS *Lafayette*. Unofficially, it was arson committed by mobsters led by Albert Anastasia on the orders of the incarcerated Luciano, after which a deal was struck by the government which brought the Mafia onside and led to, among other things, the relatively trouble-free American invasion of Sicily. They really did rule more than New York's dark side.

Miller apparently telephoned Fralick when he realised things had dragged on too long without any word, and was told to rush over immediately. He arrived to find Flowers was dead.

According to Jimmy Jones, writing many years later, he said, in broken sobs, to newspapermen, 'They have killed my champion.'

Who are 'they'? Who did he mean?

If that outpouring of emotion did happen it suggests that Miller, for all his weaknesses, had a notion that something suspicious had happened. But then he had 'squawked' loud and long without foundation about loaded gloves when Tiger had lost to Delaney. And he had no evidence.

When the reactions poured in, Mickey Walker also said something that does not quite sit right. He sent his condolences to Willie Mae and Verna Lee, though he was unsure how many children Tiger had at home in Atlanta.

May God have mercy on his soul. It doesn't seem possible that Tiger is dead. He was the cleanest fighter I ever met.

It is too bad that some of us were not there with him when his toughest fight came along.

Did Walker know, or suspect, more than we know now? Certainly he would have known when to keep his mouth shut about what he saw or knew but just on this one occasion, in his sorrow for the demise of an honest brother fighter, did his guard slip? Nobody, as far as I can see, followed that up and offered him the chance to say more but the likelihood is that, if lapse this was on Walker's part, he would not have been stupid enough to expand on it.

Fralick announced the cause of death as 'lymphaticus', which is an inflammation of the lymph tissue, particularly the thymus, and where death had occurred it had either been in children – or in those who had undergone anaesthetic treatment. However, more recent medical evaluation does not accept lymphaticus as a genuine condition. In 1954, in the *British Medical Journal*, H. B. Dodwell referred to it as a myth. Nobody seemed to have questioned Fralick in any depth. It was simply assumed that he knew what he was doing.

Jimmy Jones, however, said when recalling the story in *Ring* in 1975 that Miller claimed to have had an autopsy performed on Flowers' body. Given the speed of subsequent events that does not appear to have been the case. Maybe he asked for one but was refused or ignored. Strangely, Miller appeared before the New York State Commission with what he said was evidence that not only had the Tiger been given too much ether but had also been operated on after he was dead. That has never been explained. If it were the case, why would anyone have done that? We just don't know.

Jones added that Miller was a lone wolf with plenty of enemies – and also said the *New York Daily Mirror* did try to unravel some deeper background to the story but got nowhere.

Inevitably, perhaps, the frustrated writers of the *Afro-American* continued to rake up the story of the deaths of Flowers and another great Harlem entertainer, the singer Florence Mills, and claimed that if they had been treated by black physicians they would have survived. In an article published on 21 February 1931 the reasoning ran that if Flowers and Mills had been under the care of an African-American, the doctor would have known the impact of their deaths would have on the community – and on their own careers – and therefore they would have been meticulous in their attentions. In other words, the newspaper believed these were examples of white negligence in dealing with black people.

The body of the first African-American middleweight champion of the world was taken from Fralick's clinic on West 70th to the H. Adolph Howell Funeral Parlor at 2332 Seventh Avenue in Harlem. It was the same chapel of rest where earlier in the month the body of Mills had been laid, ready for burial. Mills, weakened by tuberculosis, had not survived surgery for the removal of her appendix. She was thirty-two.

The house in which Flowers recovered following his first win over Harry Greb was only three blocks away. Just around the corner, was the Zion African Methodist Episcopal Church where, it was said, Flowers had sometimes worshipped. It was the oldest black church in New York, which had given shelter to escaped slaves and had built a reputation for improving the secular education as well as the spiritual welfare of African-American people. Certainly, he had worshipped at the First Methodist Church, which was perhaps more closely linked to his religious philosophy, three blocks west along 140th Street.

His body was placed in a silver casket for the people of Harlem to come to the funeral parlor and pay their respects between 4 p.m. and 7 p.m. on the day after death. However, Walk Miller told Willie Mae Flowers, who had not even known her husband was undergoing surgery, not to come, that the body would be brought to her in Atlanta. She accepted his advice.

The *Chicago Defender* reported that thousands stood in the November rain waiting to pay their respects. Some of the Harlem people did not have time to go before the parlor was closed and the body sent on the 750-mile journey south to Georgia. They complained, but were appeased by the assurance that it was the wish of Tiger's widow that he 'go home' as soon as possible.

> Many accompanied the body last night to the railroad station, where the silver casket was placed in the baggage car of the 8.40 train and sent away to his home in Atlanta. Walker Miller, who discovered and managed Flowers through his entire career, accompanied his old friend on the last sad journey.

The train pulled into Atlanta railway station at 5.30 p.m. on Friday, 18 November 1927. The coffin was taken to his home in the mansion at 1010 Simpson Road, and was left open to allow local people to pay their respects over a twelve-hour period on the following Sunday, from 9 a.m. to 9 p.m., before the funeral service and burial on the Monday. They filed past in their thousands, the lines stretching out through the grounds of the house.

'Flowers' death has stilled Atlanta,' said the reporter for the *Chicago Defender*.

CHAPTER 17

No Ordinary Fighter, No Ordinary Man

News of the death of Tiger Flowers drew tribute after tribute from the boxing world. Floral bouquets by the dozen and around five hundred telegrams were delivered to the shattered Willie Mae in Atlanta.

Jack Kearns, manager of Mickey Walker, was stunned and, it appeared, genuinely sorrowful.

> I was talking to him only a few days ago. At that time he was complaining of pains in his head, and I told him not to worry about it. He was a great fighter, and a fine, loveable fellow.

Tex Rickard, who had promoted the Tiger's greatest fights and who would himself die before the decade was out, said, 'He was of the old fighting school. He never argued about opponents and he was always willing to fight.' Gene Tunney, the classy, under-valued heavyweight champion of the world, said,

> I am proud to have called Tiger Flowers my friend. As a man he showed to the world that he could carry and keep his religion in the pursuit of the profession of boxing. He was deeply religious but he did not parade it... He was an inspiration not only to the youth of his race but to all boys and young men – to live cleanly, speak softly, trust in God and fight hard and fair.
>
> Tiger Flowers was a credit to his calling, his race and his country. The Negro race have lost a bright and shining standard bearer, the boxing game a real champion, and we of boxing have lost a friend.

The always astute Paul Gallico wrote in the *New York Daily News*,

> What I liked about the Tiger was that when he signed a contract to fight, he fought. He never loafed, never tin canned, never stalled, never clinched, never stopped punching, never, from bell to bell, stopped trying to give back in thrill and entertainment full value for what he received in pay. How many of us are that honest?

Ed Sullivan, in the *New York Evening Gazette*, said Broadway was terribly shocked by the Tiger's sudden passing, that it was only the previous Saturday night that fans had watched him knock out Leo Gates at the Commonwealth Sporting Club.

> Tiger Flowers was one of the nicest fellows I have ever met. You will find that to be a general opinion… Every memory of the Tiger is a pleasant one. Every regret is a sincere regret that he has passed on. None of us can expect anything more than that when we 'cash in our checks'.

Sullivan wondered whether Flowers had developed, through his Bible, a philosophy that had allowed him a benign tolerance of the foibles of the white man. It was interesting that Sullivan chose to consider it as a possibility, though his interpretation was limited to Flowers' Christianity and not the influence of black rights pioneers like Booker Washington. Most writers, or anyone else responding to the news, were content to trot out the pointless, insulting cliché that he had a white heart, or was pure white inside. Jack Kearns did that, so did Gene Tunney, Jock Malone, Nat Fleischer and others.

His old conqueror Jack Delaney apparently struggled to find words when the news was telephoned to him. Eventually he said,

> I always liked Tiger Flowers. Win or lose, he was always a sportsman. He came to my dressing room after one of our fights and told me he wished me good luck, even though he had lost. It is too bad.

Pete Reilly, Delaney's manager, said,

> What a pity that is. I have never met a more generous, likeable fighter. My heartfelt sympathy goes to his relatives in their loss. Boxing can well mourn him, for he was a credit to the game, and his race.

Pete Latzo, the former welterweight champion who had fought the Tiger in his home town of Wilkes-Barre, Pennsylvania, only six weeks before, said, 'He was my friend and I am sincerely grieved at his passing. They don't come any finer than the Deacon.'

Mike McTigue wanted fighters to get together in some form of tangible support in order to honour him. He did not express anything more specific, just said, 'Words are useless.'

Jock Malone, who fought him four times, most recently only three months before, said, 'He was a first class fighting man and a gentleman. Oh, I used to try many a trick on him, but he'd always come back with a grin, and that paint-brush right of his and give me liberal interest.'

At the next show in Madison Square Garden, ring announcer Joe Humphreys paid him tribute before a hushed crowd. 'He was a credit to the game and he was a credit not only to his race but to any race. He was a good champion, more than a good champion. He was a good man.' The *Miami News* editorial was genuine and thought out.

> In Atlanta, where he amounts to a subject for worship among his race, he is an active member of the church, more than ordinarily religious, and has given freely from his comparative wealth to charities – white and Negro. Never ostentatious, Flowers added many substantial friends by his modesty and retirement. His most pretentious possessions were fine automobiles, of which he was enthusiastically proud – one for himself, and one for his family – and a palatial home which he built in a modest section of the city's outskirts. Businessmen who knew him say he was wise in his investments and will leave a comfortable estate.

The obituary in the *Brunswick Pilot* described him as a steady and ambitious man, and predicted wholesale mourning among both black and white communities, adding that his father was highly respected.

Back in Atlanta, the *Constitution* stuck to the 'whitest colored man in the ring' line... '... the followers of ring affairs and those connected with it will miss 'Tiger' Flowers because he was a square shooter and was loved by the white man and colored man alike.' The writer also said he gave 'a large part' of the good-sized fortune he made during his career to colored churches in Atlanta and further afield in Georgia.

A 'poet' in Atlanta named Thomas Jefferson Flanagan wrote an excruciating tribute in rhyme that would, in other circumstances, have been a piece of comic genius. It began:

> All plumed for battle-royal, with
> Heart as white as winter snow,
> The gallant knight, firm in his faith
> Went forth to meet his foe.

A far more talented artist, the singer, Porter Grainger, recorded a spiritual tribute entitled 'He's Gone Home', which was released by Columbia Records. Grainger was a jazz pianist and vocalist who earlier in the year had recorded the enduring "Tain't Nobody's Business If I Do' and the slightly less classic 'Dying Crapshooter's Blues'.

British sports writer Trevor Wignall called Flowers 'the best-liked Negro fighter since the time of Peter Jackson', while Nat Fleischer, who edited the *Ring* from an office in the Garden provided by Rickard, would later reflect,

Deacon Tiger Flowers was no ordinary fighter. He was no ordinary man.'
As a man he showed to the world that he could carry and keep his religion
in the pursuit of the profession of professional boxing.

Thomas T. Taylor, the former pastor at Butler Street, wrote a letter of tribute
in March 1928.

> To my way of thinking he was one of the finest young men of our day.
> Loveable in disposition, sweet spirited and clean in life... I soon became
> personally interested in him and did advise him how to retain his sweetness
> of life. I advised him to be honest, prayerful and never to neglect reading
> his Bible.
>
> I believe in quality first and then position. Tiger qualified morally and
> religiously for every place of honor that came to him... A splendid life was
> cut short, a race's monument of thrift and sobriety was removed in the
> passing of our brother, Theodore (Tiger) Flowers.

Perhaps the most touching tribute also came through Henry Grady Edney.
The more I read his book, the more I seemed to be listening to the voice, not
of Edney, but of Willie Mae Flowers in the months after her husband's death,
badly wanting to tell the world of the man she had lost, whom those who
knew him through boxing, or who considered themselves his friend, knew
only superficially. Edney's book has been dismissed as unreliable in some
quarters. I understand that. However, I would contend that it is of value
simply because of the fact that it was written with Willie Mae's blessing and
input. Edney wrote,

> While his race suffers much by his departure, his sweet, hospitable home
> misses his genial smile which illumined it.
>
> There is great consolation for all concerned in the fact that he had utmost
> faith in the great God who created him, and loved him with his 'whole soul,
> mind and strength' – and was able to pass through the valley of the shadow
> of death without fear.

As Ed Sullivan wrote, none of us can hope for more than that when our time
comes.

CHAPTER 18

The End For Squawk, a New Start For Willie Mae

And then, as detailed at the beginning of this story, after the emotion and heartbreak of Tiger Flowers' death, funeral service and burial, with unseemly haste Walk Miller produced the will that purported to give him power over the boxer's estate. Willie Mae Flowers defended herself and her lawyers managed to foil him, and perhaps the incident revealed more about the nature of the relationship between her husband and his manager – and about Miller's character. He considered he was not merely Flowers' professional guide but the owner and director of his personal fortune, and that whatever money the Tiger had earned was, in some way, only loaned him by Miller. In one way it was the master and slave relationship personified, yet in another it was a product, not of the black/white divide but of lord and serf – I have heard a modern-day manager joke more than once that a boxer 'takes seventy-five per cent of my money'.

However, Miller's attempts to blacken the name of the man who had risen from poverty to the middleweight championship of the world in order to get his hands on his assets failed. He was removed as trustee of Verna Lee's investment fund. He was not empowered to decide the future of the estate, although what happened to the New York will he purported to have discovered remains unknown, as does the contents of the safe box to which he referred in the days after the funeral. Miller's behaviour, especially given its timing, and the reports of his unfeeling harassment of Willie Mae, appear to have made him leave Atlanta and return to New York. He had no friends there either. He could no longer afford his office on 42nd Street. Willie Mae and Verna Lee remained, for the time being, in their home.

When the Edney biography was written Willie Mae was obviously extremely proud of her home, as it is described in great detail. Edney is, as usual effusive in his flattery but his account is illuminating.

Situated on a high hill, the acreage comprising some ten city lots, and with a wonderful view, it is indeed beautiful. The structure is of the old English design, with broad tile verandas. There are fourteen rooms, elegantly furnished, many of the hangings and decorations being imported.

Edney considered the paintings on the walls of the rooms to be masterpieces and noted the presence of state of the art radios and Victrola phonographs as well as a piano and violins. He went on,

> He loved music. His very soul feasted on it, and he spent much time when at home playing favorite selections on the violin, while Mrs Flowers accompanied him on the piano.

Again, it's impossible to ignore Willie Mae's own voice here, for the praise is close to anguished loss. Verna Lee, we learn, had her own playroom for entertaining friends. Theodore planted many of the shrubs and trees in the garden himself. 'He shared a great deal of joy in their contemplation with Mrs Flowers. Nothing was spared in the construction of his home. It was his castle - and the castle of his family, for whom he worked.'

Which makes it, in my view at least, highly unlikely that he would have entrusted it, in the event of his sudden passing, to the care of someone outside of his family – even though he had been naïve enough to consider Miller to be a genuine friend and, according to Jimmy Jones, at times seemed to display an almost childlike trust in him. The truth of that impression may well have been that Flowers knew how he was expected to behave in public, with Miller as with any other white man, but that did not extend to allowing his manager to take away all that he had worked for and built.

No longer able to stay in New York, Miller managed a few triers, using Madam Bey's facilities in Eddyville, near Kingston, about ninety miles up the Hudson River on the offshoot called the Wallkill, towards the Catskills and Albany. It was the middle of nowhere but at least in Madam Bey's, top class boxing people sometimes drifted in and out, drawn to its peace and quiet when they needed to train away from prying eyes. They brought with them the sniff of success, the reminder of the big time and the promise of the big break. Max Schmeling, still two years away from becoming heavyweight champion, was just one top class fighter who trained there. Most days, though, it was populated by ham-and-egg triers – the kind Miller was reduced to handling, men like Billy Grime, who had travelled from Australia in search of a fortune only to discover he was no more than a preliminary fighter in New York. Grime, and the scufflers like him, earned peanuts. Miller's cut amounted to pocket change. His scheme to get his hands on Flowers' fortune had been foiled. What he had been such a short time ago meant nothing now – or maybe it did. Maybe he owed someone and couldn't pay. Maybe he knew something it would have been better not to know. Or perhaps it was something more trivial or even spontaneous that led to his being found dead across a bed in his room at the gymnasium with a bullet in his heart and two in his head, a pistol positioned in the crook of his left elbow, on 17 September 1928.

At first the police thought they had wrapped it up as a suicide resulting from his money worries. Doctors spoiled that convenient theory by declaring that either of the bullets in his head would have killed him instantly, and given that there was only one gun, it was, in the circumstances, impossible to shoot himself in the head twice, without taking into account the bullet in his heart. Even the police had to admit suicide was therefore a less than likely scenario. A full investigation was ordered but produced nothing. Walk Miller, born Walker Valentine Miller and sometimes called Squawk, just didn't matter anymore.

The first United Press International reports out of New York accepted the first police verdict of suicide and declared his action was 'because of despondency over financial affairs'.

In the Atlanta white press, he was given a reasonable send-off, his attempts at purloining the Flowers estate conveniently put aside. 'The death of Walk Miller, manager of prize fighters, removes from the sports world one of the foremost figures of the squared circles that the South has known in recent years.'

In a retrospective in *Ring* magazine in March 1952, Miller's achievement in guiding Flowers to the world title was recognised. The writer, Ted Carroll, called Miller 'the hustling Southerner' and described it as 'one of the standout managerial jobs of all time'.

Walk Miller did not get his hands on Flowers' fortune and did not evict Willie Mae from the mansion, but the row rumbled on and sorting out the estate took a long time.

In the *Pittsburgh Courier* of 27 November 1928 a writer named Rollo Wilson suggested Flowers had overstretched himself financially when he took on the project of building the family mansion. He also claimed Miller had persuaded him to move up the housing ladder, with the added encouragement of Willie Mae, and the manager had then somehow managed to use the property to raise three mortgages of his own. It might seem to us odd that he was able to do that but a white man in Georgia could do many things with a black man's property that seem incredible to us now. Wilson's article was inflammatory to the point of suggesting that, far from being distraught, shocked and confused, Miller encouraged Fralick to use general anaesthetic when a numbing of the specific areas to be treated would have done. Wilson also suggested Flowers might even have been going blind. Unfortunately he supplied no evidence to back up his theories.

As late as September 1929, almost two years after Theodore's death Lula Flowers filed a court petition to have the executor, an African-American real estate operator, H. W. Akin, removed from the position. The *Atlanta Constitution* reported,

According to the petition, Flowers willed in fee simple to his mother the property known as 938 Simpson Street and $1,000 in cash. The petition sets out that there was an outstanding indebtedness of $2,000 against the property and that Fulton County tax collectors have served notice of their intention to bill the tract for 1928 taxes unless some move is made to pay...

In other words, Theodore left his mother her house, but he had not completed the payment for it – there was still $2,000 left on a mortgage – and the house was tied up as an asset to pay his outstanding tax issues from his last year of earnings. There is no suggestion that he had not paid his taxes up to the point of his death. However, it would seem there were issues outstanding from the financial year in which he died.

The petition served by Lula Flowers also mentioned other properties that were being rented out. This may well have been a reference to the farms mentioned in Edney's book and in press cuttings from early in the decade. Lula contended that nothing was being done to clear up the mess, that she had no idea where the rental money was going, and by implication was worried she would lose her home.

Petitioners contend that Akin has not filed an appraisal, nor an inventory of the property as required by law, although he had held the post for more than a year. They also contend he has not made an accounting of rentals which it is stated aggregate at least $250 a month net.

The outcome of the case, whether it was heard or not, was not reported, or at least is not available now, but Lula appears to have faced a prolonged struggle to keep what was left to her. We do know, from an *Atlanta Constitution* report of the progress of the case, that the attorney for the administrator denied any involvement in the rentals, saying the original petition made no reference to them. By the time of the 1930 census Lula was back with her husband, Aaron, in Brunswick, living in Bartow Street with their son Carl, his wife Viola, and children Verdine and Carl Jr. Carl was still a baker, but no longer with his own shop. Aaron was labouring in the docks. It seems the Flowers fortune had evaporated into thin air, or vanished deep into someone else's pocket.

Willie Mae and Verna Lee left the main house in either 1929 or at the latest early 1930. Perhaps they could not afford to pay for it. Perhaps there was not enough money left to look after their day-to-day living expenses. Perhaps it was frozen by the procrastinations of the executor of the estate, who steadily helped himself to large chunks of it in fees without releasing enough funds for the family to live. Or perhaps Willie Mae simply could not bear to live there once her husband had gone.

However, Andrew Kaye also raises the question of whether or not she was hounded out by the Ku Klux Klan, which although declined from its peak of a few years before was still active, or by a similar racist group. A report out of Atlanta, reprinted in the *Milwaukee Sentinel* of 27 January 1929 suggests his inclination was right, that whatever the title of the organisation or individuals behind it, violent racist repression was the cause of Willie Mae's flight.

> A police guard tonight was ordered placed around the $60,000 mansion here of the late Tiger Flowers, Negro, and former middleweight champion. The action was taken after the Flowers family reported to police that the home had been threatened with dynamiting unless it was vacated at once. The home is occupied by the fighter's widow and family. The alleged threats were anonymous.

In other words, it is likely that Willie Mae and Verna Lee Flowers were the victims of so-called white-capping, where African-Americans were forced out of their homes to make way for whites, or just to keep a particular road or area free of people with any other skin colour.

Kaye wrote that the word was that Willie Mae had travelled somewhere out west but he had been unable to track down her whereabouts. I had more luck.

I found Verna Lee on the US census taken on 12 April 1930. She was recorded as Berna Lee Flower and was living, aged eight, in a rooming house at 818 East 33rd Street, Los Angeles… and she was with her mother and stepfather. Willie Mae was now Willie Mae Crawford, married to Usher William Crawford, a baker from Georgia. Perhaps Crawford had been a colleague or employee of Theodore's brother, Carl, back in Atlanta. Perhaps he had owned, or had run, his own premises. Maybe he had courted Willie Mae and took her away when it was too uncomfortable or dangerous for her to continue to live in Atlanta. She and Theodore had enjoyed their visit to Los Angeles to the point where a local newspaperman had suggested they might return and buy property there. Perhaps the welcome they had received on that trip persuaded her that Los Angeles could provide her, and Verna Lee, with a fresh start. There is no sign, however, that she had any of the Tiger's fortune, for the three of them were living as lodgers in the house of Lucie Warner, who earned a living as a cook for a private family. Lucie's parents, brother, sister and nephew also lived there.

It is not unusual for details of families, particularly African-American poor families, to alter from census to census. In her quest for a new life Willie Mae might have been reluctant to give too much away – but for whatever reason she said her father was born in the West Indies. Lewis Spellars, as far as is known, and according to the 1900 Census, was born in Georgia. She was a year out in her age at the time of her first marriage, though that's a common and minor inaccuracy. She was not working. Verna Lee was attending school. Usher, who said he had first married when he was twenty-two, which would have been around 1916, had a job in a bakery. He was thirty-six.

In the June 1930 edition of *Ring* magazine, under a section entitled In California, by Theron Fiske, there is a strange, unexplained one-sentence reference that asks even more questions. Fiske got her name wrong, but the rest is plain. 'Flo Mae Flowers, widow of the late Tiger Flowers, former middleweight champion, is living in Los Angeles, stranded and an invalid.'

What type of invalid? Physical, or psychological? If the latter, was it as a result of the trauma she had suffered with the loss of her husband, and then her home, or is the unthinkable possible, that Walk Miller's tempestuous threat to have her committed to an asylum had some basis to it? Was she psychologically fragile during her marriage, or at least the latter part of it? And was, after all the slaughtering of his reputation, Walk telling the truth? Did Flowers believe Willie Mae to be incapable of looking after Verna Lee and the home and therefore trusted his manager to take care of his business if the operation went wrong or some other tragedy fell? All we can say is that there is no evidence beyond this single paragraph that points towards that.

We cannot even assume that Fiske had his facts straight. After all, he would have written it at the latest around the time that the census was taken, as *Ring* magazine usually worked at least a month in advance of its publication date. Therefore, far from being stranded, she was sharing accommodation with her new husband and her daughter. Fiske also got her name wrong. It's not therefore, beyond the bounds of possibility that he completed his hat-trick of errors in a single sentence by claiming she was an invalid. The 1930 census form does not indicate anything of the sort. However, she was in Los Angeles. Fiske at least got that bit right.

Final proof that Willie Mae had been educated at Tuskegee comes, surprisingly, in the 'society' page of *The California Eagle*, a newspaper for African-American readers, of 1 September 1931.

Mr and Mrs Willie Mae Crawford entertained the Los Angeles Tuskegee Club members at the club's monthly social on last Tuesday evening, August 22nd, at their home, 689 East 53rd Street. This was a very interesting meeting as each member reminiscented [sic], and much amusement was caused by the disclosure of different activities and experience of classes, classmates, schoolmates and instructors, while at Tuskegee Institute. Our hostess, Mrs Crawford, gave reminiscence of her once-wealthy station in life as the wife of the late 'Tiger' Flowers of Georgia, whose tragic death shocked the world, and also reminiscences of events leading to the untimely death of the former world's middleweight champion. Following the many different disclosures, a delicious luncheon was served.

Oh, to have been a fly on the wall at that gathering.

By 1932 Willie Mae and Usher had moved on to 892 East 49th Place, Los Angeles. According to the voter lists they were Republican supporters.

By 1936 Willie Mae was at 1406 East 21st Street, listed as a housewife, although Usher was not at home – and that was once again the situation in

1938. She still voted Republican, which was the traditional African-American vote of the time. That address, 1406 East 21st Street, is in what is now known as the historic south-central district of Los Angeles, a few blocks from the Santa Monica Freeway. It sounds grander than it is. In truth it's a poor, tough place to be.

The evidence that Willie Mae and Usher parted is confirmed in the 1940 census. She and Verna Lee were living in a rented home at 1273 West 36th Street, Los Angeles, and Willie Mae was once again using the name Flowers. On either side of them were a carpenter and his family and a Japanese couple and their children, who would, within a year or so, see their lives changed by the attack on Pearl Harbor. Intriguingly, Willie Mae declared that she was working forty hours a week as a psychic reader at a spiritual science church. Verna Lee did not have a job. Both women lopped a little bit off their ages – Willie Mae was thirty-nine again instead of forty-three, Verna Lee seventeen instead of eighteen. In the 1948 Los Angeles telephone directory, Willie Mae was still using the name Flowers, and was still on West 36th Street, but at no. 1428.

Verna Lee grew up, married a man named Alfred Alexander Jackson and had eight children, four boys and four girls, and continued to live in Los Angeles and its surrounds, including Gardena, which isn't far from the Ascot racetrack arena where her father boxed Eddie Huffman back in the glory days.

Back in Atlanta, the house that Tiger built was pulled down around the turn of the 1960s to provide the site for Fire Station 16, which housed the first black firefighters employed by the city. His grave in Lincoln cemetery was unmarked for many years before a headstone was placed on it. And the authorities eventually named two roads after him in the Dixie Hills community of north-west Atlanta: Tiger Flowers Drive, which is not near to where he lived, and Flowers Place, which is close by where the house stood.

A horse called Tiger Flowers raced in 1930, for a while other African-American boxers called Flowers took the name Tiger. We had Tiger Flowers, Baby Tiger Flowers, Young Tiger Flowers – and a Tiger Flowers Gym was opened in Baltimore in 1945. Today 'Tiger Flowers' is a rock band named, according to the relevant website, in his honour.

Roll forward to August 2011: After a gap, I returned to this manuscript, wondering once again what happened to Verna Lee and Willie Mae, mulling over all the questions the Tiger Flowers story had left unanswered. The previous winter I had been given an address for one of his nieces and had written to her, asking for her co-operation, but had received no reply. This time, idly googling his name yet again, the search engine produced a new tribute facebook site to the great man – with two email addresses at the foot of the page.

I emailed them both, explaining why I was interested, and within days received welcoming, enthusiastic emails from both people, who were members of the Flowers family in Georgia. When I explained in more detail that I was looking for information on what had happened to Willie Mae and Verna Lee, a response came back that astonished me. It referred to Flowers, then said, 'I recently spoke to his only daughter who is residing in California.'

Verna Lee Flowers is, or was at the time of writing, alive, aged ninety.

I begged for the opportunity to speak to her, or have my questions relayed to her. Sadly, although initially it seemed a telephone conversation would be possible, the trail dried up. I was told her telephone number had been lost. Further questions met with a blank.

I tried one more email in February 2012. Again, no response.

Then in May 2012 I came across a short tribute to Flowers in response to a youtube video. It was written by his great-granddaughter who spoke of caring for Verna Lee Jackson, her mother's mother and the Tiger's daughter. I wrote a letter on the public response system but again, no reply.

Finally, an email came back from Georgia suggesting I talk to Tiger's great-granddaughter. After an explanatory email conversation, she emailed me again. 'Hello Bob, how are you? Well, I wanted to inform you that I've talked to my grandmother. You can talk to her directly.' And she gave me her telephone number.

I called on a Monday and a woman answered but sounded much younger than the old lady's voice. I explained who I was, what I wanted and asked if it was possible to talk to Mrs Jackson. 'This is Verna Lee,' she said, and I told her it was a privilege to talk to her, that I had been hoping to do this for a long time. She listened to what I wanted to talk to her about.

'You're writing a book for yourself?' she said. I said, yes, it was for myself, and for history, and it meant a great deal to me, that I knew a lot about her father's career and life but would love to know her memories of him and anything she felt she could share with me.

'I don't know,' she said. 'I will have to talk to the family about this. What's today? Monday. Ring me Friday.'

I asked what time was best, if this time, 11 a.m. Californian time was all right. 'Any time,' she said. 'I seldom go anywhere.'

And that was that.

I explained the conversation to her granddaughter and we had a courteous, pleasant exchange of emails that eventually established that Verna Lee herself was reluctant to talk to me, as her mother had felt exploited by Henry Grady Edney way back in 1928. Her argument, as relayed to me, was that Edney had made $20,000 from the book – that's about a quarter of a million dollars now – and Willie Mae had not received a penny. Before Verna Lee talked to me, therefore – and if she talked to me – she required a legal letter entitling her to a percentage of the profits of this book. I had already explained that, as much as I would love it to be a bestseller, the truth was that its appeal would be mostly confined to a relatively small number of boxing people interested in the sport's history. The situation was different in 2012 to that which had existed when Edney's book had appeared in 1928. Then Tiger Flowers' name had been known and respected all over the country and his tragic death would have multiplied the appeal of the story. Now Flowers was all but forgotten.

I considered offering a one-off fee for an interview but that in itself carried with it potential problems. If I offered a realistic, inevitably fairly low fee then the possibility was that somewhere down the line someone would consider Verna Lee to have been ripped off. If I pitched the offer high, then it could seem that I was lying about the potential sales for the book.

I also thought about the idea of a percentage offer on any potential profits but again it seemed an unrealistic situation. How easy would it be to persuade someone that this book, for all the years of research and effort, would very likely be released on a very small print run? How much grief would be in store as I attempted to assure people that the figures I was giving them over sales were accurate? How hard would it be to convince anyone of the truth that I researched and wrote this book because the legend of Tiger Flowers fascinated me, and because I wanted to immerse myself in a subject that was not governed by the restrictions of writing for money, of earning a living – that writing for television and newspapers provided that, and this project was an emotional release from that type of commitment – and not because I believed it was the key to untold wealth?

Therefore, with regret, I had to let it go and be satisfied with what I had. Was it the right decision? I don't know.

CHAPTER 19

The Legacy

Although Tiger Flowers was elected to the Georgia Sports Hall of Fame in 1976, almost fifty years after his death, and to the International Boxing Hall of Fame in 1993, many boxing fans haven't even heard of him, and even those who know about him might struggle to get beyond the fact that he was black, a southpaw, beat Harry Greb to win the world middleweight title, lost it to Mickey Walker and died after an operation. It is the way history sometimes works. While it's right to celebrate the lives of those who have gone before us sometimes the greatest make little noise and what they really were is lost in half-remembered anecdotes that say very little. If this book does anything, I hope it revives a little interest in Theodore 'Tiger' Flowers and puts him closer to his rightful place in history.

And if we settle back on the colour of his skin briefly, once again, it is fair to say that his attitude took the cause of the black man in sports forward. Flowers built a bridge that led from Jack Johnson to Joe Louis, from the day when an African-American athlete was despised and whose success provoked anger and violence, to the time when a man with African blood became, as with Louis in the fight with the German, Max Schmeling, in 1938, the celebrated representative of the nation. It was a gradual progress but Flowers played his part in it. Each of us can change the world. Flowers would probably have laughed if anyone had suggested he had improved the way life was, especially in the Deep South, but changes sometimes happen slowly and with subtlety. Flowers did, whether he knew it or not, make a significant and positive difference, for his own family, for the people of Atlanta and Georgia, for boxers, and for the black people of America.

As we know the success of Joe Louis was just one more step along the way towards the achievement of the Civil Rights movement and, eventually, the arrival of a black President, but in his turn Louis was tolerated as his rise began to take shape partly because of the example set by Flowers, who had not been in his grave ten years when Joe won the heavyweight championship.

That same year Paul Gallico published *Farewell to Sport*, his reflections on his own career up to that point which was then to take him into other areas of writing. In one chapter, Gallico addressed the difficulties black boxers had faced up to the arrival of Louis – and in doing so launched a withering attack on the attitudes that still prevailed.

> Fight managers, the most shameless, rapacious, and unmoral crew in the world anyway, lose practically every last vestige of decency when dealing with Negro fighters.

Gallico was generalising, of course, but felt the world was afflicted by a ridiculous prejudice that the black man was innately inferior, less sensitive to pain, thicker skulled and stupid with money.

> The Negro of course is a poor, misguided fool ever to go into the profession of prizefighting because except in the rarest of instances the rich rewards are not for him, and from the point of view of sportsmanship and a square shake, he is whipped before ever the bell rings.

Gallico's testimonial played its own small part in changing people's minds because his book *Farewell to Sport* reached a substantial audience.

In spite of a rose-tinted editorial by Nat Fleischer in *Ring* in 1941, which claimed that Flowers' victory over Greb enabled 'the bars of prejudice' to disappear as if by magic, the lot of the black boxer did not, could not improve overnight because of the achievements of or examples set by Flowers or Louis. Through the thirties and forties and well into the fifties, for one spurious reason or another, talented black fighters had to stand in the shadows and watch white men with far less ability box for world championships. Men like Charley Burley, Jimmy Bivins, Holman Williams, Elmer 'Violent' Ray, Eugene Hairston, Lloyd Marshall, Eddie Booker and plenty of others were either avoided by the fighters that mattered, robbed of decisions they deserved or just ignored full stop.

However, Fleischer was right when he said that Flowers' example did make a difference in that, in many states at least, 'mixed matches were no longer taboo'.

Getting on for sixty years ago, in *Ring* magazine in June 1954, Ted Carroll had no doubts of the place of Tiger Flowers in this fight to provoke and force change. He wrote,

> Flowers was really the man who cleared the atmosphere of the clammy climate left by the Jack Johnson era... Tiger's publicised piety made him welcome in many towns which at that time frowned on boxing in general and mixed bouts in particular and he became a countrywide sensation... Flowers came upon the scene at a time when a man such as he was most needed and his career was a history-making one.

Johnny Salak, writing in *Ring* magazine in May 1950, said,

> The Tiger unconsciously became a benefactor to the other boxers of his
> race by establishing a precedent which could not be ignored. From that day
> the Negro boxer has made huge strides and rapid advancement in boxing.

Through each stage of this book, I found myself considering the possibility
that I was missing something, that the Tiger might have had a second side,
a flip side. I kept asking myself, am I being naïve here, might this man have
walked a different path by night to the sober, Christian one he trod by day?
Was a part of him cold, calculating, cynical? Did he play Miller's publicity
game for effect? Well, there is no evidence of that – and there were enough
wise and sceptical people around in New York and on his travels who would
have said or written something to cast a little doubt on his piety. As far as I
have been able to tell, nobody did.

The only slight niggle is the Miller will and its reference to the woman
Matty Jarrett. It is flimsy, poor evidence, and barely worth considering, but
it is possible that, even though we have no idea who she was, she might
have existed. However, even if she did, does it really offer the possibility of
a more sinister, if you like sinful, side to Flowers? If we accept the tenuous
argument that not only did Jarrett exist, she was a potential romantic link,
then all that Flowers stood for could be open to question. In the two years of
research I committed to this book, nothing came to light that suggested she
was anything more than a ruse on the part of Miller, designed to destabilise
Willie Mae and the Flowers family. Even then, if I am wrong and Miller did
not invent her, nobody is perfect and the best of men or women can slide off
a self-constructed pedestal without turning into the devil incarnate.

However, the more persuasive argument is that Jarrett was dreamed up by
a panicking Miller, who suddenly realised that the financial gravy train had
just run off the end of the track without warning. Similarly there is nothing
else to suggest Miller might have been right in his assessment that Willie
Mae was psychologically unstable and, without Tiger, could not cope with
the strain of ordinary life. There is no evidence of that in her testimonies as
used by Henry Grady Edney, although the 1930 reference in *Ring* magazine
did describe her as an invalid. However, that short report contained at least
two other inaccuracies, which casts doubt on the statement that she was not
well. The fact that by 1940 she was a psychic reader, acting for or through
a church, might tell us that she had never recovered from the death of
Theodore, or might tell us that she had a sense of the mystical as well as her
earlier Methodism. Perhaps that elusive conversation with the ninety-year-
old Verna Lee could have shed light on that, and other issues. But perhaps
not. If there is ever a second edition of this book, any member of the Flowers
family is welcome to contribute.

In the end, by accident or design, Tiger Flowers was robbed of so much, of seeing his daughter grow up, of his home, of whatever enjoyments his eventual retirement from the ring would have brought. If he had lived, he would most likely have gone home to Georgia and remained there among his friends and family. It is unlikely the Ku Klux Klan, or an offshoot of it, would have pressured even an ageing Tiger out of his home. Instead of moving west, Willie Mae would have stayed in Atlanta, and Verna Lee would have been raised there under her father's guidance in comparative wealth rather than in less affluent circumstances in Los Angeles. But who knows, perhaps she had no complaints, that there was a flip side. That life was good in spite of losing her father when she was six years old, and that Willie Mae, too, prospered and reached new levels of fulfilment in whatever direction her life took after 1940. I hope so.

A Place In History

Attempting to evaluate how good Tiger Flowers was in terms of the best middleweights in history, or how he might have fared against modern champions, are pointless exercises. Better to look at the facts of his career and leave it at that. He twice beat Harry Greb, who is still regarded as one of the ring's legendary fighters, pound-for-pound, but as we know Greb was past his peak with serious visual problems when they fought out their two fifteen round championship contests. He beat world title claimants like Johnny Wilson, Lou Bogash and Jock Malone, twice drew with one light-heavyweight champion in Maxie Rosenbloom, lost another horrible decision to another in Mike McTigue and was twice knocked out by a third, Jack Delaney. On the downside Flowers was stopped or knocked out more often than almost any other world middleweight champion. Flowers crammed in a huge number of fights into a comparatively short space of time, and in almost every one of them he appears to have tried to entertain and give his customers value for money. People wanted to see him box probably because of the fact that in attacking so relentlessly he took risks, and occasionally paid for them, and they respected and admired him because he fought wherever he was booked to fight. He attracted crowds because he was a curiosity, a devout, serene man in a corrupt sport, but also because it appears that he did not hide his personality in the ring, he gave of himself openly. Watching him must have been 'edge of the seat' stuff.

It is fair to say Flowers was probably not as accomplished as the best middleweights of all time – Greb in his peak years, Ray Robinson, Carlos Monzon, Marvin Hagler and way back Stanley Ketchel – but he was a man who learned his trade, who overcame the kind of prejudice in and out of the ring that would have demoralised most people, and who improved his skills to an astonishing degree from a wild youngster with a leaky defence to a man cunning, strong and persistent enough to beat the world's best. That made him remarkable.

In an interview with columnist Mike Katz for the *New York Daily News* in 1985, trainer Ray Arcel, by then in his mid-eighties, named the best twelve fighters he had ever seen. They were Henry Armstrong, Jack Dempsey, Roberto Duran, Tiger Flowers, Harry Greb, Pete Herman, Benny Leonard, Joe Louis, Willie Pep, Ray Robinson, Barney Ross and Mickey Walker. That's a prodigious group – and Flowers is right up there among them.

In their 2012 pamphlet honouring their choice of the 100 best boxers in history, the venerable *Boxing News*, which has been around for more than a century, ranked Flowers at eighty-eight, which is at least some level of acknowledgement of his achievements. It may be that he is just beginning to be recognised for what he did accomplish, but these things are not fixed in stone. Opinions alter with the years. Now it is considered heresy not to rank Ray Robinson as the number one pound for pound boxer in history. Yet in 1958, for his book *Fifty Years At Ringside, Ring* editor Nat Fleischer had Robinson, who was then still boxing but with his best days behind him, only the fifth best middleweight in history, behind Stanley Ketchel, Tommy Ryan, Harry Greb and Mickey Walker. Tiger Flowers, widely considered to have been robbed against Walker and who twice beat the faded Greb, was not in Fleischer's top ten. We can never rely on statistics alone to evaluate how good a man was – they need to be applied to a situation to have relevance. However, wherever we rate him Flowers was certainly one of the most prolific and successful middleweights of all time. Records of old fighters are still being researched, and so the following stats are no more than a guide.

World middleweight champions with most fights:
Harry Greb 301, Ray Robinson 202, Jock Malone 190, Jeff Smith 185, Mickey Walker 164, George Chip 161, Ken Overlin 159, Al McCoy, Tiger Flowers and Vince Dundee 157.

World middleweight champions or claimants with most wins, including newspaper decisions, according to the last of the *Ring Record Books*, plus one modern record taken from www.boxrec.com:

Harry Greb 265, Ray Robinson 175, Jeff Smith 139, Tiger Flowers 133, Ken Overlin 132, Jorge Castro 130, Jock Malone 128, Vince Dundee 122, Freddie Steele 120, Mickey Walker 115.

Flowers also covered a thousands of miles each year, travelling by road and rail, which in itself took an enormous amount of stamina, dedication and ambition. The distance Tiger Flowers travelled by road and rail to fight, not including unspecified trips back to Atlanta, or other excursions:

1922	8,200
1923	9,600
1924	18,130
1925	13,181
1926	10,250
1927	18,268
Total	77,629

The distances Flowers covered in his boxing career are all the more remarkable given the difficulties he would have encountered as a matter of routine – in many of the towns and cities he fought he would have had to seek out the places where he was welcome to sleep and eat. His manager, Walk Miller, may well have stayed in a 'white' part of town to do their business while more often than not Flowers would have sought his shelter among the black communities. Decades later Muhammad Ali charted graphically similar problems he encountered on the road because of the colour of his skin. Ali had the capacity to make a noise about it and have writers highlight it. Flowers' way was to avoid conflict wherever possible, to accept the presence of social obstacles as God's will and move on. He said once he never had a fight outside the ring.

APPENDIX 2

The Rest of the Cast

And so we know what happened to Tiger Flowers and Walk Miller, but what of the rest of the players in this extraordinary drama?

Theodore's parents, Aaron and Lula, lived into old age. Aaron was eighty-eight when he passed away in 1957, while Lula died at seventy-eight in 1949. Carl Flowers, the Tiger's elder brother, also lived until he was eighty-eight.

Tex Rickard, who changed the face of boxing in the 1920s and promoted Flowers' world title wins against Harry Greb, died in Miami on 6 January 1929 of peritonitis. He was fifty-nine.

After his boxing career petered out Rufus Cameron, who gave Flowers his first boxing lesson, lived in Los Angeles, where he died on 24 November 1943, aged fifty-six. Perhaps he kept in touch with Willie Mae in Los Angeles. Or perhaps the big city just swallowed them up.

William 'Battling' Gahee, one of the men who fought Flowers several times on the merry-go-round of the black circuit, worked for many years at the Champion Spark Plug Company in Toledo, Ohio, and died after an illness lasting a year in a veteran's hospital in Dearborn, Michigan, in June 1948. He was in his mid-fifties.

James J. Johnston, known as Jimmy, or The Boy Bandit, who managed Mike McTigue and some say had an unhealthily close relationship with the New York State Athletic commissioners, also had spells as manager of Ted Kid Lewis, Johnny Dundee and the heavyweight Bob Pastor, who fought Joe Louis for the heavyweight title. Johnston died in 1946. Nat Fleischer wrote of him,

> James J, who never took a drink and hated smoking, clung fondly to the good old British custom of four o'clock tea to the very end. His feuds, capers and wisecracks kept him in the spotlight.

William 'Young' Stribling died on 3 October 1933, of injuries sustained in a motorbike accident two days before in Macon, Georgia.

Chuck – or Charles Frederick – Wiggins, one of the toughest men Flowers ever fought, was an alcoholic down-and-out when he fell 40 feet down a stairwell in downtown Indianapolis in 1942. He died in hospital of a fractured skull, aged only forty-three. Jack Dempsey once called him the greatest street fighter in the world.

Mickey Walker's long career ended in 1935, although he had one comeback fight in 1939. He ran restaurants in his hometown of Elizabeth, New Jersey, and then New York City and turned his hand to art, becoming a successful painter in oils in what was known as the naïve style. Walker had studied drawing at two colleges before moving into boxing. In his fifties he had a painting entitled Main Street in the Metropolitan Museum in New York. When asked if he could live his life again, would he have chosen to be an artist. 'No, I would choose fighting,' he said. 'Fighting and all the fun that went with it.' Walker was almost eighty years old when he died in 1981.

Jack 'Doc' Kearns, who managed Walker and ran with him in their glory days, whose real name was John Leo McKernan, did make it to eighty years old before he passed on in July 1963. Near the end of his life he denied any involvement in a fixed fight – then qualified his statement by saying,

> Fixed, that is, where I lost a fight. But I will admit this, I'm a winner, not a loser. I'd do anything to win and I won't lose. And you can draw your own conclusions.

Benny Yanger, who gave the controversial decision to Mickey Walker that cost Flowers his world title, died in a car wreck on the shores of Lake Michigan in 1958. After the Walker-Flowers fight, he never refereed another contest in Illinois.

Bob Sage, the Boxing Barrister who found the Tiger too good for him in the summer of '27, would go on to be a practising judge in Detroit but in 1940, after sinking around $35,000 into an ill-fated sports park venture, he shot dead two business partners, brothers Alfred and Ralph Nadell, during an argument in his chambers. A third associate, Maurice Smiley, survived gunshot wounds to his chest. Sage then shot himself, but the bullet passed out of his cheek. He left the building, and two weeks later his body was found in the Detroit River by two men hunting ducks at a place called Mud Island.

Pete Latzo, the former welterweight champion who fought Flowers in 1927, kept in touch with boxing through the Veterans Associations in New Jersey, where he lived after he retired from the ring. He passed away in Atlantic City in 1968.

Joe Lohman died in Toledo, Ohio, at the age of seventy-three, in 1971 while Jimmy Darcy, alias Valeri Trambitas, passed away in Portland, Oregon, in 1972. Lou Bogash stayed in boxing as a referee after his career was over and lived out his life in his hometown of Bridgeport, Connecticut, where he died in 1978.

Light-heavyweight champion Maxie Rosenbloom, who beat Flowers on a foul in 1926 and twice drew with him in 1927, settled in Los Angeles, where he did some acting and ran nightclubs, both in L.A. and San Francisco. He played an ex-fighter reduced to telling the same old stories in a bar in *Requiem For a Heavyweight*, written by Rod Steiger. He died of a bone disease at sixty-eight in 1976.

Leo Gates, Flowers' last opponent, also fought as Joe Wilson and Young Clay Turner. After his career ended in 1928 he was a police officer in New York until 1949. He died eight years later at fifty-seven.

Jack Delaney, the man who twice so dramatically knocked out Flowers at Madison Square Garden, succeeded Paul Berlanbach as world light-heavyweight champion in July 1926 but relinquished his championship in June 1927 to chase the heavyweight crown. He lost a fifteen round decision to the New Zealander, Tom Heeney, in March 1928, and it was Heeney who was given the shot at world champion Gene Tunney. Even during his career Delaney had a tendency to live on the edge, disappearing at times on three-day benders, and his lifestyle eventually caught up with him. He had not reached fifty when he died in Katonah, New York, in 1948.

Johnny Wilson fought until 1926 and lived for almost sixty more years. He died in Boston in 1985, aged ninety-two. Wilson was referred to in the 1970 cult movie *Zabriskie Point*. The heroine, Daria, is in a small town bar when an old man, who may or may not have been the real Johnny Wilson, approaches her and asks

'Do you remember Johnny Wilson?'
'Johnny Wilson? No.'
'That's me. I was middleweight champion of the world in the 1920s.'
'Middleweight champion of the world?'
'That's right.'
'That's great.'
'Thank you.'

The Known Ring Record of Theodore 'Tiger' Flowers

Middleweight

Atlanta, Georgia, born Camilla, Georgia, February 1893
5 foot 10 inches.

1918
no date Bill Hooper w ko 11 Brunswick, Georgia
no date Kid Fox w ko 2
no date Battling Henry Williams w pts 20
no date Battling Hazel w ko 8
no date Rufus Cameron w pts 10
no date Battling Mims w pts 15

1919
no date Battling Mims w pts 10
no date Roughhouse Baker w ko 3

1920
no date Eddie Palmer w ko 3
no date Sailor Darden w pts 15
no date Tiger Moore w ko 2
Mar 17 Bill Hooper w pts 20 Brunswick, Georgia
no date w pts 10 Battling Mims
Sep 27 Bill Hooper w pts 10 Auditorium, Atlanta, Georgia
Nov 9 Battling Mims w pts 10 Auditorium, Atlanta, Georgia

1921
May 2 Chihuahua Kid Brown w ko 8 Business Men's Athletic Club, Atlanta,
    Georgia
no date Chihuahua Kid Brown w ko 2
May 23 Jim Fain w ko 4 Business Men's Athletic Club, Atlanta, Georgia

no date Whitey Black w ko 1 Georgia
Jun 14 Battling Troupe w ko 4 Business Men's Athletic Club, Atlanta, Georgia
no date Battling Mims w pts 10 Georgia
Jul 12 Jack Moore w ko 2 Pekin Theatre, Savannah, Georgia
Aug 8 Panama Joe Gans l ko 6 Auditorium, Atlanta, Georgia
no date Kid Williams w ko 3 Georgia
Sep 26 Chihuahua Kid Brown w ko 3 Auditorium, Atlanta, Georgia
Oct 18 Battling Gahee w pts 10 Business Men's Athletic Club, Atlanta,
    Georgia
Oct 24 Whitey Black w pts 8 Memphis, Tennessee
Nov 8 Battling Gahee w pts 8 Memphis, Tennessee
Dec 15 Panama Joe Gans l ko 5 Auditorium, Atlanta, Georgia

1922
no date Jack Ray w ko 2 Georgia
Jan 11 Battling Burke w ko 4 Nashville, Tennessee
Jan 30 Kid Norfolk l ko 3 Auditorium, Atlanta, Georgia
Feb 21 Gorilla Jones w rsf 9 Ciudad Juarez, Mexico
Mar 7 Jim Jam Barry drew 15 Ciudad Juarez, Mexico
Mar 21 Chihuahua Kid Brown w ko 1 Ciudad Juarez, Mexico 153
Mar 28 Jim Jam Barry w ko 5 Ciudad Juarez, Mexico
Apr 11 Billy Britton w pts 15 Ciudad Juarez, Mexico
May 9 Lee Anderson l ko 7 Ciudad Juarez, Mexico
May 16 Frankie Murphy w pts 15 Ciudad Juarez, Mexico
Jun 5 Sam Langford l ko 2 Ponce de Leon Ballpark, Atlanta, Georgia
Jul 4 Kid Norfolk drew 8 Memphis, Tennessee
Jul 26 Jamaica Kid l rsf 2 Covington, Kentucky
Aug 22 Andy Palmer w pts 15 Ciudad Juarez, Mexico 160
Aug 30 Kid Paddy w ko 1 Ciudad Juarez, Mexico
no date Kid Davis w ko 1 Ciudad Juarez, Mexico
Oct 10 Battling Gahee w pts 8 Memphis, Tennessee
no date Eddie Palmer w pts 8 Memphis, Tennessee
Dec 13 Eddie Palmer w rsf 10 Coliseum Arena, New Orleans, Louisiana 164
Dec 22 Frank Carbone w dis 10 Ciudad Juarez, Mexico

1923
Feb 21 Bob Lawson w pts 8 Nashville, Tennessee
Feb 28 Battling Mims w pts 8 Nashville, Tennessee
Mar 19 Jack Ray w ko 3 Central Garage Arena, Nashville, Tennessee
Apr 20 Jamaica Kid nd – w 12, Coliseum, Toledo, Ohio
May 8 Kid Norfolk l ko 1 Springfield, Ohio
May 15 Sailor Tom King w pts 15 Ciudad Juarez, Mexico
May 25 Panama Joe Gans nd - w 12, Coliseum, Toledo, Ohio

Jun 20 Rufus Cameron w pts 10 Bijou Ring, Nashville, Tennessee
Jul 3 Tut Jackson w pts 12 Auditorium, Atlanta, Georgia
Jul 18 Tut Jackson w pts 12 Springfield, Ohio * did not weigh in.
Jul 30 Whitey Black nd – w 10, Detroit, Michigan
Sep 4 Jamaica Kid w pts 10 Auditorium, Atlanta, Georgia
Sep 17 Fireman Jim Flynn l rtd 5 Mexico City
Nov 27 George Robinson drew 12 Auditorium, Atlanta, Georgia
Dec 6 Rufus Cameron w ko 4 Albany, New York
Dec 28 Sailor Darden w pts 12 Auditorim, Atlanta, Georgia

1924
Jan 23 Herbert Moore w ko 2 Nashville, Tennessee
Jan 31 Sonny Goodrich w pts 12 Bellinger Theatre, San Antonio, Texas
Feb 18 Bob Lawson w rsf 10 Coliseum, Toledo, Ohio 165
Feb 25 Battling Gahee nd 12 Barberton, Ohio
Mar 3 Jamaica Kid nd – w 10, Fremont Theatre, Fremont, Ohio
Mar 19 Bob Lawson w ko 6 Nashville, Tennessee
Mar 29 Lee Anderson w pts 12 Commonwealth Sporting Club, Harlem, New
    York
Apr 9 Dave Thornton w ko 2 Nashville, Tennessee
Apr 19 Jimmy Darcy w pts 12 Commonwealth Sporting Club, Harlem, New
    York 163
Apr 29 George Robinson w pts 12 Auditorium, Atlanta, Georgia 161
May 3 Ted Jamieson w pts 12 Commonwealth Sporting Club, Harlem, New
    York
May 14 Willie Walker w rsf 7 Commonwealth Sporting Club, Harlem, New
    York
Jun 14 Joe Lohman w pts 12 Commonwealth Sporting Club, Harlem, New
    York 165
Jun 20 Battling Gahee nd – w 10, Fremont Theatre, Fremont, Ohio
Jun 27 Jamaica Kid nd – w 10, Grand Rapids, Michigan
Jul 3 Lee Anderson w dis 11 Auditorium, Atlanta, Georgia 163
Jul 21 Jamaica Kid w dis 3 Covington, Kentucky
Aug 2 Jack Townsend w rsf 11 Commonwealth Sporting Club, Harlem, New
    York
Aug 12 Oscar Mortimer w rsf 6 Soledad Roof, San Antonio, Texas 171
Aug 21 Harry Greb nd 10 Legion Amphitheatre, Fremont, Ohio 161 ½
Sep 1 Tut Jackson w rsf 8 League Park, Martins Ferry, Ohio
Sep 15 Jamaica Kid nd – w 12 Columbus, Ohio
Sep 22 Lee Anderson w pts 12 Columbus, Ohio
Sep 29 Tut Jackson w ko 2 Auditorium, Canton, Ohio 167
Sep 30 Battling Gahee w rtd 4 Weller Theatre, Zanesville, Ohio

Oct 11 Jamaica Kid w rsf 8 Commonwealth Sporting Club, Harlem, New York 168

Oct 21 Cleve Hawkins w ko 3 Auditorium, Atlanta, Georgia 165 ½

Oct 23 Joe Lohman w dis 4 Moose Arena, Hamilton, Ohio

Nov 1 George Robinson w pts 12 Commonwealth Sporting Club Harlem NY 159 ½

Nov 10 Hughie Clements w rsf 2 Arena, Philadelphia, Pa.

Nov 10 Jerry Hayes w ko 2 Arena, Philadelphia, Pa.

Nov 27 Clem Johnson nd – w 12 Auditorium, Canton, Ohio

Dec 1 Battling Gahee w rsf 2 Columbus, Ohio

Dec 9 Johnny Wilson w rsf 3 Madison Square Garden, New York 159 ½

Dec 15 Jack Townsend w rsf 5 Arena, Philadelphia, Pa. 170

Dec 26 Frankie Schoell drew 6 Broadway Auditorium, Buffalo, NY161 ¾

1925

Jan 1 Joe Lohman w rsf 3 Rink Sporting Club, Brooklyn, New York 168

Jan 5 Billy Britton w rsf 4 Mechanics Building, Boston, Massachusetts 165

Jan 7 Dan O'Dowd w rsf 6 Marleville Gardens, North Providence, Rhode Island

Jan 16 Jack Delaney l ko 2 Madison Square Garden, New York 161 ½

Jan 27 Tommy Robson w rsf 8 Mechanics Building, Boston, Massachusetts 169

Jan 29 Bill Savage w ko 2 Providence, Rhode Island

Feb 2 Ted Moore nd – w 12, Sussex Avenue Armory, Newark, New Jersey

Feb 4 Jamaica Kid w rsf 10 Dayton, Ohio

Feb 14 Jackie Clark w rsf 5 Commonwealth Sporting Club, Harlem, New York

Feb 16 Lou Bogash l dis 3 Mechanics Building, Boston, Massachusetts

Feb 26 Jack Delaney l ko 4 Madison Square Garden, New York 166 1/4

Mar 16 Sailor Darden nd – w 12 Coliseum, Toledo, Ohio 165

Mar 20 Lou Bogash w pts 10 Boston, Massachusetts 167

Apr 29 Sailor Darden w ko 5 Savannah, Georgia

May 4 Battling Mims w ko 5 Macon, Georgia

May 18 Pal Reed w pts 10 Mechanics Building, Boston, Massachusetts

May 26 Lou Bogash w pts 12 State Street Arena, Bridgeport, Connecticut 167 ½

Jun 5 Jock Malone nd – w 10, East Chicago, Illinois

Jun 8 Lee Anderson w pts 10 Shibe Park, Philadelphia, Pennsylvania 166

Jun 20 Lee Anderson w dis 3 Commonwealth Sporting Club, Harlem, New York 164

Jun 26 Jack Stone w ko 4 Elizabeth, New Jersey

Jul 20 Pat McCarthy w pts 10 Braves Field, Boston, Massachusetts 168

Jul 24 Lou Bogash nd – w 10, Aurora, Illinois 165

Aug 21 Allentown Joe Gans nd – w 10, Grand Rapids, Michigan
Aug 28 Jock Malone w pts 10 Braves Field, Boston, Massachusetts
Sep 7 Ted Moore w rsf 6 Taylor Bowl, Cleveland, Ohio
Oct 23 Jock Malone nd – w 10, Auditorium, St Paul, Minnesota
Oct 27 Chuck Wiggins nd – d 10, East Chicago, Illinois
Nov 30 Benny Ross w pts 6 Broadway Auditorium, Buffalo, New York 163 ½
Dec 10 Frank Moody w pts 10 Boston, Massachusetts 165
Dec 23 Mike McTigue l pts 10 (s) Madison Square Garden, New York 163 ½

1926
Feb 26 Harry Greb w pts 15 (s) Madison Square Garden, New York 158 ½
    (world middleweight title)
Apr 16 Allentown Joe Gans w pts 10 (s) Armory, Wilkes-Barre, Pennsylvania
    168
Jun 18 Young Bob Fitzsimmons nd – w 10, Boyle's Thirty Acres, Jersey City,
    New Jersey, 166 ½
Jun 28 Ray Neuman w pts 10, Braves Field, Boston, Massachusetts 171
Jul 11 Lee Anderson w ko 2 Coliseum, Ciudad Juarez, Mexico
Jul 24 Eddie Huffman w pts 10 Ascot Park, Los Angeles, California
Aug 10 Battling Jim McCreary w dis 3 Auditorium, Atlanta, Georgia
Aug 19 Harry Greb w pts 15 (s) Madison Square Garden, New York 159 1/4
    (world middleweight title)
Sep 16 Happy Hunter w ko 3 Memphis, Tennessee
Oct 15 Maxie Rosenbloom l dis 9 Mechanics Building, Boston,
    Massachusetts
Nov 22 Eddie Huffman w pts 10 Coliseum, Chicago, Illinois 168
Dec 3 Mickey Walker l pts 10 Coliseum, Chicago, Illinois 159
    (world middleweight title)

1927
Jan 6 Tut Jackson w ko 2 Grand Rapids, Michigan 166
Jan 22 Leo Lomski l pts 10 Wrigley Field, Los Angeles, California 167
Jan 25 Lee Anderson w pts 4 Denver, Colorado
Feb 18 Lou Bogash w pts 10, Boston, Massachusetts 167 ½
Mar 29 George Jones w ko 1 Auditorium, Atlanta, Georgia 168
Apr 29 Chuck Wiggins w pts 10 Broadway Auditorium, Buffalo, New York
    170 ½
May 13 Chuck Wiggins nd – w 10, Grand Rapids, Michigan
May 27 Eddie Huffman w pts 10 Mechanics Building, Boston, Massachusetts
    171
Jun 17 Bob Sage w pts 10 Detroit, Michigan
Jul 4 Maxie Rosenbloom drew 10 Comiskey Park, Chicago, Illinois 167
Jul 28 Bing Conley w pts 10 Amusement Park, Norwalk, Connecticut 169 ½

Aug 3 Chuck Wiggins drew 10 Taylor Bowl, Cleveland, Ohio 170

Aug 10 Harry Dillon w pts 10 Ice Coliseum, Portland, Oregon 167

Aug 16 Jock Malone w pts 6 Dugdale Park, Seattle, Washington 166 ½

Sep 1 Joe Anderson w pts 10 Madison Square Garden, New York 163

Sep 30 Pete Latzo w pts 10 Wilkes-Barre, Pennsylvania 168

Oct 17 Joe Lohman nd – w 10, Auditorium, Canton, Ohio

Nov 9 Maxie Rosenbloom drew 10 Olympia Stadium, Detroit, Michigan 168 ½

Nov 12 Leo Gates w rsf 4 Olympia Boxing Club, New York, NY 171 ½

Sources

It has become a fad – and a requirement of some publishers – to supply exact sources of every single reference and quotation in a book but I do not subscribe to it on the grounds that, aside from a very few people in what amounts to a clique of 'boxing historians', readers neither care about that nor bother to read or follow up the reference. Therefore, it is a costly waste of space. However, I have included sources for each chapter because it is right to acknowledge the original and so that if anyone wants to research further they can find the relevant document or extend their reading easily enough.

Introduction

Herman Skip Mason, *Black Atlanta In the Roaring Twenties*

Chapter 2

Atlanta Constitution; Associated Press; Atlanta Independent.

Chapter 3

Henry Grady Edney, *Theodore Tiger Flowers*; Andrew M. Kaye, *The Pussycat of Prizefighting, Tiger Flowers and the Politics of Black Celebrity*; www.ancestry.com, the US Census from 1860 to 1920; Nat Fleischer, *Black Dynamite Vol. 5*; Booker T. Washington, *Up From Slavery*; W. E. B. Du Bois, *Souls of Black Folk*; John Dittmer, *Black Georgia in the Progessive Era 1900–20*; Douglas A. Blackmon, *Slavery By Another Name*; Donald Grant, *The Way it Was In the South, The Black Experience in Georgia*; *The Savannah Tribune*; Anthony Summers, *The Secret Life of J. Edgar Hoover*; Archie Moore, *The Archie Moore Story*

Chapter 4

Henry Grady Edney, *Theodore Tiger Flowers*; *The Brunswick Pilot*; Elbert Hubbard, *The Scrap Book*; Nat Fleischer, *Black Dynamite Vol. 5*; Nigel Collins, *Boxing Babylon*;

New York Graphic; The 1920 US Census; *Atlanta Constitution*; Psalm 144; James Butler, *Kings of the Ring*; *Ring* magazine

Chapter 5

James J. Corbett, *The Roar of the Crowd*; *New York Sun*; Adam Pollack, *In the Ring and Out James J. Jeffries*; Adam Pollack, *In the Ring and Out Marvin Hart*; *San Francisco Bulletin*; *San Francisco Post*; *Police Gazette*; B. Bennison, *Giants on Parade*; *Richmond Planet*; *Daily Mirror*; *Atlanta Constitution*; Stan Shipley, *Bombardier Billy Wells*; *New Orleans Times-Democrat*; *Los Angeles Times*; *The Times*; *Chicago Defender*; *Chicago Tribune*; Randy Roberts, *Papa Jack*; *New Orleans Daily Picayune*; *Baton Rouge State Times*; Gene Tunney, *A Man Must Fight*; Paul Gallico, *Farewell to Sport*; Jack Dempsey, *Massacre in the Sun*; *New York Daily News*

Chapter 6

Atlanta Constitution; Henry Grady Edney, *Theodore Tiger Flowers*; Jaclyn Weldon White, *The Greatest Champion that Never Was, The Life of W. L. Young Stribling*; Andrew Gallimore, *A Bloody Canvas, the Mike McTigue Story*; Clay Moyle, *Sam Langford, Boxing's Greatest Uncrowned Champion*; James Butler, *Kings of the Ring*; Jimmy Jones, *King of the Canebrakes*; *Ring* Magazine

Chapter 7

Atlanta Constitution; Henry Grady Edney, *Theodore Tiger Flowers*; Nat Fleischer, *Ring* magazine; Geoffrey C Ward, *Unforgiveable Blackness*; Nat Fleischer, *Black Dynamite Vol. 5*; *New York Herald Tribune*; *El Paso Times*; *El Paso Herald*; *Toledo Times*; *Atlanta Journal*; *Springfield Sun*; Muhammad Ali & Richard Durham, *The Greatest, My Own Story*; *Fremont News*

Chapter 8

Jack Kearns, *Oscar Fraley: The Million Dollar Gate*; Mrs Tex Rickard: *Everything Happened To Him*; Jim Brady: *Boxing Confidential*; Hyman Segal: *They Called Him Champ*; Langston Hughes: *The Big Sea*; John Jarrett: *Champ in the Corner, the Ray Arcel Story*; Jack Dempsey: *Massacre in the Sun*

Chapter 9

Atlanta Constitution; *New York Age*; *Ring* magazine

Chapter 10

Henry Grady Edney, *Theodore Tiger Flowers*; Bill Paxton, *The Fearless Harry Greb*; James Fair, *Give Him To the Angels*; *Toledo News Bee*; *Lima News*; *The Afro-American*; *New York Evening Independent*; *Columbus Citizen*; *Fremont Daily News*; *Akron Press*; *Toledo Blade*; *Pittsburgh Post*; *Sandusky Register*; *Elyria Chronicle Telegram*; *Grand*

Rapids Herald; Atlanta Journal; Atlanta Georgian; Ring magazine; *Modesto Evening
News; Columbus Dispatch;* Peter Benson, *Battling Siki; Atlanta Constitution*

Chapter 11

Peter Heller, *In This Corner; Afro-American; Reading Eagle; Atlanta Constitution;
Brooklyn Daily Eagle; New York Daily News; Boston Globe; Associated Press;* Paul
Gallico, *Farewell To Sport;* Gilbert Odd, *Debateable Decisions; New York Sunday
American;* Nat Fleischer, *Black Dynamite Vol. 5; New York Herald Journal; New
York Age; Lewiston Sun; Boston Daily Advertiser; Norwalk Hour; Chicago Defender;
Oakland Tribune; St Paul Pioneer Press; Boston Evening Transcript;* Gareth Jones, *The
Boxers of Wales, Vol. 2*

Chapter 12

Norman Hurst, *Big Fight Thrills;* Marcus Griffin, *Wise Guy – James J. Johnston, A
Rhapsody in Fistics;* Andrew Gallimore, *A Bloody Canvas, the Mike McTigue Story;*
Bob Mee, *Mickey Duff – Twenty and Out;* Nat Fleischer, *50 Years At Ringside;*
Gene Tunney, *A Man Must Fight; Time* magazine; *New York Daily News; Chicago
Defender; New York Evening Graphic; New York Evening Post*

Chapter 13

Gene Tunney, *A Man Must Fight; The Afro-American;* James Fair, *Give Him To the
Angels;* Bill Paxton, *The Fearless Harry Greb; Ring* magazine; *Chicago Defender;
Pittsburgh Post; Washington Post; United Press; Associated Press; New York Graphic;*
James Butler, *Kings of the Ring; Savannah Journal;* Henry Grady Edner, *Theodore
Tiger Flowers; New York Mirror*

Chapter 14

Los Angeles Referee; Associated Press; Henry Grady Edner, *Theodore Tiger Flowers; Ring*
magazine; Paul Gallico, *Farewell to Sport;* American Film Institute records; James
Butler, *Kings of the Ring; Boston Globe; Cohocton Tribune;* James Fair, *Give Him To
The Angels; Universal Service; Pittsburgh Post; Milwaukee Sentinel; New York Evening
Graphic; Chicago Defender; United Press International; Washington Post; Indianapolis
Recorder;* Oscar Fraley, *Jack Kearns, Million Dollar Gate;* Charley Rose, *Life's A
Knockout; Chicago Telegraph-Herald; New York Times; Pittsburgh Press; Afro-American;*
Trevor Wignall, *Prides of the Fancy; St Petersburg Times;* Mickey Walker, *The Toy
Bulldog*

Chapter 15

Afro-American; Los Angeles Record; Los Angeles Times; United Press; Milwaukee Sentinel;
Henry Grady Edney, *Theodore Tiger Flowers; Ring* magazine; *Pittsburgh Press;
Associated Press; Ottawa Citizen; Chicago Defender*

Chapter 16

Ring magazine; www.ancestry.co.uk; *New York Times*; *Associated Press*; *New York Journal American*; *British Medical Journal*; *Afro-American*; *Chicago Defender*

Chapter 17

Atlanta Constitution; *New York Evening Gazette*; Henry Grady Edney, *Theodore Tiger Flowers*; *Miami News*; *Brunswick Pilot*; Trevor Wignall, *Prides of the Fancy*; *Ring* magazine; Nat Fleischer, *Black Dynamite Vol. 5*

Chapter 18

Henry Grady Edney, *Theodore Tiger Flowers*; *Ring* magazine; *United Press International*; *Atlanta Constitution*; *Milwaukee Sentinel*; US Census 1930 and 1940; Los Angeles Directories; *California Eagle*.